Don Wildmon

The Man
the Networks
Love to
Hate

Don Wildmon

The Man
the Networks
Love to
Hate

by
Donald E. Wildmon
with Randall Nulton

BRISTOL
BOOKS®
WILMORE, KY 40390

DON WILDMON: THE MAN THE NETWORKS LOVE TO HATE
Copyright © 1990, 1989 by Donald E. Wildmon and Randall Nulton
Published by Bristol Books

Don Wildmon, American Family Association, P.O. Drawer 2440,
Tupelo, MS 38803, 601/844-5036

First Edition, November 1989
Second Edition, January 1990

Scripture quotations are from the *New American Standard Bible,* © 1960, 62, 63, 68, 71, 72,
73, 75, 77 by The Lockman Foundation. Used by permission.

Library of Congress Card Number: 89-81449
ISBN: 0-917851-39-0
Suggested Subject Headings:
1. Mass Media—Religious Aspects—Christianity
2. Television
Recommended Dewey Decimal Classification: 261.52

BRISTOL BOOKS
An imprint of Good News, A Forum for Scriptural Christianity, Inc.,
308 East Main Street • Wilmore, KY 40390

Contents

This book is dedicated to the supporters of the
American Family Association—people who are
making a difference!

1

Time to Come Out Swinging!

Well, it's finally happened, I thought. *They're going to bring incest into millions of American homes.*

I then reread the article in the *Memphis Commercial Appeal* TV section to make sure my eyes had not been playing tricks on me. Sure enough! "MS. PLESHETTE PLAYS A SEXY WOMAN WHO HAS A LOVE AFFAIR WITH HER TOUGH BOXER SON...."

Memphis television columnist Larry Williams went on to explain that CBS had purchased the movie rights for Pete Hamill's controversial novel *Flesh and Blood*—a book known for its graphic descriptions of incestuous passion. Starring Suzanne Pleshette (best known for her TV role as Bob Newhart's wife in a popular 1970s CBS situation comedy) and Tom Berenger, the video version of Hamill's story was scheduled to air as a four-hour, made-for-television miniseries the following spring.

I wish I could say that I was surprised. But I was not! That's because during what Grant Tinker, president of MTM Productions,[1] had cynically dubbed "the year of the stewardess—the worst ever on network television,"[2] virtually every form of sexual immorality had been portrayed on the small screen.

Adultery. Teenage sex. Homosexuality. Even mate-swapping. It was all there in living color during prime time.[3] That year sexual intercourse and allusions to sex were dramatized with record frequency on all three major networks.[4] And incredibly, almost nine out of ten times the partners were not married.[5]

That's no misprint. Nine out of ten times!

Rarely was there even the slightest hint that infidelity or

premarital sex might be improper. Instead, it was almost always presented as normal, acceptable and even wholesome conduct.

Needless to say, I had figured that it wouldn't be long before sex between a parent and son or daughter made its way into a telecomedy or teledrama plot. And since television history appeared to be in the making, I wanted to make certain I knew as much as possible about *Flesh and Blood*. After reading the newspaper TV section I decided to head for the library and check out Mr. Hamill's book. I wanted to read for myself the story CBS executives felt warranted four hours of prime time on the public airwaves.

First, however, I looked up what the critics had said about Hamill's contribution to American literature. My instincts had told me to expect the worst: that *Flesh and Blood* possessed little or no socially redeeming value. I soon learned my hunch was right.

The *New York Times* called it "a savage novel which makes *Rocky* [the 1977 Oscar-winning boxing movie starring Sylvester Stallone] . . . look like a fairy tale." My heart grew heavy as I read how "son and mother make love repeatedly, dominated by their reprehensible need for each other." The *Times* reviewer also pointed out that this relationship is in no way condemned but rather is described as if mother and son do nothing wrong.

Newsweek magazine's review didn't make me feel any better. It spoke of "the spoiled innocence of a Lolita-like mother-son motel trek across the country."

This advanced billing almost made me ashamed to pick the book off the library shelf. But I did. And believe me, I quickly discovered that the critics hadn't been kidding.

I noticed that one provocative scene in particular seemed to set the tone for the entire book—a scene the author serenely sets on Christmas morning. So you'll better understand just what I'm talking about, let me give you a toned-down synopsis of the disturbing passage. Kate, the mother, and Bobby Fallon, her son the boxer, happen to be home alone enjoying the holiday. Outside, a gentle snow falls. Inside, blinking Christmas tree lights coupled with Frank Sinatra love songs playing on the stereo create a perverse, surreal romantic atmosphere. It isn't long before lustful thoughts turn to lustful action.

However, because it's their "first time," Bobby is somewhat

self-conscious and nervous. So Kate quickly thinks up a clever scheme to put him more at ease.

"Let's play a game," she suggests. "Call me Mary. You'll be Joe."

Her blasphemous charade works (remember, it's Christmas morning) and the stage is set for "Mary" to alluringly lead "Joe" by the hand into her cozy apartment bedroom. Still, Bobby (alias "Joe") is a bit uptight as his mother's clothes begin to drop to the floor.

"Nuthin' to worry you, Joe," she whispers in his ear. "Door's locked, if that's what's got you."

Then, after some more seductive dialogue designed to coax him into bed, "Mary" concludes, "It's all right, Joe. Everything is all right. Now and forever."

Naturally, or more appropriately, unnaturally, "Joe," who by now has swallowed her sensual bait—hook, line and sinker—quietly responds, "I love you, Ma."[6]

In addition to making this lascivious love affair a major theme, Hamill throws in a couple of non-incestuous, yet adulterous heterosexual bedroom scenes for good measure. He also includes vivid descriptions of fellatio and other male homosexual behavior. Meanwhile raw profanity peppers the dialogue with scatter-gun frequency. For example, the word f--- appears no less than 90 times.

On top of all this, the book's fight scenes, which are filled with blood-spattering violence, left me feeling nauseous. While scoring merciless knockouts almost every time, the protagonist develops a rage that manifests itself in a consuming desire to kill his opponents. As a result he must be restrained from literally beating some defenseless foes to death.

These liberal doses of gratuitous sex, profanity and violence adorn a plot which features the fictional Bobby Fallon, a poor Irish-American street fighter from the seamy side of Brooklyn. Fallon is serving two years in the homosexual-infested New York State Penitentiary when he is "discovered" by a famous boxing manager. His crime? Punching a police officer during a drunken barroom brawl.

After his release he trains at a run-down Brooklyn gym and impressively fights his way up the contender ladder. Soon he becomes a nationally acclaimed boxing sensation—"the great white hope of the heavyweights."[7] Finally, near the book's end, he's ready for a climactic multi-million dollar shot at the title.

Please don't misunderstand! I don't claim to be a connoisseur of pugilistic prose. However, I do know enough about boxing to recognize a worn-out plot line when I see one. Hamill's hero—"the hard-luck kid who beats the odds"—had been standard fare for many a fictional fight story. And that probably posed a marketing problem for him and his publisher, Random House.

You see, Hamill needed some way to make his story different. He had to find a memorable ingredient so reviewers wouldn't label his book "just another ho-hum boxing novel." He knew he needed a hard-hitting "left hook" to grab reader attention and knock the critics off their feet. So as *Newsweek's* review speculated, "for shock and presumably for sales . . . Hamill plunged from Oedipal overtones into graphic, unsubtle incest." I agreed. In my opinion, the incestuous, exploitive twist was Hamill's "left hook." I believe he threw this literary punch to attract more readers and sweeten his royalty check.

Similarly I came to believe that CBS executives had purchased the rights to what Rena Pederson of the *Dallas Morning News* had called a "gutter-language rip-off of the boxing hero genre" for the very same reason. In fact, that fall the CBS Network had been proudly promoting itself with the on-air motto, "Turn Us On: We'll Turn You On." I suspected that they planned to "turn viewers on" by exploiting the abundant violence and warped sexual subplot. They presumably hoped that this unusual right and left combination would make *Flesh and Blood* the movie a big audience ratings winner.

Of course, I knew CBS would have to scale back much of *Flesh and Blood's* sex, violence and profanity for television. Still, no matter how much the writers, producers, directors and CBS program practices personnel toned it down, the incest would still be incest. That was simply too integral to the overall plot to be cut or changed.

So with all this in mind, I made a major decision. The time had come to take a stand . . . to draw the line and say, *Enough is enough!* I would try to stop CBS from being exploitive in airing yet another form of perverted sex. If that didn't work, it was time to use every resource at my disposal to attempt to turn what CBS executives thought would be a financial success into a financial disaster.

Fighting *Flesh and Blood* became top priority for me and my organization, then called The National Federation for Decency. To phrase it in boxing vernacular, the time had come to lace up some eight-ounce gloves, step into the ring, put up my dukes and come out swinging.

But before I give a round-by-round account of the action, let me place this battle in context.

The Titillation Sweepstakes

It was the end of what a *TV Guide* magazine cover story had labeled "The Year TV Turned to Sex."[8] More specifically, the calendar read December 1978.

At the time, network executives had saturated the prime-time television schedule with programs based upon what they perceived to be an inexpensive, easy, can't-miss formula for luring viewers. Called "jiggly" or "T and A" (short for the derogatory expression, "t--s and a--es") programming by television industry insiders, the basic ingredients were relatively simple.

1. Build the program around one, two or more beautiful, shapely women (acting ability not necessarily required).

2. Use any pretext to present the voluptuous heroines in lacy lingerie or revealing swim wear.

3. Shoot scenes with alluring camera angles and lots of lingering close-ups.

4. Inject large doses of sexual subject matter into the program's plot and dialogue.

Essentially this "titillation sweepstakes"[9] (as Federal Communications Commission Commissioner Margita White angrily called it) had really started in earnest the previous year. That's when an ABC program called *Charlie's Angels* soared to number one in the prime-time audience ratings by employing this formula. It starred three female make-believe detectives who seemed to do much of their undercover investigative work at resort pool sides, in steamy health spas, on breezy ocean beaches or aboard luxuriant yachts.

Charlie's Angels' secret for success, according to *Time* magazine, was due in part to the fact that "typically . . . at least one

co-star strips down to a bikini in the first ten minutes." Why?
". . . To keep males in a state of gape-jawed passivity and expectation thereafter."

The rest of ABC's 1978 "jiggly" line-up was led by *Three's Company*—a situation comedy *Newsweek* called little more than a "libidinous . . . confection of one-liners and double-entendres about a ménage à trois."

One thing I had learned about television—when one show in a certain genre hits it big, the other networks scramble to produce copycat shows.

Flying High—the weekly series that had prompted Grant Tinker's "worst year ever" diatribe—headlined the *Charlie's Angels* clones over at CBS. It focused primarily on the sexual exploits of three airline stewardesses. But as soon as *Flying High* got off the ground, a flock of critics directed turbulent remarks at it, including Patricia D. Robertson, president of The National Association of Flight Attendants. Pointing out that CBS used "every stereotype and cliché" to portray her organization's members as "brainless sex goddesses," she called the show "demeaning and inaccurate."[10]

The CBS program *The American Girls* drew even more wrath from critics—especially newspaper writers who cover the television beat. And it was easy to see why. According to *Broadcasting Magazine*, the pilot episode "centered on a white slave ring through which scantily-clad women were auctioned off to a group of international dealers."

Not to be outdone by the competition that year, NBC aired its share of shows that NBC executives admitted were "high on skin and low on mental stimulation.[11] Most notable was *Rollergirls*. It focused on a roller-derby team of "flaky women in tight T-shirts and short-shorts who spent most of their time inhaling for the cameras" as *TV Guide* columnist Sally Bedell described the show in her critically acclaimed book, *Up the Tube: Why We See What We See . . . Like It or Not!*

But as much as I had been frustrated by the plethora of sexually exploitive weekly serials, the TV movies bugged me the most. Their longer format had given producers and directors additional latitude. Indeed, not only could they incorporate every dimension of the "jiggly" formula, but they could also be much more forthright in their use of immoral plot lines involving illicit behavior. This behavior would more often than not be presented as fashionable, healthy and, in the case of adultery, even beneficial to one's marriage.

Of course, total frontal nudity and explicit camera shots of actual intercourse were still taboo.[12] But seductive visual suggestion techniques utilized by highly skilled producers, directors, camera operators and video editors usually left little to the viewer's imagination. There was rarely any doubt about the sexual activity the characters were, had been or would soon be performing.

For the record, here's a brief rundown of what I'm talking about: NBC had kicked off its 1978 made-for-TV movie lineup by "setting a new standard for titillation." That was *Newsweek's* conclusion as it described *Loose Change*—a six-hour, three-part "let-it-all-hang-out memoir of the 60s counter-culture." Before viewers had watched even a half hour of this February miniseries, they had already witnessed two salacious sex scenes. Neither of the two California-Berkeley coeds who lose their virginity in the revealing vignettes express even the slightest bit of remorse. Instead, they both jubilantly speak of no longer being "private."[13]

NBC regressed even further a few weeks later. In *Death of Her Innocence,* boarding school teenagers took part in the most sexually explicit scenes I had yet seen on television. *TV Guide's* movie critic, Judith Crist, sarcastically noted that this telefilm might have been more appropriately titled, "My Most Memorable Academic Experience or How I Lost My Virginity and Muffy Got Pregnant and Had an Abortion and Died and I was Sad."

Now how's that for an uplifting story line?

Shortly after *Death of Her Innocence* NBC aired *Betrayal.* It presented two lesbian sexual encounters and numerous "therapeutic sex" scenarios between a manipulative psychiatrist and his insecure patients.

Other typical 1978 NBC movie offerings included *Thou Shalt Not Commit Adultery, Sex and the Married Woman, Secrets of Three Hungry Wives, Sharon: Portrait of a Mistress, Kathie: Portrait of a Centerfold* and *Three Desperate Women*—one of the all-time "jiggly" classics. Described by *TV Guide* as "idiotic," *Three Desperate Women* featured "television's now inevitable three females as convicts stranded in the wilderness . . . wearing low-cut, two piece, bare-midrifted prison garb." Such a plot would be hard enough to swallow if set in the late 1970s, much less during—get this—the Civil War!

Meanwhile ABC launched its slate of 1978 movies amid a much deserved whirlwind of controversy. Six young actresses who played college sorority sisters in February's *The Initiation of Sarah* risked their careers to tell what had happened during production. An official protest against ABC, filed by the Actors Union, charged that the actresses had been told to pose nude and wear nothing under robes—robes that were subsequently blown up by wind machines.

The protest continued by noting that the actresses had been "embarrassed numerous times," especially when the camera had "unnecessarily lingered on them in humiliating positions." The six had also fumed about being expected to wear oversized bras stuffed with foam rubber. The protest concluded by charging that "unbeknownst to the ladies, several scenes were filmed for the private viewing pleasure of network officials."[14]

After such an inauspicious start I could understand why ABC's movies got worse as the year went on. In March ABC aired what *TV Guide* had called the "crassly exploitive" *Little Ladies of the Night*. Instead of educating viewers about an American tragedy, ABC, as *TV Guide* pointed out, presented a "tawdry, superficial, lip smacking exploitation of teenage prostitution."

Scheduled between *How to Pick up Girls, Three on a Date* (featuring several Playboy Playmates), *A Guide for the Married Woman* and several other movies in the "jiggly" genre, ABC sank deep into the cesspool of immorality with their video version of Joyce Haber's novel, *The Users*. Jaclyn Smith, one of Charlie's three famous angels, starred as a devious part-time hooker who used her body to get to the top of Hollywood's power structure. Her husband's character, played by Tony Curtis, was a practicing bisexual. Said *TV Guide*, "This presentation demonstrates how trash can be made even trashier in another medium."

Still, as bad as all this sounds, NBC's and ABC's 1978 movie offerings were tame compared to CBS's. Our fall 1978 National Federation for Decency monitoring study, meticulously conducted by hundreds of volunteers, indicated that CBS incorporated even more immoral sexual content into their movies.[15]

True to it's "We'll Turn You On" motto, CBS became particularly adept at transforming soft-core pornographic novels, such as *Flesh and Blood,* into tawdry visual turn-ons. For instance, CBS's *Once Is Not Enough,* based on the novel by Jacqueline Susanne, was called "star-studded trash" by *TV Guide.* It featured a lesbian love scene—complete with caressing and kissing, some additional bed scenes (all adulterous affairs), a graphic shower scene and enough sexually suggestive dialogue to fill a small book.

The Pirate, which aired only a few days before I found out about *Flesh and Blood,* was even worse. After calling this adaptation of Harold Robbins's novel "four hours of awful . . . trashiness brought unadulterated to the screen," *TV Guide* sarcastically concluded, ". . . the only missing items are credibility, taste and a kitchen sink. But there's enough adultery, double-dealing and jet set life to compensate."

As you've now certainly gathered, I was far from the only one fed up with this steady diet of "sleaze tease" (as several popular television columnists liked to call it) served on network television night . . . after night . . . after night.

The press from coast to coast was buzzing about the phenomenon. *Newsweek,* in its 1978 cover story, "Sex and TV," even took a rare editorial stand, calling the trend "tragic . . . and disturbing . . . because these programs are designed to pander to prurience in the most cheaply exploitive manner."

Scores of high profile individuals, some within the entertainment industry itself, were also voicing their displeasure. "The heads of the networks are parasites and tasteless mercenaries," huffed Kathleen Nolan, president of the Screen Actors Guild after she learned what had happened during the *Initiation of Sarah* shooting. She then said, and I didn't disagree, "They've trashed up the airwaves almost beyond repair."[16]

Many nationally recognized citizen groups and organizations were speaking out as well. The National Parent-Teachers Association (PTA), for obvious reasons, was particularly critical of what they called television's "sexploitation" proliferation. And even The National Organization for Women (NOW) got into the act. I rarely have agreed with NOW on anything, but on this issue we saw things eye to eye. This voice of America's feminist movement called "jiggly" programming "a discouraging trend because it depicts women as empty-headed sex objects."

So you see, much condemnatory talk was aimed at the network brass during the fall of 1978. But unfortunately, that's all most of it was—TALK! Except for my own fledgling organization, very few individuals or groups were taking any action.

Into the Ring with CBS

Once I decided to step into the ring and fight *Flesh and Blood*, I wasted little time letting CBS know that they had more than one boxing match on their hands. I threw the initial two punches—a one-two combination—soon after my informative library excursion.

First, I wrote letters to 250 television sponsors and 50 major advertising agencies. My advice? "Read the book before you place any advertisements on this miniseries. See for yourselves what CBS has deemed to be appropriate entertainment for America's family rooms!"

To make sure there would be no misunderstanding, I informed advertisers that they would face consequences if they rewarded CBS's moral irresponsibility: The National Federation for Decency would strongly encourage people not to purchase their products. I also pledged that a complete list of *Flesh and Blood* sponsors would appear on a continuing basis in NFD's monthly newsletter.

My second punch was more direct. I asked NFD financial support partners, other NFD members, friends and all concerned citizens to write letters of protest to CBS Television President James Rosenfield.

Experience had taught me that the three big networks essentially ignore complaint letters. In fact, protest letters had been such a waste of time, I hadn't even been publishing network addresses in my organization's informational material.This time, however, I wanted the top CBS decision-maker to receive a loud and clear message: CONDONED INCEST HAS NO PLACE ON NETWORK TELEVISION!

I wanted Rosenfield to realize that his network had gone too far. He needed to understand that lots of frustrated folks besides Don Wildmon were—to quote a famous phrase from the movie

Network, which CBS had just aired—"mad . . . and not going to take it anymore!"

Apparently my call to action hit a responsive chord all across America. People started writing, first by the dozen, then by the hundreds, and after a couple of months, by the thousands. Indeed, almost every day I received copies of original, personal letters concerned viewers had sent to Mr. Rosenfield.

Most searing in my memory are the letters from women who had been incestuously abused in their childhoods.[17] Many poured their hearts out as they wrote about the resulting confusion, hurt, anguish and psychological trauma. Typically these emotionally-charged letters ended with a vehement plea for Mr. Rosenfield to change his mind.

CBS responded to the flood of mail they received by not responding. Oh sure, everyone who wrote got a reply assuring them that *"Flesh and Blood* will be appropriate for television . . . maintain contemporary standards of decency and good taste . . . and adhere to the high standards viewers have come to expect of CBS programming."[18] But that's what the CBS audience services department almost always said. Their letter read almost word for word like countless CBS "complaint letter" replies I had already seen.

What I wanted to know was whether they planned to feature the incestuous relationship in the movie. CBS, however, had been conveniently avoiding that subject. They also were being unusually secretive about when, specifically, they planned to air *Flesh and Blood.* As a result, I couldn't help but conclude that CBS fully intended to portray the incest . . . and intended to show it explicitly.

I became convinced that this indeed was the case on March 8, 1979. That day I received a call from an NFD supporter who had just talked to someone at CBS who inadvertently let the cat out of the bag. According to my friend, CBS had tentatively scheduled *Flesh and Blood* to air on May 9 and 10.

That news was significant because May 9 and 10 happened to be right smack in the middle of the next television "sweeps."

"Sweeps" is a four-week period each May, November and February when the networks tend to pull out all the stops and schedule special programs and movies they believe will get unusually high ratings.

Why? Because during "sweeps" nightly viewer totals carry extra importance in determining how much each network can charge for their commercial spots. Simply put, bigger "sweeps" audience ratings—ratings generated by projected winners like *Flesh and Blood*—mean more advertising revenue during the rest of the year.

But the air dates weren't the only slip CBS made that fateful March day. Later that evening I happened to watch part of a CBS made-for-TV movie called *Coach*. Its story involved a fictitious high school that had accidentally (due to computer error) hired a beautiful woman (Cathy Lee Crosby) to serve as boys' basketball coach.

That irony could have made it a fun, light, comedic drama appropriate for its targeted pre-teen and adolescent audience. Unfortunately CBS had a different idea. Not only did Miss Crosby endeavor to teach the boys winning basketball, she also instructed them in the basics of another extracurricular activity.

You guessed it . . . SEX!

By movie's end she had had sexual relations with several boys. In fact, one graphic scene focused on a steamy lovemaking session with the team's star player. I say steamy because it took place in the locker room shower.

I don't know about you, but where I come from they still call that sort of thing statutory rape! And I couldn't help but wonder, *If statutory rape fits CBS's definition of "high standards," "decency" and "good taste," just how far are they going to go with* Flesh and Blood?

As it turned out I only had to wait a few more days before CBS, again inadvertently, gave me my long-awaited answer. It seems that the *Coach* shower scene had stirred up a spontaneous storm of protest from shocked viewers. Local CBS affiliates all over the nation were inundated with *Coach* complaints.

As fate would have it, most of the CBS affiliate owners and managers were meeting the very next week at the National Association of Television Program Executives (NATPE) Convention in Las Vegas. Many had been embarrassed by *Coach* and had taken a lot of heat—especially from angry parents. So naturally, as the *New York Times* reported, the "organized letter-writing campaign against *Flesh and Blood* generated some concern amongst nervous network affiliates."

James Rosenfield, in response to questions posed by some of the station owners, first tried to dismiss the furor over *Flesh and Blood* as much ado about nothing. "We don't pay attention to complaints from people who have not yet seen the show," he said. But that answer wasn't good enough. Like me, many affiliate people were concerned about the book's incestuous subplot, and they kept pressing. Eventually Rosenfield revealed what I had been trying to find out all winter.

"If you haven't read the book," he explained, "you wouldn't recognize the allusions to incest in the film."[19]

I had my doubts about Rosenfield's claim that the incest would be presented in a subtle manner. But even if that were true, I still felt strongly that CBS had no business *alluding* to incest at all—at least not in the book's favorable context. So I decided to hit CBS with another one-two combination.

This time I asked viewers across the country to join me in tuning CBS out during the May "sweeps" period. I also announced that the National Federation for Decency would protest by picketing dozens of local CBS affiliates on May 1.

CBS countered by altering their strategy. The next week James Rosenfield announced that *Flesh and Blood's* airing was being postponed until fall. Though he didn't say why, an industry publication reported it was "because of shaky affiliates and fear of pressure groups."[20]

Then on March 27 George Zurich, CBS Director of Communications, told CBS affiliate stations that *Flesh and Blood* "will be neither salacious nor sensational in any way and will not, as has been reported in the press, 'feature a case of incest.'"[21]

That same promise soon began appearing in Audience Services Director Marjorie Holyoak's "complaint letter" replies. Meanwhile, Mike Silver, special projects director in the CBS press information office, was assuring newspaper reporters that "CBS is not putting anything on the air that would be as offensive as that [incest]."[22]

At the time, it looked like we had won a major victory. Contrary to Mr. Rosenfield's defiant "we don't pay attention to complaints" remark, it appeared that the efforts of several thousand concerned letter writers had paid off. CBS had gone on record stating that they would be pulling the incest. And that good news had made me feel like celebrating. I even decided to cancel our May 1 picketing.

However, on May 2 I wished I hadn't. That's because in *Torn Between Two Lovers* CBS made it clear that they were back to business as usual. This made-for-TV movie featured a young woman who was both "happily married and helplessly in love with another man." Or so CBS's full page *TV Guide* ad had described her dilemma. According to the promo, she resolved it by "breaking all the rules" because "sometimes . . . that's the only way to win."

Later that week CBS aired *Anatomy of a Seduction*. It depicted an affair between an attractive 40-year-old woman and her best friend's 20-year-old son. Again, the relationship was treated positively, as if the characters were actually doing the right thing.

As May dragged on CBS continued to feature one kind of infidelity after another in a steady stream of titillating "sweeps" movie specials. That made me wonder if my *Flesh and Blood* victory celebration was premature. After all, I reflected, the task of getting CBS to change its mind about the incest had been much easier than I had anticipated—almost too easy!

The more I thought about it, the more suspicious I became of CBS's quick about-face following James Rosenfield's recalcitrant Las Vegas comments.Then I remembered the reputation CBS had garnered for what the Federal Communications Commission had called "false and misleading statements to the public." Only months before, the FCC had severely reprimanded CBS officials for "a pattern of negligent conduct" and "repeated instances of deception" during promotion of four "Heavyweight Championship of Tennis" matches in 1975, 1976 and 1977.[23]

I couldn't help but wonder, *If they've lied before . . . they could lie again.* Consequently, as spring turned to summer, I developed a strong gut feeling that CBS might not be fighting fair. Somehow I sensed that CBS might be preparing to hit the American public with a sneaky "left hook". . . below the belt!

Unfortunately in August I found out my premonition had been right. It was then that I learned, despite all the statements to the contrary, CBS intended to include the incestuous subplot and had planned to do so all along. Indeed, it became crystal clear that their

Flesh and Blood "will not feature incest" promise had been part of a mendacious strategy to quiet the protest effort. Then they hoped, I believed, to air the movie—incest and all—before an effective protest could once again be mounted. The CBS ploy might have worked were it not for one unforeseen circumstance. Pete Hamill and *Flesh and Blood* Executive Producer Gerald Abrams (employed by Paramount Studios) weren't cooperating. In fact, the running feud Abrams (who had been candidly telling reporters that his movie "includes a not-so-subtle suggestion of incest"[24]) and Hamill were having with CBS had become the talk of Hollywood.

Reported extensively in the press, the squabble erupted when, according to syndicated columnist Marilyn Beck, CBS did "additional tampering" with the "controversial" Christmas morning incest scene. *Newsweek* explained that "worried network censors" had cut Bobby's "choked-up 'I love you, Ma' confession" along with "footage showing the mother passionately kissing her son and then starting to undress, as both move into the bedroom."[25]

Surprise, surprise!

As a result, noted Ms. Beck, Hamill and Abrams were "incensed that CBS should bow to pressure that has been applied by The National Federation for Decency."[26] The revised scene, which *Newsweek* reported "concludes with Berenger ('Bobby') frozen at the bedroom door as Ma glides seductively inside, after reassuring him that 'It's all right . . . Everything is all right,'" was totally unsatisfactory to the producer and writer. They, of course, wanted the scene to come to life as it was originally written. To them, anything less was a compromise of artistic license. Said Hamill (brace yourself for this one), "It [the CBS incest scene revision] makes it vulgar, cold, dirty, devoid of emotion."[27]

Still, the revised scenario, which *Newsweek* said "anyone past puberty will quickly decipher," was totally unsatisfactory to me—especially since CBS had led thousands of us to believe that the incestuous theme would be removed entirely. And so, even though barely a month remained before the newly-announced October air dates, I decided to make one more stand against *Flesh and Blood*.

First I wrote again to potential *Flesh and Blood* sponsors and reminded them of my earlier pledge. Then, once again, primarily through the *NFD Journal*, I asked people to write and call both their local CBS affiliates and CBS's New York headquarters. I also encouraged the many pastors on my mailing list to urge their congregations to get involved. Finally, to add an extra punch, I printed a protest petition that concerned TV viewers could easily reproduce and circulate.

Though my mailing list was still rather small, I'm pleased to say that enough churches, civic groups (such as the 200,000-member Georgia PTA which pledged to help promote a sponsor boycott) and individuals took action to make *Flesh and Blood* the most protested movie ever shown on network television until that point. When it was all over, network officials admitted receiving 10,000 individually written, original complaint letters.[28] However, I have good reason to believe that the actual figure was considerably higher.

In addition to my write and call campaign, dozens of disappointed citizens held their own *Flesh and Blood* demonstrations. For instance, two Amarillo, Texas, women (one had been an incest victim as a child) organized a "Pray In" in front of KFDA (Channel 10). Some 300 Texas Panhandle residents joined the rally in an effort to peacefully persuade their station not to air the miniseries. Two hundred frustrated television viewers attended a similar protest in Orlando, Florida.

In Savannah, Georgia, 400 people gathered for a protest rally at CBS affiliate WTOC. WTOC station manager Jess Mooney told them, "You have two alternatives. Change the channel or turn it off."[29] That heartless attitude did not set very well with many east Georgia folks, especially when they remembered that WTOC had been licensed to "serve the public interest." So two days later, more than 1,000[30] people showed up at another impromptu demonstration. Promoted at the last minute primarily by word-of-mouth, to my knowledge it was the largest group ever assembled in one place on behalf of constructive television.

Speaking through a portable sound system, rally organizer Dr. Cecil Hodges lamented, "We will not tolerate any efforts on the part of television to encourage, either directly or indirectly, our sons to commit sex with their mothers." Pastor of a 5,000 member Savannah Baptist Church, Dr. Hodges was one of 75 pastors attending the demonstration. "This kind of degrading televised filth [incest]," he said, "is despicable, diabolical and intolerable."[31]

But despite all the demonstrations . . . despite all the phone calls . . . despite the record number of letters from people admonishing CBS to not show the incest . . . CBS went right ahead and did it anyway. As a matter of fact, *Newsweek's* review noted that after the famous Christmas scene, the incestuous affair "is practically spelled out in neon *throughout* the rest of the film" (emphasis mine).

"The steamy odyssey to Las Vegas," added *Newsweek* as it cited examples, is "replete with cheek-to-cheek dance embraces and bed-top nuzzlings."

Since those two fateful October nights in 1979 when the controversial miniseries finally aired, I've often been asked, "Who won the fight over *Flesh and Blood?*" Well, that's hard to answer. But I will say, obviously, since CBS broke their promise, the thousands who joined me in voicing their displeasure did not win. CBS succeeded in imparting a subtle message to millions of viewers, both young and old, that, as Steve Nicely, TV critic of the *Kansas City Times,* summarized, "incest is harmless and possibly even a beneficial experience."

But even though CBS got away with, as Nicely not so nicely described it, "a crime against its mass audience on a par with the crime of incest committed by relatives on their own flesh and blood," CBS certainly did not win either. Actually, I'd have to call the whole tussle a draw.

Why? Though some TV journalists praised *Flesh and Blood* for its acting and production quality (I didn't necessarily disagree), the movie still took a beating in the press. Rena Pederson of the *Dallas Morning News* said that CBS deserved the "Hypocrite of the Year Award" for the presentation.

"Down deep, at its core, *Flesh and Blood* is trash presented as a lure for a big audience," added Bill Barrett of the *Cleveland Press* as he summed up the feelings of a host of television writers. He concluded by echoing Steve Nicely's harsh criticism: "It is sick sex offered for money . . . a blatant exploitation of a morally reprehensible condition." Unfortunately, as is usually the case with after-the-fact reviews, CBS hardly even felt the sting of the critics' words.

But there are two more very good reasons why I call the fight a draw. The protest effort's fine support allowed us to flex our muscle like never before and land a couple of hard-hitting punches.

First, primarily because of strong local protest campaigns, numerous CBS affiliates, including KTVA, Anchorage, Alaska; WCPO, Cincinnati, Ohio; WBTW, Florence, South Carolina; and several Texas stations, refused to air *Flesh and Blood*. KLBK in Lubbock, Texas, decided to delay airing until 10:30 p.m. after, according to the station manager, receiving more than 1,000 letters. And KDFW in Dallas, thanks to a large protest ad in the *Dallas Times Herald* paid for by a suburban Dallas church, did some extra editing on the incest scenes.

At the same time, dozens more local CBS affiliates that did take the network feed as is weren't particularly happy about it. Speaking on behalf of what he believed to be "the great preponderance of affiliates," Robert E. Schmidt, chairman of the CBS Television Network Affiliates Association, sounded as if he were me. "What are the socially redeeming qualities of showing this [the incest]?" he rhetorically asked network officials.[32]

Still, the damage caused by the ill-will between CBS affiliates and the parent company was relatively minor. It was our second connecting blow that really left its mark.

Because of the protest, advertisers avoided *Flesh and Blood* like a plague. Leonard Lavin, chairman of Alberto-Culver, one of *Flesh and Blood's* few sponsors, told an NFD supporter that his company purchased time for $30,000 per minute. Normally, CBS could have expected to get $150,000-$200,000 or more per minute for a movie like *Flesh and Blood* during the fall of 1979.

In other words, CBS had to practically give commercial time away to get any sponsors at all. In fact, I later learned from one of television's largest advertisers that the twelve movie promos appearing during *Flesh and Blood* were probably free spots that CBS had not been able to fill.

Based on all the information available, I conservatively estimated that CBS lost approximately $4 million in advertising revenue on *Flesh and Blood*. However, that was not our most significant accomplishment.

CBS had been served notice that their defenses were not impenetrable. They had learned that the people of America who object to the behavior and values constantly promoted by their programming were no longer going to roll over and play dead. They had discovered that we could stay in the ring with a giant network, trading punch for punch for several rounds of action. And CBS also learned that sooner or later they were going to have to start listening to us, whether they wanted to or not.

As I reflect on the sickening Christmas scene in *Flesh and Blood* for which CBS paid so dearly, I remember another Christmas season scenario a few years earlier that radically changed the entire course of my life. Indeed the decisions I made that Christmas eventually made me the man the networks love to hate.

2

The Struggle for Decency Begins

The final weeks of 1976 were no different from any other December in my 10 plus years as a pastor. The rush of holiday activity at my church—First United Methodist of Southhaven, Mississippi—once again crowded my schedule. And of course, that meant fewer evenings to enjoy with my family.

I guess that's why I had been looking forward to a rare night off just before Christmas. For a change, my date book had shown no prior commitments: no Sunday school program rehearsal . . . no year-end board meeting . . . no marriage counseling session. It simply read: *Spend Time With Kids!* And that's just what I intended to do.

On that particular day a bone-chilling arctic air mass pushed its way deep into the heart of Dixie. So shortly after a filling supper, I lit a crackling fire in the den's fireplace. Then I kicked off my shoes, unknotted my tie, stretched my arms and legs and sat down in my favorite recliner.

It sure feels good to be home at this special time of year, I thought as I let myself relax. *Home . . . with the woman I love and the children who have so enriched our lives.*

As usual, our children had scattered following the meal. However, as the fire worked its magnetic magic, somehow I knew they'd soon be joining me in what was now the coziest room in the house.

Sure enough, Mark, my five-year-old bundle of energy arrived a couple minutes later. One hand clutched a large white notepad, the other a box of Crayolas. He gave me a quick smile just before he belly-flopped to the floor in front of the fire. With his feet sticking straight up in the air, he started a masterpiece that was certain to be displayed at the Wildmon family art gallery—the refrigerator door. Charlie Chu, our gray Pekinese, followed close behind. Heading straight for a comfortable patch of carpet close to Mark, he plopped down for a winter's nap.

Next came my 10-year-old bookworm, Donna. She whisked by, grabbed a half-read *Nancy Drew* mystery off the coffee table, curled up in her favorite corner of the love seat and soon was lost in the exciting world of her literary heroine.

As soon as my wife, Lynda, and my seventh-grade daughter, Angela, finished the dishes, they, too, made a beeline for the family room. Angela grabbed the newspaper off the couch and rifled through it until she found the comics. Lynda gathered up several remaining sections and started bargain hunting. I watched her zealously flip a few pages and figured it wouldn't take her eagle eyes long to find every "can't miss" Christmas special in nearby Memphis, Tennessee.

Tim, my warm-blooded eighth-grader, sauntered in last. Often times he headed outside to visit friends after our evening meal. But that frigid night he wasn't going anywhere. "Yankees who put up with this weather all winter have got to be nuts," he exclaimed with a shudder to no one in particular. Then I heard him mumble something about "moving to Hawaii" as he found his favorite spot on the couch.

Tim's "spot" just happened to be located in front of our Curtis-Mathes console television set. Consequently his next words, "Hey Dad, can we watch TV?" came as no surprise.

Normally I would have given Tim the usual grilling: "Have you finished your homework?. . . Have you taken the garbage out? . . ." all the stuff conscientious fathers are supposed to ask their kids before saying yes. But it was Christmas vacation, and none of the kids had pressing school work. Earlier I had thought about suggesting a table game we could play together as a family. But to be honest, the idea of being lazy in my recliner for an hour or two was awfully inviting.

So I responded with an enthusiastic, "Sounds like a good idea. Why don't you see what's on?"

As the TV picture filled the screen, we found ourselves witnessing the romantic overtures of an attractive married couple. Unfortunately it quickly became apparent that they weren't married to each other. When the seductive dialogue stopped and mouth met mouth, it didn't take a genius to figure out what the actor and actress were about to do. I didn't wait to see what happened. I asked Tim to change the channel.

I'm afraid that I can't even begin to tell you about what we saw next. That's because we only had the show on for a half minute or so before it had filled our cozy den with an outburst of offensive expletives.

Tim's third try seemed to be the charm. He had found my favorite kind of program—a "Whodunit?"—and in no time I was wrapped up in a well-written and well-acted story. A quick look around the room revealed that everyone else, including little Mark, was hooked on this suspenseful mystery as well.

But then the scene changed. Without warning, we suddenly found ourselves watching a scenario similar to those found in grade B Hollywood slasher films. To my horror, one character, brandishing a hammer, was literally beating the life out of a terror-stricken, defenseless victim who had been bound and gagged.

This time I told Tim to turn the set off. I'd guess that it took him about 10 seconds to get up, cross the room and push the knob. But as far as I was concerned, that was 10 seconds too long. This graphic brutality had not been a welcome holiday guest in our family room. I especially had not wanted such savagery imprinted on my five-year-old's consciousness right before bedtime.

When Tim first suggested that we watch TV, I had thought that my family might laugh together or that we might all hold our breath in suspense. Ideally, I had hoped to find a program that would teach us something positive about the fascinating and complex world we live in—a program that would mix some mind-stretching nourishment into the entertainment.

Instead our three choices on the prime-time television menu (these were the days before cable TV) were promiscuous sex, crude profanity and gratuitous violence!

The three big networks had simultaneously served my impressionable grade-schoolers and junior-highers mind-poisoning junk food. And the implications of that made my stomach churn with righteous indignation.

Look What Happened While We Looked the Other Way
As I turned my gaze from the blank screen back to the peaceful, flickering flame, I was no longer feeling peaceful. It greatly upset me to think that we couldn't find a single program appropriate for family viewing, and the more I reflected on what I had just seen and heard, the angrier I became.

Now it's not as if my eyes were suddenly opened. I realized that movies had become much more violent, profane and sexually explicit during the late 1960s and early 1970s. I had also noticed the dramatic increase in pornographic publications on newsstands and behind convenience store check-out counters. And naturally, I had been disappointed to see television undergoing the same metamorphosis as motion pictures and many periodicals.

However, up until that point my credo had always been: I'll just look the other way. After all, this is a pluralistic society. The Constitution guarantees freedom of speech, freedom of expression and freedom of choice. Therefore, if people want to produce vulgar movies, publish pornographic magazines or create television programs containing gratuitous violence and exploitive, immoral sex, that's their business. I don't have to go see them, buy them or watch them. As long as this stuff doesn't directly affect me or my family, why be concerned?

Of course, all those years while I conveniently "looked the other way" I never dreamed my family would one day be affected by the very things I was ignoring. And that prompted me to do some serious thinking about the electronic marvel known as television—especially its impact and influence on my family, my church congregation and American society in general.

Initially I acknowledged that television had positively contributed to my family's cultural and educational development. I remembered a hot summer Sunday night in 1969 when I had even canceled church so no one would miss astronaut Neil Armstrong's famous "one small step for man: one giant leap for mankind."

Seven summers later, thanks to ABC, we had all enjoyed our front row seats for the Montreal Olympic Games. I smiled when I recalled how Lynda and the girls were absolutely mesmerized by the gold medal performances of a graceful Romanian gymnast named Nadia.

Then my thoughts fast-forwarded through that fall's campaign and election coverage. I remembered the keen interest Tim had taken in Jimmy Carter's bid to unseat Gerald Ford, making me wonder if I might be raising a future politician.

Next I thought about Mark's favorite shows. *Sesame Street* had taught him the alphabet and how to count. *Captain Kangaroo* and *Mr. Roger's Neighborhood* had exposed him to many people, places and things. These fine programs had also helped reinforce principles of good behavior such as the importance of sharing.

Indeed, television was a remarkable invention with almost limitless potential to benefit people everywhere. But something had gone very wrong.

At that point I shifted my weight, crossed my feet and focused my mind on the stimulus of my vexation. I started thinking about how prime-time television entertainment had changed since my older kids were toddlers.

Foul four-letter words and other expletives were seldom employed in mid-1960s dialogue. But I had watched enough television to know that what we had just heard was standard fare in the mid-1970s. In fact, it occurred to me that if a viewer didn't know any better, he or she would assume that profanity is an integral part of normal and proper communication.

The dramatic increase of prime-time beat 'em up, shoot 'em up, crash 'em up and blow 'em up scenes had me wondering whether multitudes of viewers might mistakenly believe that violent behavior is appropriate for ventilating anger and dealing with problems.

Then my thoughts centered on network television's portrayal of sex. It dawned on me that the adultery we had seen was not the exception to the rule, as it had been a decade earlier. Rather, it had become the norm. More often than not, when the three big networks depicted or suggested a sexual relationship, it involved two unmarried people. In fact, I almost couldn't remember when I had last seen a program which expressed the idea that sexual intimacy and marriage go together.

The belief Lynda and I shared and hoped to instill in our children—that sex is a beautiful and special gift designed by our

Creator for enjoyment within his well-specified parameters—was almost never reinforced. Instead, prime-time television's underlying message was just the opposite. And that message seemed to be:

1. Sex is inherently funny . . . something to snicker at (i.e. the heavy emphasis on sexual innuendo and double entendre in the newer situation comedies).

2. Sex is something to engage in indiscriminately and frequently for one's personal pleasure.

3. A woman's self-worth is measured by her physical features and sex appeal.

I knew that this message, reinforced night after night, had to influence people's thoughts and actions—especially young people's. And I couldn't help but wonder, *Is there a correlation between TV's message and America's skyrocketing divorce rate, the recent surge in teenage pregnancies and the ever-increasing spread of sexually-transmitted diseases?*

Of course, I knew television didn't cause all these problems. However I had to believe that television contributed to them since it was society's only major new medium of influence in the last generation.

Then I thought again about my "look the other way" philosophy and I realized it had one major flaw. Its effectiveness depended upon my ability to keep my family in a narrow world isolated from society. And of course, that wasn't possible. The changes in TV's attitudes toward morality were now coming into the sanctity of my very own home. Television's increasingly violent and exploitive messages were already influencing the community and neighborhood we called home. I also realized that these changes were going to influence the views and values of my children's friends, including the young men who would soon be dating my daughters.

I wrestled with that thought while I got up to throw another log on the fire. As I poked at some burning coals with my fireplace tongs, I made a simple and logical decision. No longer would I look the other way. No longer would I sit idly by and ignore the excessive sex and violence on television. I made up my mind to do something I had never done before . . . something that involved exercising my constitutionally guaranteed right of free speech.

That's it, I thought. I would take action. I would preach a

sermon on television and challenge my church members to be better viewers.

But to effectively challenge my 500-member congregation to become more selective TV viewers, I knew I'd need to dig up some facts on the subject at the Southhaven library.

As it turned out, I didn't have to dig very deep. A quick look in the card catalog and *Reader's Guide to Periodical Literature* indicated that a veritable mountain of material had been written about television's influence on viewers—especially young ones.

Rare was the woman's, news or general interest magazine that had not run a major article citing what *Newsweek* had called "the overwhelming body of evidence drawn from more than 2,300 studies and reports." That evidence, said *Newsweek* in its cover story, "What TV Does to Kids," demonstrates that television's impact "is decidedly negative."

At the time, much of that "overwhelming body of evidence" came from a wide array of scholarly studies—including a $1.8 million research project conducted by the U.S. Surgeon General's office—focusing on TV violence. And according to Victor B. Cline, a University of Utah psychologist widely known for his expertise on media violence, these studies continually reached the same conclusion. "Televised and filmed violence," he summarized, "can powerfully teach, suggest—even legitimize—extreme antisocial behavior."

"In some viewers," added Cline in his *Ladies Home Journal* article entitled, "TV Violence: How It Damages Your Children," "it can trigger specific aggressive or violent behavior." Then he noted that research done by scores of behavioral scientists had shown "a definite cause-effect relationship between violence on TV and violent behavior in real life."

Naturally information like this got my attention; especially when I learned that, at 1976 levels, the average child in Mark's kindergarten class could expect to witness some 13,000 TV killings by the time he or she is old enough to enter high school.[1] Add to that the fist fights, muggings, beatings and even simulated rape featured during prime time, and I couldn't help but think, *No wonder the Federal Bureau of Investigation says that my wife and kids are 50 percent more likely to be victimized by violent crime today than they were 10 years ago!*[2]

What few remaining doubts I had about television's indelible power were dispelled when I learned who America's young people had named as their personal "heroes." That fall, *Senior Scholastic Magazine* surveyed 27,000 kids Tim's age and asked them who they idolized the most. Rather than name a political figure, scientist, sports figure or writer, as *Senior Scholastic* had suggested, the vast majority of respondents listed TV personalities. In fact, five of the top six vote-getters were Hollywood stars.[3] The sixth was Romania's young gymnastics sensation, Nadia Comaneci—the girl made famous by ABC's Olympics coverage.

To my chagrin, the number one "hero," by a wide margin, was Charlie's most famous angel—Farrah Fawcett Majors. Interestingly, the same week *Senior Scholastic* had taken its survey, Farrah's *Charlie's Angels* role had required her to go undercover (or maybe I should say *uncovered?*) as a pornographic magazine centerfold candidate. According to *Newsweek,* she had been used as "male bait" while gathering evidence against the bad guys. As usual, she had manipulatively gotten what she wanted by being slinky, sexy and seductively suggestive.

A study conducted about that time by the Cambridge, Massachusetts-based Project on Human Sexual Development confirmed what my instincts had already told me. It found that television ranked just behind parents as "the highest authority for teaching children the facts of adult sexual behavior."[4] Consequently I couldn't help but wonder what Mrs. Majors's actions were teaching millions of impressionable young girls about "adult sexual behavior."

That winter countless girls Angela's age made the "Farrah look" hairstyle the rage in beauty shops across America. Meanwhile the famous Farrah pin-up poster became the country's hottest pop art item. Its record setting sales of more than $2 million eclipsed the old poster sales mark set by fellow ABC actor Henry Winkler,[5] "The Fonz" on *Happy Days*.

I mention "Fonzie" because I learned that he had started one of the greatest mass television audience stampedes ever. Immediately following the *Happy Days* episode in which he got a library card, America's libraries were inundated with an unprecedented 500,000 library card requests.[6] That made me think, *If this mythical Hollywood hero can trigger a run on America's libraries, what*

*does his constant braggadocio about his sexual adventures teach
young viewers about "adult sexual behavior"?*

My Church Goes Cold Turkey

At any rate, once I put together some statistics, quotes and
thoughts such as I've outlined here, I preached my sermon. But I
didn't stop there. My research convinced me that helping my
church members become more selective TV viewers should be a
high priority, and I knew it would take more than a 20-minute
message for my point to sink in.

So I came up with a plan which followed the advice of several
network executives. I had heard them say, "if you don't like what's
on TV, turn it off." And that's just what I decided to do.

I challenged my congregation to voluntarily join me and my
family in not watching *any* television for one week. No Walter
Cronkite. No Johnny Carson. No Archie Bunker. No *Starsky and
Hutch.* No *General Hospital.* No *60 Minutes.* No Memphis State
or Ole Miss basketball games. No Saturday morning cartoons.

In other words, I asked them to go cold turkey. Of course, I
knew seven days would be a long time for some of our heavier-
viewing families, but I figured they'd survive.

In order to make it official, I designated February 27 to March
5, 1977, as "Turn the TV Off Week" at Southhaven First United
Methodist Church. That allowed several weeks to promote the
event within the church. It also gave some of our borderline and
full-fledged TV addicts some time to emotionally prepare for the
shock of silence.

But that wasn't all. I asked my church members to phone each
Memphis network affiliate on Monday, February 28 to explain why
they wouldn't be watching their station that week. I also figured if
some other folks in the north Mississippi, east Arkansas, west
Tennessee tri-state area would do the same thing, the local stations
might get the point and encourage the networks to clean up their
act.

So, drawing on some free-lance journalism experience, I wrote
a simple one-page press release outlining what my church planned
to do and why. Then I mailed it to the three big Memphis television
stations and all the area newspapers and radio stations I could think
of.

Quite frankly, I had expected my little story to be ignored and wind up in newsroom trash cans. Therefore, I was absolutely stunned by what happened the next morning. I had gone about my business as usual, beginning that particular day by visiting hospitalized church members in Memphis. Then, about mid-morning, as was my custom, I called my office to check for messages. To my surprise, my normally calm and collected secretary was practically in hysterics.

"Where have you been?" she scolded. "This phone's been ringing off the hook all morning. Channel 5 and Channel 3 both called and want to interview you for their six o'clock news. Several radio stations have called and I just got off the line with a writer who works for the *Commercial Appeal.*"

Needless to say, I hurried back to the church and spent most of the afternoon talking with reporters. I also did some live radio interviews and answered questions on a couple of call-in talk shows.

The following day things got even crazier because the Memphis correspondent for The Associated Press had sent my story out over the wire. He had headlined it, "Mississippi Preacher Leads TV Turn Off Campaign," or something to that effect. Calls began coming in from newspapers and radio stations in Florida, Pennsylvania, Illinois, Colorado . . . all over the country. I could hardly believe what was happening. My idea had seemed so simple. I certainly didn't think turning our TVs off for a few days would be considered such a big deal.

However, it seems that I had struck a nerve. As I've mentioned, television cause-and-effect impact studies had been getting quite a bit of press coverage. And unbeknownst to me, at that time the National PTA happened to be holding eight high-profile regional hearings exploring "The Effects of Television on Children and Youth." My little "Turn Off" effort represented an unusual angle on what had become a hot nationwide issue. To the reporters who called me, I represented the little guy who had decided to take on Goliath.

As the calls steadily kept coming—some 200 during that February alone—I realized I had stumbled onto a golden opportunity to do some good. Subsequently I accepted each interview request and did my best to sound the alarm about network television's increasing use of sex and violence.

But it wasn't just the media's interest in my "Turn Off" campaign that surprised me so much. It was also the letters addressed to me that filled our church post office box. Each morning for weeks the church secretary handed me 50, 100 or sometimes 200 newly arrived envelopes. And it wasn't long before their total exceeded 1,500.

Spontaneously written by business executives, teachers, truck drivers, doctors, lawyers, homemakers, factory workers—people from all walks of life—these personal notes all had one thing in common: *Support!* That's what had surprised me the most.

Let me explain.

During that memorable December night in my den I had wondered, *Maybe it's just me. Perhaps I'm the only one who feels this way about television.* After all, I had never heard anyone in my church denomination raise the issue. None of my friends or church members had ever introduced the subject in conversation. So I really had thought I might be all alone in my belief that much of television had become a negative force in society.

However, this deluge of unexpected and encouraging letters laid these doubts to rest. It convinced me that many people all around America strongly shared the same concerns.

Some folks simply said "Right on!" "Preach it, preacher" or "I'm behind you 100 percent." Others wrote lengthy letters venting what seemed to be a lot of bottled up frustration. Indeed, literally hundreds of people told me how they, too, had become disgusted by the lack of decent programming during prime time.

Lots of these friendly letter writers identified themselves as moms, dads or grandparents. They usually expressed disappointment about what television seemed to be teaching the little ones they cared about most. They especially echoed my concerns regarding the constant portrayal of sex outside of marriage.

But that's not all. Many of these people sent newspaper clippings and magazine stories they had found—articles about television and what famous, influential people were saying about it.

For example, I learned that quite a few United States senators and congressmen had already articulated many of the things I had come to believe. Minnesota Senator Hubert Humphrey had cited television as one of the key reasons for the "breakdown of the family unit" in America. And only a few months earlier, Congressman Timothy Wirth (now Senator) of Colorado had called "network programs, loaded with violence, crime and sex, a national disgrace."[7]

From this material I also discovered that several giants of the entertainment industry had not been afraid to speak out against network programming's sex and violence overkill.[8] Bing Crosby's words, written for a *Los Angeles Herald Examiner* guest column, particularly caught my eye.

This Hollywood legend had just been hospitalized for several weeks (sadly, he died a short while later). So naturally he had seen "lots and lots of TV." According to his article, that had made him "worried" about the business of show business.

"It became apparent to me," Bing said, "that very slowly and very subtly writers and producers are working in nudity, permissiveness, profanity, smutty innuendos, smutty situations . . . and scenes of semiexplicit sex into their shows." Then, after noting that moral responsibility on television "is almost indiscernible," he concluded that the effect of all this on children "can't be anything but harmful."

"They see these chic, sophisticated people behaving immorally, salaciously," he explained. "People living together without the benefit of marriage must be the thing to do, they think. Must be clever or attractive.

"Kids, you know," he continued, "are indelibly impressed by anything they see on film or television done by attractive, famous people."

Needless to say, it was reassuring to know that even some of Hollywood's all-time greats, including Red Skelton and Lucille Ball, concurred that the three big networks were not serving the best interest of America's young people. And that brings me to the most significant television-related fact that I discovered during that incredibly hectic February.

Much to my amazement, I learned that each and every American citizen is part owner of the airwaves—the same airwaves all television stations must use in order to transmit their signals. I also found out that all television stations, including ABC,

NBC and CBS affiliate stations which air network programming, are licensed by a United States Government regulatory agency called the Federal Communications Commission (FCC). That license, which must be renewed periodically, grants that TV station the privilege of using the *publicly owned airwaves* free of charge. That same license specifies that the licensee must faithfully "serve the public interest."

In other words, the entire television industry has a mandated obligation to provide satisfactory programming in the interest of the public it serves. I found this news to be somewhat ironic because of three things: (1) I qualified as part of the "public" (2) ABC, CBS and NBC weren't doing very well at serving my interest, Lynda's interest or Tim, Angela, Donna and Mark's interest; (3) I knew of at least 1,500 men and women from practically every state whose interests weren't being served very well either.

To learn what steps would help remedy this discrepancy, I didn't have to look any further than the Code of Ethics subscribed to by the National Association of Broadcasters (NAB) whose members include the big three networks. "In order that television may best serve the public interest," it directed, "viewers should be *encouraged* to make their criticisms and positive suggestions known to the television broadcasters" (emphasis mine).

That seemed easy enough. So I decided that as soon as things quieted down after the Turn Off Week, I would personally contact network officials in New York City and share my concerns. However, once again I made up my mind not to stop there. In my reading I had come across a statement adopted by the United States Congress: "Individual citizens and the communities they comprise," it noted, "owe a duty to themselves and their peers to take *an active interest* in the scope and quality of television service"(emphasis mine).

That had made it abundantly clear that the viewing public was supposed to play a vital role in America's television broadcasting system. Naturally I thought that someone ought to try and help individual citizens to more effectively do their duty. And the more I thought about it, the more I believed that that someone might as well be me.

After much prayer I sensed that the God I had faithfully endeavored to serve as a pastor was calling me to take a step of faith. So I informed my congregation that I would be leaving them to devote myself full time to the cause of decent television programming. A few months later I moved my family from South-haven to Tupelo (we had lived there eight of the previous nine years), and I became executive director of a new citizens action organization that I named The National Federation for Decency.

Learning the Networks' Language

When I got in touch with ABC, CBS and NBC during the spring of 1977, I quickly discovered that my "turn off" week had not gone unnoticed. Thanks to the widespread media coverage, the name Don Wildmon was known all along New York's famed "Network Row."[9] That meant I had no problem reaching executives with impressive sounding titles like vice president of programming, vice president of broadcast standards and practices, or vice president of public affairs, both by phone and letter.

Almost without exception, these network officials were friendly, personable and willing to listen while I voiced my criticisms and made suggestions. Then, after courteously hearing me out, most of the TV executives I talked to would inevitably reply by paraphrasing what ABC's audience information manager, Dan Rustin, had told me.

First they'd say something like "as parents, as well as broadcasters, we share your concern over the content and standards of television." Next, they'd express their intention to "act with integrity and honesty, dedicated to the improvement of . . . programs and to the maintenance of the highest tastes and standards." And finally, they'd "assure" me that their network "will not be swept by fad or surrender those durable moral values that give our nation its spiritual foundation."[10]

After repeatedly getting the same response, it became clear that network officials were using the same words I used, but we weren't speaking the same language. To Dan Rustin and his peers, "durable moral values" meant something entirely different. Just exactly what they meant, I really wasn't sure. But I did know this: While Dan Rustin was assuring me that ABC would not undermine our nation's spiritual foundation, his network was unwrapping a new show called *Soap*. "*Soap*," said *Time* shortly after its premier,

will always be remembered "as the show that broke the TV sex
barrier by spilling uninhibited promiscuity into . . . prime time."

When I started the NFD I thought that if you appealed to a
person's moral base rationally and reasonably and explained the
progressive nature of something that is abhorrent, then that person
would respond. But during my Introduction to Television course
in the school of hard knocks, I found out that didn't work. As far
as the people at the networks were concerned, they *were* being
moral. They were paying lip service to me and being nice—but
they weren't paying attention to what I had to say.

I realized I needed to find some common language in which
they knew exactly what I meant and I knew exactly what they
meant—a language which would enable me to more effectively
communicate my concerns. However, to find that mutual language
I sensed I would have to do some homework on the financial end
of the television business and on how programming decisions are
made.

So I subscribed to television industry trade publications such
as *Variety, Broadcasting* and *The Hollywood Reporter*. I also kept
an eye out for television business news in the *Wall Street Journal,*
the *New York Times* and weekly news magazines. I soon learned
that Atlanta television station owner Ted Turner wasn't just whis-
tling Dixie when he called network television "the most profitable
business in the country."

Here's a brief overview of what I learned.

Between 1960 and 1974 the pretax profits at ABC, CBS and
NBC rose an average of 38 percent per year while American
business profits as a whole grew an average of only 12 percent per
year.[11] In 1975 a nationwide recession resulted in slower network
income growth. But when America's economy bounced back in
1976, the three networks benefited from the law of supply and
demand. More advertisers bidding to buy increasingly scarce commercial time meant an unprecedented boom in both advertising
revenues and profits.

As a result, by the summer of 1977, Wall Street analysts
estimated that each ratings point (the equivalent of 1.5 million
viewers) represented an additional $35 million in advertising
revenue—up from just $12 million two years earlier.[12]

The largest financial windfall was reaped by ABC. That's

because during the fall, winter and spring of 1976-1977, ABC had consistently clobbered rivals NBC and CBS in the nightly ratings battle. In fact, primarily on the strength of new "jiggly" shows such as *Charlie's Angels* and *Three's Company,* along with the block-buster miniseries *Roots,* ABC averaged an unprecedented three ratings points per night more than CBS and three and a half more than NBC. This ratings success, translated into dollars and cents, meant an extra $100 million in advertising revenue.

En route to becoming number one, ABC had knocked powerful CBS out of its customary top spot for the first time in 20 years—a flip-flop that did not go unnoticed by Wall Street investors. As CBS stock plunged from $62 to $46 per share during the summer of 1977, I followed the articles speculating how CBS Chairman William L. Paley would respond.

You see, since Mr. Paley *personally* owned 1.6 million shares of CBS stock, he had quickly become about $25 million poorer.[13] No one was surprised when Paley wasted little time wielding "his terrible swift sword," as *TV Guide* called it, upon CBS's top two television executives, Robert Wussler and Jack Schneider. They were replaced by the bottom-line conscious trio of James Rosenfield, Gene Jankowski and Robert Daly.

Meanwhile across the street at NBC, heads were rolling as well. NBC President Herb Schlosser made NBC TV President Bob Howard the scapegoat for that network's poor 1976-1977 third place showing and replaced him with Robert Mulholland. Schlosser also made major personnel changes in NBC's highly influential programming department.

The more I read, the more I realized that the idea of "service to the public" was a network television fairy tale. In this business where top level executives had almost no job security, what really mattered was the bottom line. To post large profits, satisfy stock-holders and hold on to their jobs, network executives had turned TV entertainment into a "slum" catering to "the lowest common denominator." At least that's what former CBS News President Fred Friendly said in a *Newsweek* article entitled, "Why Is TV So Bad?"

In other words, the language spoken most fluently by the handful of top-level TV executives who ultimately decide what shows reach America's living rooms is M...O...N...E...Y!

Since I had tried everything else and gotten nowhere, I determined that the networks were not going to pay attention to what the NFD was saying until we protested by hitting them where it hurts—in the pocketbook. And that meant focusing the attention of the newly-founded National Federation for Decency on the source of the six-figure salaries of network executives and even higher salaries of the actors and actresses who had become the "national heroes" of America's young people.

That source? The advertisers that gave the networks $3 billion a year to extol the virtues of everything from tennis shoes to toilet bowl cleaner.

3

Sears Shows Me that I'm Right!

It had become crystal clear that my only alternative was to shift the focus of the National Federation for Decency to the sponsors of gratuitous sex, violence and profanity. However, if we were going to encourage advertisers to stop sponsoring offensive material, we could no longer talk about "indecent" programming in general terms. We would need to cite specific examples and support our contentions with reliable research data.

I had learned this lesson the hard way a few years earlier while lobbying to change the administrative structure within the North Mississippi Conference of my church denomination. My plan made good sense from a stewardship standpoint and dozens of my preaching peers supported it. But I hadn't done my homework. I lacked the necessary facts and figures to fortify my case, and my proposition was easily defeated. Embarrassed, I vowed never to make the same mistake again.

I knew that accurately identifying programs containing the highest levels of sex, violence and profanity, and the companies that sponsor them, would be a major undertaking. It would require monitoring every minute of prime time on all three networks over an extended time period.

In order to do the job right, I realized I'd need a lot of help. So as the fall 1977 season approached, I wrote to a dozen or so NFD members who had said, "If there is anyway I can lend a hand, let me know!" I asked if they could round up 21 adults who would commit themselves to watch television one night a week.

Why 21? I figured I would need at least that many volunteers on each monitoring team. That's one person, per network, per night.[1]

Meanwhile I developed a method for recording the amount of sexual content and profanity in programs—the two areas those first NFD monitors would concentrate on since both the National Citizens Committee for Better Broadcasting and the National PTA were already monitoring for prime-time violence.

When eight of my letters came back with affirmative replies, I made plans to meet each team coordinator and personally train the 21 adults they had recruited in the how-to's of prime-time television monitoring. Though this meant traveling to distant places such as San Diego, California; Prairie du Chien, Wisconsin; and Houston, Texas, I felt it was crucial that each monitor know exactly what was expected of him or her.

To monitor the amount of sex, I taught them how to watch for and record instances of suggested sexual intercourse and sexually suggestive comments. Then I asked them to record whether or not the sexual incident or sexual comment occurred inside or outside of marriage.

Since camera shots of actual intercourse were still taboo on network prime-time programming, I instructed the monitors to mark the categories if (and only if), in their opinion, based upon the content and context of the show, sexual intercourse occurred.

Sexually suggestive comments, I explained, ranged from obvious direct quotes, such as, "let's go to bed together" to the more subtle double entendres. To illustrate what I meant, I used examples such as this one from an early episode of *Three's Company*: While examining an old miniature golf card, Mr. Roper, the show's impotent landlord, says, "I really used to score pretty good in those days."

"Times change," his wife sarcastically sneers.

"Maybe," he replies, "I need a better course to play on."

To tabulate the occurrence of profanity, the monitor simply needed to write down each expletive spoken in the program and record the number of times each word was used.

Finally, the results from each individual program or series episode were totaled. Sponsors of each program were assigned a score reflecting the amount of time they had purchased on a particular show or episode.

In early December I put the results recorded during the previous 15 weeks (some 864.5 hours of prime-time television were monitored) into a computer. The computer, utilizing a specially designed program, processed the data and revealed the shows with the highest and lowest sexual content, as well as the highest and lowest use of profanity. The computer also pinpointed the most and least frequent sponsors of sex and profanity on television.

The results confirmed what I had already suspected. During the study, 89 percent of all sex shown or alluded to on prime-time network television occurred outside of marriage. The programs containing the highest sexual content were no surprise either. Three of the four top spots were held by ABC's *SOAP, Three's Company* and *Charlie's Angels.*

But while our research produced no surprises in the worst programs categories, our data identifying advertisers who consistently sponsored this sexual and profane content made me do a double take. Right near the top of the list for sponsorship of both sex and profanity was none other than Sears, Roebuck and Company. I could hardly believe it. In fact I was so surprised, I checked and rechecked the numbers several times in case I'd made some mistake. But I hadn't. According to our figures, Sears was the third most prolific sponsor of sex and ranked fifth as a sponsor of profanity. (To add insult to injury, Sears had also placed third in the National Citizens Committee for Broadcasting's fall 1977 violence ratings, even worse than their fourth place ranking the year before.)

What irony! Sears brought to mind images of mom, apple pie and the American way. If ever a company epitomized traditional values, Sears was it. Yet in 1977, the world's largest retailer had become one of the biggest promoters of adultery, distorted and exploitive sex, violence and profanity.

When I contacted executives at Chicago's Sears headquarters and pointed out this incongruity, they didn't seem to comprehend what I was saying. As a matter of fact, they responded to my concern with nice-sounding letters just like the ones I had received from the networks. For instance, William F. McCurdy, Sears' vice president of public relations, assured me that his company was "deeply aware of its responsibility as a major sponsor" and had a "sincere concern for wholesome programming." He also told me that the Sears advertising program meets "the highest of standards" and "every effort is made to direct our advertising dollars toward family-oriented shows."

Charles A. Meyer, Sears' senior vice president of public affairs, in turn indicated that Sears strived to avoid "programs containing excessive violence or antisocial behavior."

That all sounded well and good. But I had a listing of every single ad Sears had placed during prime time for 15 weeks. Despite the fact that Sears officials felt they were already being highly responsible in their placement of television ads, the record showed that they had room for *major* improvement.

Since the Sears people essentially told me that I couldn't possibly know what I was talking about, I came to the conclusion that I had no other alternative but to speak to them in the language that they, like the networks, understood. On March 3, 1978, I announced that the National Federation for Decency would promote a nationwide consumer boycott of Sears. I had learned that television simply wasn't going to get any better until the viewing public could communicate its disgust to a major sponsor. A boycott would send a message to advertisers that they would be held accountable for their sponsorship. Committed to my decision, I even cut up my Sears charge card.

In my letter to Sears' chairman Arthur M. Wood, I explained that we regretted having to resort to such action. But Sears' ostensibly wholesome advertising policy and its actual advertising practices simply did not match up. And as long as Sears continues its present practice of promoting violence, sex and profanity, I said, it doesn't warrant the business of Americans concerned about television's deleterious impact.

The only response Sears' corporate executives made to my boycott announcement was to contact the Tupelo Sears store manager in an effort to learn something about this "Don Wildmon fella." In fact, if Wiley Brooks, Sears' assistant national news director, had not told *Advertising Age* magazine that they did not consider my complaints to be "legitimate," I wouldn't have even known if they had received my letter. So after waiting more than a month for a reply, I decided it was time to let Sears know that I meant business. Early in April, I announced that the National Federation for Decency would be picketing Sears' retail outlets all over the country on May 12. I also published a list of almost two dozen volunteer picketing coordinators from 14 states.

Sears Pays Me a Visit

At this point, Sears' executives realized they had a genuine public relations problem on their hands. And that's when I heard from Sears vice president of public affairs, Donald Deutsch. He called and asked if we could get together on April 19 in Tupelo. I was thrilled because I didn't have any vendetta against Sears. I simply wanted them to more carefully abide by their well-worded written advertising guidelines. And I knew a face-to-face meeting would help Sears understand why their actual advertising record was one of the worst in corporate America. I was especially pleased to learn that Ms. Kelly Seaton, a senior account executive with the Sears advertising agency, Ogilvie Mather, would be joining him.

Don Deutsch's initiative to dialogue left me with one minor problem, though: Where to hold the meeting? I couldn't hold it in my office because I didn't have one. In April 1978 I worked out of the dining room of our three-bedroom house. Its furnishings consisted of an old gray metal army surplus desk, a padded metal secretary's chair that had been patched with duct tape to keep the stuffing from falling out, a used IBM Selectric typewriter, a rotary dial telephone and a pre-owned A B Dick 326 tabletop printer. Therefore, I didn't feel my work space would be an appropriate setting in which to meet two high-level executives from one of the world's largest corporations.

The next logical meeting site was the Tupelo Holiday Inn. However, I was trying to make every precious dollar count and didn't feel I could justify renting a room. At that time, financial donations to the National Federation for Decency were trickling in so slowly I couldn't even afford to pay a part-time secretary, much less rent office space or a hotel meeting room.

In the end I decided to hold the meeting in the pastor's study of a Tupelo church I had formerly served—Lee Acres United Methodist.

I waited outside the church and greeted the Sears emissaries as they got out of their rented car. No doubt the setting seemed strange to these two professionals who normally conducted their business in plush offices on the 40th floor of Chicago's Sears tower and in Madison Avenue suites. Once inside, I introduced Mr. Deutsch and Ms. Seaton to two NFD board members and my older brother, Allen, whom I had invited to the meeting.

After some cordial chitchat about the natural beauty of northeast Mississippi, Don Deutsch got down to the business at hand. He said he hoped we could better understand our respective positions and perhaps even resolve our differences. As he spoke I could easily see how he had risen from the retail sales floor to the top echelon of Sears' corporate management. He was articulate and had a natural gift for putting everyone at ease.

Like his colleagues who had written me during the previous months, Deutsch explained that Sears shared many of the NFD's concerns about television. Then he spoke of Sears' strong commitment to sponsoring wholesome, family-oriented programming.

"For more than 10 years the Sears-Roebuck Foundation has been the largest contributor to the Pulitzer prize-winning children's program, *Mr. Rogers Neighborhood*," he said as he made his case. "Sears has been principal sponsor of *Winnie the Pooh* specials on network TV and we've also consistently been one of the top two or three advertisers of televised sporting events."

"My son Mark is probably the biggest fan of Fred Rogers," I replied with a chuckle. "And it pleases me to know that you've stood behind such quality, constructive programming. Indeed, I hope Sears will continue to do so. However, our beef with you is a direct result of your prime-time network advertising record."

"Let's talk about that record," Kelly Seaton interjected as she got up from her seat on the church office couch. Then, with the aide of several slick charts and graphs, she proceeded to illustrate how Sears had concentrated their advertising on shows appealing to family audiences. Like Don Deutsch, she was extremely articulate and would have been very convincing if I hadn't known better. I had the facts and figures from our fall monitoring right in front of me.

Ms. Seaton ended her presentation by emphasizing that since January 1977 Sears and her agency had jointly made a concerted effort to improve the Sears advertising schedule. "Last year, in an effort to reduce their violence rating, Sears gave us the word not to buy any more time on *Starsky and Hutch, Baretta,* and *Kojak*," she said. "In fact, since then we've pulled more than 100 commercials from programs that are unacceptable under Sears' strengthened advertising policy. Quite frankly," she concluded, "I don't understand why we made your worst advertiser list."

"Please understand," I responded. "Every advertiser was rated exactly the same way Sears was. You graded out as the number three sponsor of sex and number five sponsor of profanity based upon the shows you were on. The shows you stayed off of had nothing to do with it."

Then I explained why their sex sponsorship rating had been so high. I noted that Sears had helped pay for the highly criticized miniseries *Washington: Behind Closed Doors*, as well as made-for-TV movies such as *Once Is Not Enough, Sex and the Married Woman* and *The Night They Took Miss Beautiful*. "I don't know about you," I said, "but I would certainly have a hard time classifying all of these programs in the category of wholesome family viewing."

"Sometimes what one person considers offensive, another may not," Kelly replied. "So much of what's on television is in the gray area."

"That indeed may be the case with some of this material," my brother Allen chimed in. "But for millions of Americans this exploitation of sex, excessive violence and profanity is no longer in the gray area. It is patently offensive."

After we had a chance to air a number of our general grievances with the sad state of network programming, I specifically criticized Sears for their frequent sponsorship of ABC's *Three's Company*, NBC's *James at Fifteen*, and ABC's *Charlie's Angels*—the second, third and fourth most sexually-oriented weekly programs on television, according to our monitoring study.

"Wait a minute," Ms. Seaton interrupted. "I know we bought time on several episodes of *Three's Company* and *Charlie's Angels*, but some of the programs you've mentioned today don't sound right. Are you sure Sears was on all of those?"

"We've worked really hard to make sure our records are accurate," I answered. "If not Sears, Allstate Insurance sure was."

"Allstate?" Don Deutsch replied with a puzzled look on his face. "Allstate isn't Sears!"

"Well, who owns Allstate?" I asked him.

"Uh . . . we do," he answered after a slight hesitation. "But I can explain. They are a completely separate division. In fact, Sears doesn't have anything to do with their advertising."

"That's right," Ms. Seaton added. "Another agency produces Allstate's commercials and does their media buying."

"That doesn't matter," I replied firmly. "The buck has to stop somewhere. Individual policy holders may be in good hands with Allstate. But Allstate, the corporation, is in someone else's hands . . . and that someone else is Sears. That means," I emphasized, "Sears must take ultimate responsibility for Allstate's advertising record."[2]

As the meeting wound down Ms. Seaton explained some of the problems her agency faces when buying network time. Some ads, she said, must run on specific dates because they feature special Sears merchandise promotions—promotions that may only last for a weekend or a week. If Sears pulled a lot of their spots on those critical days because the network programming didn't meet their advertising guidelines, the success of those in-store sales campaigns would be severely jeopardized.

"That's a problem Sears, as the seventh largest advertiser on television, can help resolve," I noted as I looked Don Deutsch in the eye. "Right now the networks can easily ignore the public that they are supposed to be serving. But they can't ignore Sears. Your $80 million advertising budget speaks much too loud.

"You have told me that Sears is deeply aware of its responsibility as a major television sponsor," I added. "We're simply asking you to show us that you really mean that."

When the meeting ended, I had a decision to make. Should I cancel the picketing and call off the boycott as Don Deutsch hoped, or should I proceed with our protest against Sears?

The choice was tough because it was impossible not to like the two Sears representatives. My instincts told me that when they talked about Sears' interest in the well-being of America's children and families, they really meant it. Unlike my discussions with network officials, when the Sears reps and I used phrases such as "wholesome, family-oriented programming" and "exploitive, immoral programming," we meant the same thing. I sensed that Sears really did want to set a good example as an influential corporate citizen and a high-profile member of America's communities. I also had a gut feeling that high-level Sears executives like Don

Deutsch would make sure they did a better job of following their advertising guidelines in the future.

However, Don Deutsch could not *promise* that changes would be made in his company's actual advertising practice. He and Seaton also gave no assurance that Sears would pull out of programs containing profanity, exploitive sex or gratuitous violence. So with no commitment for improvement from Sears, I decided to go ahead with our plans.

On May 12 I flew to Chicago to personally lead the NFD protest effort at the Sears corporate headquarters. Dorothy Nopar and Dorothy Heidecker, our Chicago picketing coordinators, had recruited about 30 enthusiastic, hearty souls and shortly after 11 a.m. we began pacing back and forth in the shadow of the world's tallest building.

At first I felt very strange carrying a placard which screamed, "BOYCOTT SEARS" in big, bold, black magic marker letters. When I had watched civil rights and Viet Nam war demonstrations on television, I had never envisioned that I would one day be doing the same thing. In my mind, carrying a sign conjured up images of rebellion, disrespect for authority and even violence. That's something good Christians just didn't do. Yet, there I was carrying a sign which exposed Sears as a top sponsor of immoral sex and gratuitous violence on TV.

I must confess that every time a car on Upper Wacker Drive honked its horn, and every time a cluster of passersby stopped to stare, I felt a bit self-conscious. However, as I wrestled with my feelings, I realized that a few cold stares and jeers from hecklers was a small price to pay if my peaceful protest could help curb the proliferation of immorality in our society.

Three's Company and *Charlie's Angels* 'Aren't for Sears'

Just before noon a reporter from one of the Chicago papers stepped up and singled me out. "Have you heard?" he asked rather excitedly. "Sears just announced that they are pulling their ads from *Three's Company* and *Charlie's Angels* because the shows don't conform to their advertising guidelines. Your comments, please!"

I didn't really know what to say because the news had caught me off guard. Sears hadn't said anything to us. And since his statement sounded too good to be true, I was a little skeptical. However, a few minutes later I knew he must be right because television news crews from the three Chicago network affiliates showed up almost simultaneously.

The timing couldn't have been better. Since it was a beautiful spring day, people were filing out of the Sears office tower literally by the thousands on their lunch break. Many, out of curiosity, stopped to see what the commotion was all about. So as the cameras rolled, our little group of 30 actually appeared as if we were several hundred strong.

But downtown Chicago wasn't the only place where there was news in the making that day. The Sears announcement had gone out over the wire services. Consequently many of our 35 picketing teams positioned at Sears stores all around the U.S. became the centerpiece of local and regional news stories. Ironically, many of our protestors were treated to cookies and lemonade by employees of the stores they were picketing. And in some cases, local Sears managers and sales personnel indicated that if they didn't have to work, they would be standing outside with the demonstrators because they wholeheartedly supported our cause.

That evening, footage shot at the Sears tower was aired on the *NBC Nightly News*. The ABC, CBS, NBC and Mutual radio networks also reported on the story. Both The Associated Press and United Press International wire services also ran detailed write-ups of the Sears announcement and its correspondence with our picketing effort. As a result, the NFD "victory"[3] made headlines in hundreds of papers across the country. At least that's how the *Washington Post* and numerous other influential publications interpreted the events of May 12.

I was elated to know that our "victory" also sent some heavy duty shock waves bouncing around Network Row. Advertisers' pulling off of shows for various reasons was not out of the ordinary. But this was the world's largest retailer and one of America's most respected corporations bailing out of two of the most watched and biggest money-making shows on television. And Sears was being surprisingly candid about their reasons.

"We feel our participation should be in shows that can be viewed by the entire family," said Wiley Brooks, Sears' assistant national news director. And as Liz Klien of the Sears news division noted, a show known for "its excessive exploitation of women's bodies" (*Charlie's Angels*) and one whose whole story line seems to be "one sexual innuendo after another (*Three's Company*) don't really qualify as family entertainment."

Sears' national news director, Ernest Arms, said it more discreetly. "Admittedly these are popular shows," he noted, "but they are not for Sears."

The first after shock came when the brand new Sears chairman, Edward R. Telling, wrote to the presidents of all three networks to explain the Sears decision. Telling said he felt that discontent voiced by "a number of organizations" concerning television programming "merits thoughtful consideration" on the part of the networks. He also outlined "Sears' increasing concern" about news reports indicating that prime-time television during the upcoming fall season "will risk offending a large segment of the public."[4] Telling had specifically been referring to the uproar over shows with names like *Wayward Girls, Scandal Hall, Coed Fever, Beach Girls, Roller Girls, Legs* and *Spa* that had been piloted and were being considered by the networks.

The second after shock to the Sears *Three's Company* and *Charlie's Angels* announcement came two and a half weeks later. Thanks to the initiative taken by Don Deutsch and some of his Sears colleagues, approximately 20 corporate advertising executives met in Chicago on May 31 to, as a Sears spokesman explained, "reflect the business community's concern about television and the way it's going."[5] Discussion focused on the problems advertisers experience in finding suitable network programming to buy time on. Input was also given on strategies citizens groups such as the PTA and NFD could employ to help "improve programming."[6]

This history-making meeting made the networks nervous because Sears had invited only the top two dozen advertisers on television—corporations such as Proctor and Gamble, Coca Cola, Eastman Kodak, McDonalds, Ford, General Motors and General Foods—those who are most responsible for network profits. As far as the Sears executives knew, it was the first time large advertisers had gotten together specifically to address the problem of antisocial programming on national television.[7]

Publicly network officials responded to the Sears initiatives with statements such as "the rise in alleged sexual permissiveness on television is an unfair charge."[8] However privately, some of them recognized that Sears had a good point. In June, shortly after becoming president of NBC, Fred Silverman, the man who got most of the credit for ABC's meteoric rise to number one, quietly admitted to his colleagues that "there is a basis for criticism in the television medium."[9]

Then, noting that "there is too much opposition by advertisers and our various publics,"[10] Silverman proceeded to swallow $4 million in red ink and ground perhaps NBC's "most sexploitive show."[11] Called *Coast to Coast*, it was created to be an airborne version of *The Love Boat*. He also amputated *Legs*—a show focusing on the love lives of Las Vegas showgirls. Described by the *Chicago Tribune* TV critic, Gary Deeb, as "a contemptible piece of trash," *Legs* had been slated to replace *Grizzly Adams,* one of the most family-oriented programs on television.

Needless to say, I responded to the positive measures Sears had taken by canceling our boycott. In the months that followed, as I realized that "The Year TV Turned to Sex" would have been much worse had Sears not acted with such integrity, I became convinced that I was right. Advertisers and their dollars do indeed represent the most effective way to improve television.

Unfortunately I quickly discovered that not every TV advertiser shared Sears' zeal for cleaning up its advertising act. In fact, I learned that there are a whole host of corporations like Miles Laboratories (Alka-Seltzer), Warner-Lambert (Rolaids, Listerine) and Heublein Incorporated (Kentucky Fried Chicken) who seemed to care very little about being good corporate citizens. I determined that they'll sponsor practically anything and everything in their pursuit of the almighty dollar.

How can I make such a condemnatory accusation? I'll let the facts speak for themselves.

During the October 1978 week when Miles Labs sponsored the sex-filled movies, *Once Is Not Enough, Lifeguard* and *The Users* I voiced my disapproval. Miles Labs chairman, Dr. Walter Ames Compton responded by assuring me that they would "avoid placing their commercials on programs . . . generally in poor taste . . . with sexual behavior contrary to the generally accepted mores of American society."[12]

In the weeks that followed, Miles helped bring *How to Pick Up Girls, Betrayal* and *The Pirate* (see chapter 1) into tens of millions of homes. Since then, Miles Labs has almost never failed to make one of our "10 worst advertiser" lists.

Like Dr. Compton, Warner-Lambert's vice president for public relations, Ron Zier, also responded to my complaints about his company with meaningless propaganda. Though he boasted of Warner-Lambert's "long-standing policy to associate its products with quality television programming that does not exploit sexuality or violence or demean human dignity,"[13] the truth made his claim look silly. That season Warner-Lambert was the number one sponsor of *Charlie's Angels*.They also had been a top sponsor of *SOAP, Three's Company* and a whole host of sex and violence-laden TV movies.

The more the NFD monitored network prime-time programming, and the more I interacted with advertisers, the more I learned about the business of television. Thanks to efforts by the NFD and other concerned citizen groups, the most exploitive programs, such as *Anatomy of a Seduction* and *Flesh and Blood,* often wound up as "distressed merchandise." At least that's what the advertising community called programs that the networks had trouble finding sponsors for.

After awhile, I noticed that the same small cluster of advertisers, Alberto-Culver and Revlon in particular, tended to appear almost exclusively on the shows that the networks had to offer for fire-sale prices. So I started calling them "Buzzard Advertisers." Like the scavenger birds that converge to eat dead and decaying animals, these companies would hover around a rotten program and buy cheap time at the last minute. Blatant promiscuity, vulgarity, gore, horror . . . it didn't matter. These Buzzard Advertisers had only one concern: reaching the most viewers for the lowest price.

But while I was spending most of my efforts dealing with irresponsible advertisers, I was not completely neglecting the power brokers on Network Row.

The Networks Strike Back

I recall the Halloween afternoon when I found that navigating my 5'9", 155 pound frame through the revolving doors at ABC's New York headquarters was a bit tricky. That's because I was carrying a tire-sized funeral wreath that I planned to give ABC president Leonard Goldenson. Handcrafted by a New York City area NFD supporter, the flowered wreath commemorated "the death of constructive programming on ABC."

The wreath's symbolism came right out of the Old Testament. People in biblical times often wore sackcloth and covered themselves with ashes to mourn the passing of a loved one. But in New York such an outfit would have looked awfully funny. So I figured that a funeral wreath was the best way to express the idea in a modern context.

Once inside I saw about a half dozen ABC employees standing in the lobby. Some were talking while others patiently waited for elevators. However, before I had taken even a few steps, I noticed that every head had turned my way.

"I'm here to see Mr. Goldenson," I told the receptionist at the information desk, trying to act as confident as I could.

"Uh . . . why do you want to see him?" the young woman nervously asked, knowing full well who I was.

"I have a gift I'd like to present him."

The receptionist paused a moment. Then she said, "just a minute," as her fingers punched some telephone numbers. While she mumbled something into her headset mouthpiece, the security guard sitting next to the front desk got up and blocked my path to the elevators. He looked like he could have played linebacker for the New York Giants. He folded his arms, furrowed his brow, looked me in the eye and scowled. Though he remained silent, his body language said, "There ain't no way you're gettin' by me, Mister," loud and clear.

Not a moment too soon the receptionist finished her conversation. "I'm sorry, sir, but Mr. Goldenson is busy and can't see you," she said, just as I had expected. "You'll have to leave the building."

"But this is really important," I feebly protested. Then with a note of sarcasm I added, "I'm sure Mr. Goldenson would cherish these flowers for a long time."

"Hey, you heard the lady," the guard impatiently groused as he stepped toward me. "Get out . . . now!"

Since the fella probably outweighed me by 75 pounds, I wasn't about to verify whether his bark was bigger than his bite. So I did a 180 degree turn and hurried for the spinning door, being sure to stay one step ahead of ABC's security man. Once outside, I walked down the steps to the Avenue of the Americas sidewalk and heard a chorus of cheers coming from the 75 men and women who had joined me that day to picket the ABC headquarters.

It was October 31, 1978, the end of the worst month in "The Year TV Turned to Sex." I figured the November "sweeps" would bring even more immorality to the small screen. So I had called for a four-week nationwide boycott of ABC programming. As mentioned in chapter 1, ABC had become the ratings king by saturating their prime-time schedule with "jiggly" programming— a move that had resulted in record revenues and profits. Consequently ABC was the natural target for a Turn Off campaign.

By that fall of 1978 our NFD mailing list had grown from a couple thousand concerned viewers in 1977 to 10,000. Of course, I knew there weren't anywhere near enough of us to put even a dent in ABC's financial armor. But I was convinced that we could once again succeed in drawing attention to television's sex and violence problems, and maybe even bring some more folks into our ranks. That's why we were demonstrating in front of the ABC building that day. (We also had sign-carrying protestors positioned outside 30 ABC affiliates around the nation.) Even though they didn't officially acknowledge our presence, I'm sure everyone inside ABC's Ivory Tower knew we were there. And I don't suppose that it made them very happy. Needless to say, I didn't think I had much of a chance of actually seeing Leonard Goldenson. Still, I at least wanted to be able to say that I had tried.

When it was to our advantage, as was the case at ABC that brisk fall day, the networks went out of their way to ignore me and the NFD. But they didn't ignore us entirely. When it was to their advantage—such as when they had captive audiences of advertisers, fellow broadcasters or influential journalists who write about TV—network executives would often use the opportunity to strike back.

Once, Gene Jankowski, president of the CBS broadcast group, used a speaking engagement at an International Radio and Television Society luncheon to take numerous pot shots at the "one man shop called The National Federation for Decency." Several hundred "movers and shakers"[1] within the radio and television industry, as well as many influential journalists who cover the broadcast media beat, listened and laughed while Jankowski called my criticism of network television "a new cottage industry." "All it takes is a television set, a mimeograph machine and an opinion," he sarcastically quipped.[2]

A few months later, Jankowski mounted a full-scale verbal attack when he set foot on my home turf to address a group of influential advertising, television and newspaper executives in nearby Jackson—Mississippi's largest media market. After labeling me "a self-styled media reformer," he issued a stern warning: "Wildmon wants to take away your freedom of choice. He wants to have you live only by his values."

Then he blasted me and my organization for failing to recognize the "constructive contribution" of many programs and for inventing an image of the television medium which, he claimed, "the average viewer would not recognize. It is a medium that appears to present scarcely anything but prurience and profanity as defined by the NFD."

According to Jankowski, "CBS is not the network of *Captain Kangaroo,* Walter Cronkite and *60 Minutes*. And it is certainly not the network that pioneered the Reading Program concept in schools and the Read More About It book program project with the Library of Congress." Instead, he contended that the NFD's followers thought CBS's entire schedule offered "nothing but raw sex and gore, punctuated by four-letter words.

"This is in spite of the plain fact that television is by far the most conservative communication medium we have," he added. "It has not even approached the boundaries long since reached by movies, plays, magazines or books."

Of course, as soon as a Jackson area journalist friend mailed me a copy of Jankowski's speech, I could see that the CBS president was doing exactly what his NBC and ABC contemporaries had done many times before. Gene Jankowski and his network comrades were, to parody a familiar advertising campaign, painting themselves as "The Dodge Boys—The Good Guys in the White Hats." He spoke for, in the immortal words of his boss, CBS Chairman William L. Paley, "a very honest organization, trying our very best to serve the public in the very best way possible."[3]

In their well-crafted scripts, Don Wildmon, in stark contrast, was the bad guy—the man in the black hat. I was the renegade outlaw who was unjustly terrorizing Dodge City. Indeed, I was a dangerous menace whose loaded six-guns were constantly blazing, indiscriminately shooting everything in sight. Of course, the whole idea was to depict me as radical, crazy and completely out of touch with reality. If they could successfully convey that image, it would go a long way toward destroying my credibility. Then fewer people would pay attention to me, they believed. In the process the networks hoped to generate sympathy and play the part of the innocent, persecuted victim.

Unfortunately most of the media opinion leaders within the sound of Mr. Jankowski's voice that night didn't know that he had conveniently forgotten to tell them that I had often complimented *60 Minutes* and *Captain Kangaroo* in my monthly *NFD Journal*. In fact, I had even mounted a petition drive to try and stop his network from cutting their daily children's show starring the "Captain," Bob Keeshan, from its one-hour format to 30 minutes. Most people in Jankowski's audience also had no way of knowing that, contrary to their speaker's intimation, I regularly published a list of "the 10 most constructive shows." I constantly encouraged viewers to write appreciation letters to consistent sponsors of non-offensive, quality programming (this list included advertisers such as Eastman-Kodak, Kraft Foods, Quaker Oats, Timex, Hallmark and Goodyear). And I mounted letter campaigns to persuade the networks to keep constructive programs such as NBC's *Grizzly Adams*, *Disney* and many others on the air.

In addition to omitting pertinent information, sometimes network executives resorted to outright lies to distort the issue and perpetuate the good guy/bad guy facade to strategic audiences. For instance, during one speech to the Association of National Advertisers,[4] CBS Television President James Rosenfield fumed about some petitions I had circulated. Quite accurately, he said those petitions included "sweeping accusations against CBS for presenting programming which depicts sexual immorality, violence and profanity as accepted and approved lifestyles."

But he incorrectly defended a few of the specific programs I had made some of those charges against. "*Flesh and Blood* did no such thing," he vehemently denied. "*Scruples* did no such thing," he added. "Nor," he concluded, "has CBS ever done so."[5] Unfortunately most of the corporate advertising and ad agency executives in attendance did not know the truth about *Flesh and Blood*. Nor did they know about one of the early scenes in *Scruples*, based upon the Judith Krantz novel of the same name. Shortly after Billy, the lead character, drops the ashes of her cremated millionaire husband from a helicopter, she seduces the young, handsome chopper pilot. Just before they have sex, Billy tells him that her recently deceased husband "would not only approve, he would applaud."[6] If that isn't a depiction of sexual immorality as an acceptable lifestyle, what is? And I could cite example after example.

The Networks Sound the 'Censorship' Alarm

Though the specifics of the networks' vindictive incantations about me varied from occasion to occasion, one accusation remained constant throughout—the charge of *censorship!*

For example, James Rosenfield, in his speech to the Association of National Advertisers, acknowledged that "we all have the right to disagree." But then, indirectly referring to the NFD, he added, "the right to disagree is not the right to censor."[7]

Rosenfield was more direct in his response to the Sears *Three's Company* and *Charlie's Angels* announcement. "When an advertiser and a pressure group get together to exert economic pressure on the networks to take programs off the air, *it becomes censorship,"* he claimed (emphasis mine).[8]

It didn't matter that Sears never even hinted that ABC should stop airing the shows. Representatives of the giant retailer had simply said, "*Three's Company* and *Charlie's Angels* aren't for Sears."

It didn't matter that I had never once said that a network had no right to broadcast a program. Oh yes, I had often expressed my opinion saying that a network had *no business* airing a particular show, followed by my rationale. Occasionally, when I had good reason, I also encouraged concerned citizens to let their protest be heard before certain programs aired. But I had never said or even implied, "you can't air that show." Rather, time and time again I made the premise by which the NFD operated abundantly clear:

1. The networks have a right to spend their money on, and subsequently air, whatever programming they choose.

2. Advertisers have a right to spend their money sponsoring any program they desire.

3. Viewers have a right to watch any program *the networks and local stations decide they can see.*

4. Individual citizens have a right to spend their money on whatever products and services they wish.

Still, although we were simply promoting the practice of selective buying, the networks constantly sounded a false alarm, crying "censorship." I say false alarm because I've always understood censorship to mean the silencing of free speech or the written word by government decree or judicial fiat. Yet we had not asked for a single law to be passed. I had also thought that censorship meant the *prohibition* of communication before the fact. Yet, we had advocated nothing of the sort.

My methods, such as boycotts and Turn Off campaigns, stemmed from my conviction that Christian stewardship extends beyond what we leave in the Sunday morning offering plate. Christian stewardship includes how we spend all of our money. As an expression of my faith, I was only trying my best not to give my dollars to companies who consistently sponsored programming which I believed to be detrimental to society. And just as others were free to voluntarily join me in being better stewards of their resources, the networks were still free to air any show they wanted—including shows featuring exploitive sex and violence. I was simply letting them know that they would have to do it without my money.

The louder the networks chanted "censorship," the more I wondered just whom the networks were trying to kid. Whenever I tried to use economic clout to influence them, they would howl like wounded wolves. But they seemed to have no qualms whatsoever about applying financial pressure to get what they wanted.

For instance, in 1978 the three big networks added yet another minute of advertising to each prime-time hour. Westinghouse Broadcasting (Group W), claiming that the move meant more network profits at the expense of local stations, protested by threatening to run public service announcements instead. ABC, CBS and NBC responded by threatening the Group W-owned affiliate stations with the loss of NFL football—a big revenue producer. Faced with the prospect of losing millions, the Group W stations were bound to comply reluctantly with the network scheme.[9]

Not only did the networks play financial hardball, but many high ranking network officials also had publicly supported other boycotts . . . especially the National Organization for Women-sponsored boycott against states that hadn't ratified the Equal Rights Amendment. In fact, the Director's Guild Association, whose members provide most network TV programming, actually passed a resolution urging its members "and all members of this industry, [television/motion pictures] not to spend production money in those states."[10]

As far as I was concerned, all the squawking about me seemed rather hypocritical. Nevertheless it was very successful and it accomplished exactly what I believe network executives hoped it would. It generated a groundswell of sympathy toward them and widespread animosity toward me.

Of course, my being from Mississippi certainly didn't hurt the networks' cause. I mean, anyone who watches much television soon learns that Mississippians tend to be stereotyped as backward, ignorant bumpkins. Maybe I'm exaggerating a little bit, but not much!

To make matters worse, I was a minister from Mississippi who had named his organization The National Federation for Decency.

That conjured up images of a Bible totin', Scripture quotin', hell fire and damnation Elmer Gantry type who could perceive "pornography" in the Sears Roebuck catalog. In other words, I represented a network publicist's dream come true.

Needless to say, it didn't surprise me to read what supposedly sophisticated journalists were calling me in some of America's most respected and influential publications. I was the "Tupelo Terror," a "puritanical blue nose," a "Puritan prude," a "stupid redneck," a "nutcase" and the "reincarnation of Senator McCarthy." Here's my personal favorite: One syndicated columnist said I was a "mad fool starting his own version of the Spanish Inquisition."

I quickly learned not to let the negative stories and ridiculous name calling bother me. The frequent and ofttimes mendacious attacks by the networks didn't upset me either. Indeed, the louder network executives yelped, the more certain I was that our efforts were hitting the bull's-eye.

However, one aspect of the network propaganda campaign really irked me: their double standard. They'd think nothing of capitalizing on their ready access to the broadcast and print media, cut me to pieces and then cry "censorship." Then they'd turn around and practice what they accused me of doing. Not once did they give me an opportunity to tell my side of the story.

Taking their cue from the network brass, local television and radio stations frequently repeated the sweeping accusations, many of them false, against the NFD. But again, I was almost never allowed to answer the charges. As far as I was concerned, this use of a public medium to condemn a group of people without permitting them to respond was censorship in its ugliest form.

In the fall of 1978, the Academy of Television Arts and Sciences invited me to serve on a "Sexuality on TV" panel at their annual meeting. I enthusiastically accepted, thinking that I would finally get to tell both the press and people within the television industry where I was coming from. But a few days before I was to leave for Los Angeles, Ken Belsky of the Academy notified me that my invitation had been withdrawn. That seemed very strange because I was amply qualified to sit on that panel. I had done more research about the subject than just about anyone in America.

Though I'll probably never know for sure, I suspect that one of the networks had exerted pressure to censor my appearance.

Why? Perhaps network executives realized they would be cutting their own throats. If they gave me a forum in which to logically articulate my position, too many people might agree that it made sense.

A few months later, *TV Guide* sent Ed Williams, one of their free-lance writers, to Tupelo on assignment. At first I wasn't too excited about the interview, figuring he would try to make me look like a silly monkey, just as several other entertainment-related publications writers had already done. But as the interview progressed, I could see he was really listening to what I said. When I explained the premise by which the NFD operated, he wrote it down. When I reminded him of the networks' mandate to serve the public interest, he wrote it down. When I explained that voluntary selective buying was as American as apple pie, he wrote it down. And when he left, I sensed that, for once, I just might get a fair shake.

But no dice! Soon another *TV Guide* writer appeared on my doorstep. Oh yes, Ed Williams had written his story. In fact, this writer told me later, it was a good article. Though Ed indicated that the *TV Guide* editors claimed to be looking for a different angle, I got the impression that part of the reason they pulled his story was because its tone was too positive. It didn't fit the Don Wildmon image the television industry had been projecting.

The second story, which *TV Guide* ultimately ran, was more accurate than most. However, it gave a lot of readers the idea that the real reason I had launched my "vigilant . . . crusade" was to pad my personal bank account. At least that's what much of the hate mail I received afterwards intimated.

To say that the *TV Guide* experience disheartened me is an understatement. I began to wonder if I ever would get to address a national audience without my words being severely edited, adulterated or censored entirely.

Turmoil on the *Tomorrow Show*

That's why I was stunned the following August when I was invited to appear on NBC's late-night *Tomorrow Show*. It seems that the sparring over *Flesh and Blood* had attracted the attention of the program's host, Tom Snyder. So his producer had arranged for me to appear on September 5, 1979, along with Lee Rich, president of Lorimar Telepictures and an outspoken critic of the NFD.

Though I could hardly believe one of the three networks was finally giving me an opportunity to clarify my position on national TV, I wasn't surprised that the invitation came from Tom Snyder. He had always impressed me as kind of a maverick—a man with an open mind who didn't necessarily toe the company line on every issue.

Still, I suspected that someone high up in NBC's chain of command might find out and pull the plug on my appearance. Subsequently I wasn't surprised when I got a call a few days prior to show time indicating that Mr. Rich suddenly had some "scheduling difficulties." Nor was I surprised when Mr. Rich canceled out again just before we had been rescheduled on September 13.

Since it had become obvious that my appearance was dependent upon his appearance, I decided that I wasn't going to let this golden opportunity pass me by. As executive producer of *Dallas*, as well as many other programs and made-for-TV movies I had criticized, Mr. Rich was considered to be one of the most powerful men in Hollywood. And by that time I had learned enough about the handful of men in Rich's elite peer group to know that a big ego usually accompanies that power.

So I decided to capitalize on that weakness. I mailed out several press releases calling him a "leading producer of television sex and violence." Then I conjectured that he was "afraid" to debate me.

My not-so-sneaky strategy worked. The story received just enough press coverage to embarrass Lee Rich. And, lo and behold, two weeks later, I was seated less than a foot away from this short, stocky man on *The Tomorrow Show* set.

I suppose the producer thought our diametrically opposing viewpoints might set off some fireworks, so he had placed our chairs inches apart to heighten the tension. It's one of the oldest tricks in the television talk show business.

At any rate, after a brief introduction, Tom Snyder, as I had hoped, gave me ample opportunity to articulate both what the NFD really stood for and what we were trying to accomplish. So I emphasized, "We have consistently said that we are not opposed to TV sex and violence per se. We are opposed to the excessive and gratuitous use of it."

Then, after explaining our concern about many of the values network prime-time television was reinforcing night after night (such as sex portrayed and alluded to approximately 11,500 times per year, 88 percent of the time in a context outside of marriage),[11] I concluded, "The purpose of this public medium should be to uplift, to inspire, to encourage, to try and build a better society. Not to tear down the one we have."

At that point, Snyder (whom I had met for the first time on the set that night just before the cameras rolled) asked me to explain why the NFD "goes after the sponsors" of programs which exploit sex and violence.

"It's regrettable that we've had to do this," I answered. "But this was the only avenue left where our voice could really be heard.

"We learned early on that the only language network executives seem to understand is money," I continued. "So our whole philosophy, Mr. Snyder, is this: The advertiser's money is their money. And if an advertiser wants to spend their money on *Portrait of a Stripper*, which CBS is airing tonight, then they have that right. After all . . . this is America!

"But we also believe that our money is our money," I stressed, trying to emphasize the words *our money*. "And we certainly have the right not to spend our money on products manufactured by companies that consistently promote what we call low values."

"Now you quarrel with that," Snyder noted as he smoothly shifted his attention to Lee Rich.

"Yes I quarrel with it," the studio president replied, giving himself a moment to think. Then, after begrudgingly agreeing that I, as a private citizen, could express my opinion about television and spend my money where I liked, he said,"The place where I walk away is on the basis of any kind of blackmail.

"I was in the advertising business for many years," he explained with some feeling, "and the way you get to an advertiser is by hitting them in the stomach with threats that you aren't going to buy his product. One letter like that frightens an advertiser.

"Now I believe Rev. Wildmon has the perfect right to say 'I'm not going to buy your product,'" he went on with conviction. "But not to threaten them, not to threaten them."

As Lee Rich spoke I realized that he was well aware of the fact that he didn't have a very good argument to counter mine. That's why he had turned to terms like *blackmail* and *threaten*. He was using these buzz words like red flags to intentionally mislead viewers by distorting the issues. It also made my decision to not buy a particular brand of toothpaste sound as if I was lobbing a brick through a corporate headquarters window, so I interjected, "we have the right to spend our money wherever we so choose."

"Yes, but you don't have the right to spend your money any way you want," Lee Rich answered, this time his voice revealing some agitation. I knew he was getting flustered because about two minutes earlier he had agreed that I had a right to spend my money any way I wanted. Now he said I didn't. "You have the right to say anything you want," he stumbled on, sounding more and more confused, "But you cannot blackmail an advertiser by threatening him, 'I am not going to buy your products.'"

"That is the third or fourth time you've used the word blackmail," I noted.

"And I will continue to use it," Rich stubbornly replied.

As the studio president's comments became more and more contradictory, Tom Snyder surprised me by jumping in on my side. "Why can't Don say, if in his heart of hearts he feels something should not be on television for morality reasons or violence reasons, 'we are not going to buy the products of companies who have sponsored this program?'" he asked Rich.

"That is an American right," I interjected before the man sitting next to me could answer.

Rich, knowing that he was cornered, responded the only way he could. "You have a right to do that," he said. "I'm not saying you don't." But then, when Snyder and I tried to pin him down further, Rich backpedaled again.

"You use a form of blackmail with advertisers," he blurted out once more without explaining what he meant. "You cannot, you cannot do that," he huffed as if I were guilty of some major crime. "You just cannot do that!"

Then Rich gave his expert advice on what people should do if they object to a television program. "Nobody has to watch a show on television," he said. "You can always turn it off. Turn it off if you don't like it."

As Rich offered this grand solution for improving television, I thought, *I wish I had a dollar for every time I had heard someone say I should simply "turn it off."* But before I had a chance to offer my standard comeback—"that's like pulling down the kitchen shade when there's a man outside exposing himself, and then pretending he's not there"—the show's host cut away for a station break.

As the producer handed Tom Snyder some messages and the soundman readjusted my microphone, I decided to try to trap the Hollywood mogul sitting inches away into making another series of contradictory comments—comments that I believed would convince even more viewers that I wasn't just a lunatic from Mississippi. For bait, I'd quote two statements—one by veteran actor Tony Randall, the other by Lee Rich himself—reported by Kay Gardella, TV critic for the *New York Daily News*.

"Have you ever heard of a man named Tony Randall?" I asked Rich as the videotape rolled again.

"Yes, I've heard of Tony Randall," he replied, seemingly perturbed that I would ask such a stupid question.

"Tony Randall recently said that if the networks had their way, they'd put pornography on tomorrow."[12]

"Oh that's not so," Rich shot back defensively, "I don't care whom you're quoting. He's wrong!"

Rich had taken the bait. Now all I had to do was push the trap door button. So I asked him, "Do you produce a program called *Dallas*?"

"Yes, I produce *Dallas*," he responded. But this time he had calculated my next move, and beat me to the punch line. "And I told Kay Gardella that I'd put as much sex on *Dallas* as I can possibly get away with," he said, "because that's what the public wants and I'm going to try and give them what they want."

I hoped no viewer would miss the contradiction in Rich's denial of Tony Randall's "pornography" statement and his "I'm going to put as much sex on *Dallas* as I can get away with" affirmation. However, before I could point out this incongruity, Tom Snyder broke into the heated discussion to challenge Rich's ridiculous comment.

"Lee, what if they say the public wants to smoke pot?" he asked. "Let's put a few more pot-smoking scenes on."

"I don't put pot on!" Rich contended.

"But what if that's what the public wants?" Snyder asked with detectable cynicism.

"I have to work under all the rules and regulations put down by the networks," Rich countered, trying to defend his irresponsible declaration. "And they are very, very critical and they are very on the ball."

"I'll tell you something," Snyder said, looking his television acquaintance in the eye. "I thought I'd be in your corner on this one. But strangely enough I'm not.

"You see, I'm in a little competition with programs called news magazines," he continued. "There is a certain one airing on another network and every week you get the sexy star and you get the male strippers and you get the T and A under the aegis and guise of news broadcasting. I want no part of that competition."

The show's host wasn't finished. "There was a schedule airing Saturday nights on this network," he went on. "Wall-to-wall sex from start to finish. That's not the way I want to win hearts and minds and educate the people of the United States."

The more Tom Snyder talked, the more I wanted to pinch myself to make sure I wasn't dreaming. Not only was he helping me make my case, he was also candidly criticizing the network which wrote his paycheck. To my knowledge, this was the first time a person associated with any of the three major networks had publicly agreed that I had a good point and that my protest methods were honorable.

While listening to Snyder, I noticed that Mr. Rich appeared to be restless. In fact, I could actually see his face turn color as anger welled up inside of him. At least that's what his expression told me was happening.

That, of course, was not hard to understand. I mean, his assumed ally in the television business, Snyder, was taking sides with "the blackmailer." And since it was happening on national TV, I'm sure he found that doubly embarrassing. Consequently I figured Lee Rich soon would completely lose his composure. As it turned out, I was right. It happened just after both Tom Snyder

and I verbally jumped all over him when he contended that viewers
should be pleased even if only "one program out of five is good."

"You insulted me in this press release that you sent to
newspapers all over the country," he groused as he grabbed the
evidence from his sport coat pocket. "You called me a leading
producer of sex and violence," he continued as he flashed the paper
in my face. "Then you said I was afraid to debate you when I was
in the hospital. You owe me an apology."

Though Lee Rich's ice cold demeanor toward me when he
walked into the studio tipped me off, I now realized my news
release had accomplished its intended purpose and more. It had
made him absolutely livid.

But before I had a chance to respond, he shook the release in
my face again, this time even more vehemently. "You sent this out
for publicity," he fumed. "That is the only reason. You owe me an
apology."

I did my best to remain calm as I quickly gathered my thoughts.
"I was never told that you were in the hospital," I explained after
a brief pause. "And if that indeed was the reason for your scheduling difficulties, I fully apologize for my accusation. However," I
added, "I'm not going to apologize for the first part."

"That I'm a leading producer of TV sex and violence?" Rich
shot back. "Is that not what you called me?"

"Yes, sir!"

"Why did you call me that?"

This is bizarre, I thought. *The man has just admitted—somewhat proudly—that he tries to incorporate all the sex he can into
some of his programs. Now he's chastising me for having the nerve
to call him what he is.*

"Did you make the movie *Helter Skelter*?" I asked, knowing
that *Newsweek* had called it "lurid, sensationalist exploitation with
no redeeming value other than a lust for Nielsen points."[13]

"Yes, sir, I did!"

"Do you know how many people died when that program was
run?"

"Ah, that is malarkey!"

"No, sir. I'm talking about several deaths."[14]

"I tell you what I would do then," he huffed. "I would take it to the courts. That is malarkey. I am not a leading producer of TV sex and violence. You owe me an apology!"

By this time Lee Rich had worked himself into a frenzy. In fact, I was afraid he might even try to hit me. That's how mad he was. Fortunately Tom Snyder cut in to announce another station break and give him a chance to cool down. I was a little disappointed because I didn't have a chance to say what *Newsweek* had said about *Helter Skelter*. But in the end I guess it didn't matter because Lee Rich had all but made my point for me.

A few minutes later it was all over. I glanced at my watch and could hardly believe that an hour had flown by. As a matter of fact, I learned later that Tom Snyder's producer had bumped another guest because our segment was so lively. Though I was not surprised by anything that was said in the heat of the moment, listening to Lee Rich convinced me of one thing: If the Lorimar president's outlook represents the elite few who actually decide what airs, these guys would put just about anything on television, regardless of its potential damaging impact on viewers, if they thought it would make money. It was almost as if they were bowing to the god of money.

Bowing to the god of Money

Consequently I hardly batted an eyelash when I learned a short while later that CBS planned to headline their upcoming February "sweeps" line up with *The Exorcist*. One of the most controversial films ever released by Hollywood, it graphically tells the tale of a demon-possessed twelve-year-old girl and the struggle by two Catholic priests to exorcise the evil entity living deep within her.

I say graphically because the girl's face is grotesquely made up to look like it's swollen with blood, pus and welts. Her tongue darts in and out of her mouth in a serpent-like manner and she (or rather he, the demon) frequently screams obscenities in a gravelly bass monotone.

In addition to this horrifying imagery, the movie also includes an unhealthy mix of violence and sex. For instance, *Newsweek's* review notes that the crazed girl "grabs a psychiatrist in the groin, hurls her mother's boss to his death from her window, vomits (pea soup) on a priest and in the most curdling scene of all, masturbates with a crucifix."[15]

I remembered how, when the movie was released theatrically, the media was filled with news stories describing how queasy moviegoers routinely fainted or threw up in their seats.

Many news stories also reported that clergy, psychologists and psychiatrists suddenly had to deal with a rash of *Exorcist* viewers who were convinced that either they or their children were possessed by demons. After placing two terrified viewers "under restraint" and treating several others suffering from *Exorcist*-related trauma, Chicago psychiatrist Louis Schlan said, "There is no way you can sit through that film without receiving some lasting negative or disturbing effects."[16] Los Angeles psychiatrist Judd Marmor was especially concerned about the movie's potential to elicit irrational, destructive reactions from the "many disturbed people in our society."[17]

Tens of thousands of Americans who, like me, agreed with these eminent psychiatrists, were outraged that CBS planned to bring this nightmarish movie into the nation's homes. In fact, by the air date 7,000 callers had registered their objections with WCCO-TV, the CBS affiliate in Minneapolis/St. Paul. KOIN-TV in Portland, Oregon, fielded more than 4,000 calls. Similar protests occurred all over the nation.

Yet, as usual, CBS callously ignored a large segment of the public they are supposed to serve. Why? Because *The Exorcist* had been Hollywood's fourth biggest money maker ever. And as CBS Entertainment President Robert Daly told *Broadcasting Magazine*, "we thought it would clearly average a 40 share or above." A 40 share means that 40 percent of the people watching television at that particular time are tuned to that program. And a 40 share during the highly competitive "sweeps" period means money. *Lots of money.*

So for the sake of ratings points, CBS aired this "freak show," as *TV Guide* had described it, without even touching most of the gruesome scenes. Indeed, "the TV version retains the graphic shocks," *TV Guide* warned in its preview. "Only the profanity has been exorcised."

If that wasn't bad enough, in an effort to cash in on the publicity generated by *The Exorcist* television premier, CBS aired the movie's sequel, *Exorcist II: The Heretic* the very next night. Though it was preceded by the usual "viewer discretion is advised" warning, I wondered if anyone at CBS with decision-making power possessed any common sense at all. That's because CBS led into *Exorcist II* with two half-hour animated kids specials featuring Popeye and Bugs Bunny.

This irresponsible and somewhat diabolical programming decision was like an accident waiting to happen. Sure enough, tragically, but not surprisingly, it had deadly consequences.

Let me explain. When CBS abruptly shifted from animated slapstick geared for children to shocking satanic horror, 24-year-old Patricia Frazier and her four-year-old daughter, Khunji Wilson, as they had done the night before, kept right on watching. Little Khunji had only been frightened by the "scary" movies. At least that's what she told her preschool classmates. However, Patricia, who had a history of mental instability, could not get her mind off of what she had seen. And after a few days she convinced herself that her daughter was possessed by a demon just like the girl in the movies.

So what did this young Wichita Falls, Texas, mother do about it? She did the very same thing she saw the priest do on TV.[18] Patricia stabbed her unsuspecting girl several times with a butcher knife. Next she cut open Khunji's chest cavity and sliced the veins connected to the heart. Then, mimicking the movie scene, she literally pulled the child-sized heart out of her limp body. And finally, when she finished the gruesome, murderous ritual, she wrapped the organ in a blood-soaked wash cloth.[19]

At the trial, video tapes of *The Exorcist* movies were shown to the jurors. And according to the *Wichita Falls Times*, Patricia Frazier's defense lawyer and "several witnesses," including a Wichita Falls psychiatrist, said they "believe *The Exorcist* caused Frazier to cut the heart out of her four-year-old daughter."[20]

Though the young mother was eventually found not guilty of murder by reason of insanity, that didn't help her child. Precious Khunji was still dead. Dead because CBS executives had contemptuously refused to heed the warnings of numerous psychologists, psychiatrists and tens of thousands of concerned citizens. Dead because of CBS's insatiable thirst for ratings and money.

When a Texas NFD supporter first told me about this heinous crime—a crime that could justifiably be laid at CBS's doorstep—a gnawing feeling of disgust and revulsion burned deep into my soul. The shocking scenario reminded me of Lee Rich's closing remarks on the *Tomorrow Show*.

Echoing his peers in the top echelon of the industry, he had emphatically stated, ". . . I will stand up and defend television as long as I can breathe." Then, noting that the medium's good points far outweigh the bad, he reminded viewers to look up and down the program schedule and think of all the "wonderful things" he and others are doing.

Though with the exception of *The Waltons*, I couldn't think of anything *wonderful* that Lee Rich had produced, what he said didn't really bother me. It's what he didn't say that bothered me. I was getting sick and tired of listening to these guys take most of the credit for television's positive contribution to society, without ever accepting any blame for television's negative impact.

As usual, CBS officials made no apology whatsoever for airing *The Exorcist* and its sequel. When I confronted CBS with this cause-and-effect television-related killing in Wichita Falls, they refused to accept even a smidgen of blame.[21]

I suspected that if Khunji had died because of the Three Mile Island nuclear disaster, CBS might have devoted an hour special to her death, or turned her story into a made-for-TV movie. Or if she had died in the back end of a burning Ford Pinto, the victim of an exploding gas tank, all of America would have known her name; especially after *60 Minutes* finished exposing the tragic incident and pinning much of the blame on Ford.

But since CBS had played a pivotal role in provoking her killing, the network never even mentioned it. Just too incriminating, they probably thought. Reporting the truth might incur the wrath of even more lunatics like the "Mississippi preacher," a whole host of expert psychiatrists and psychologists and the 11,000 callers in Minnesota and Oregon.

With everything to lose and nothing to gain, it's not surprising that CBS censored the story of Khunji's death. Chances are pretty good you're now learning about the Wichita Falls "demon" murder for the very first time (unless you happen to live in northeast Texas or southern Oklahoma where the story received extensive local coverage.)

I know I sound bitter. But that's how I felt at the time. CBS had no business showing the two *Exorcist* films. Then, after what the experts feared actually happened, CBS completely denied their responsibility. To me, it seemed as though CBS was trying to get away with murder—literally.

So I made a little bit of noise, including reporting extensively on the incident in the *NFD Journal*; sending press releases and radio spots exposing the tragedy; and asking individuals and churches to help promote the observance of a Khunji Wilson Memorial Week. I figured if I could focus some attention on what had happened, the networks might think twice before again airing something that conceivably could provoke violence and even death.

Little did I realize what was brewing behind the scenes at the networks during my little call to accountability effort. At the time CBS held an exclusive option to buy network television rights to 1978's Oscar-winning "best picture," *The Deer Hunter.*

This violent and torturous film is famous for one nerve-racking scene in which American prisoners of war are forced by their Viet Cong captors to play Russian roulette with a loaded pistol. After screening the film, CBS officials decided not to exercise their option. Shortly thereafter, ABC and NBC also turned it down because they found that scene and several others to be "troublesome."[22]

Why? I speculate that all three said "no go" not because they found the scenes troublesome, but because they realized they'd be asking for trouble if they aired it. Big trouble!

You see, several people had already blown their brains apart mimicking *The Deer Hunter* Russian roulette scene they had seen in movie theaters or on the Home Box Office (HBO) cable network. In fact, as I write this, the Russian roulette death toll among *The Deer Hunter* viewers has reached 50. That's just from theatre, cable, independent station and video rental showings. I'd hate to even imagine what that figure might be if one of the three big networks had brought the film into virtually every home in America.

My fuss over Khunji Wilson may or may not have influenced their decision. If it did, I doubt CBS, ABC or NBC would ever admit it. But that doesn't matter. The point is, there are probably people alive today because the three big networks didn't show *The*

Deer Hunter. I'd like to think something good came out of little Khunji Wilson's tragic death. Maybe she didn't die in vain after all.

But it still wasn't enough. So far we had basically just been a nuisance to the networks, seeing minor victories only here and there. *What will it take to make them listen?* I asked myself. What will it take to stop them or make them scale back? I knew that if we were really going to change things we would need allies.

From 'Pipsqueak' to 'Ayatollah of the Airwaves'

As Khunji Wilson Memorial Week concluded and the fall 1980 television season began, I took a mental inventory of how the NFD had grown and what we had accomplished during the past three and a half years. For two thirds of that time I had been the NFD's only staff member. But thankfully, financial contributions eventually increased enough so I could hire a full-time assistant director and part-time secretary/office manager.

I also had been able to turn my dining room back into a dining room. The previous fall the NFD headquarters had moved into two second-floor rooms in one of downtown Tupelo's oldest office buildings. I always wondered what corporate executives were thinking when they visited us because the wall plaster was full of cracks, the ceiling leaked almost every time it rained and the old green carpet was so worn in places that you could actually see the sagging floor boards underneath. But since the cheap rent—$125 per month—kept our overhead expenses to an absolute minimum, the three of us didn't mind the musty smell and the roaches.

Larry Durham, my assistant, had assumed many of my responsibilities since coming on board. He kept busy recruiting and training our volunteer monitoring teams, which now included some 800 individuals in 16 states. Circulation of our tabloid-style

NFD Journal had grown by leaps and bounds as well. In fact, in just two years it had increased to over 100,000.

Thanks in large measure to the journal, tens of thousands of concerned citizens had become directly involved in the effort to make television programming more constructive. Most had articulated their disapproval to the networks or specific advertisers via letter or telephone. Several thousand more had helped the cause by attending demonstrations or walking picket lines.

As a result, many advertisers in addition to Sears had made major improvements in their TV sponsorship policies and practices. We had also succeeded in making many advertisers think twice before buying time on some of the more exploitive programs.

During those first three and one half years, as far as I knew, the networks never once failed to exercise their right to air what they said they were going to air. But quite often we had made them pay a price for their decisions to present destructive programming. Most recently, our protest had focused on the ABC movie, *The Woman's Room,* which *Chicago Tribune* TV critic Ron Alridge had called "a vicious . . . ruthlessly cynical attack on traditional marriage in America, male-female relationships, and much of family life." Inside information from advertisers suggested that our efforts had cost ABC about $2 million in ad revenue.

With all this in mind, I knew I should feel more encouraged. But I was having a hard time feeling positive about what we had achieved because my work constantly reminded me of what we *hadn't* achieved. And that made me feel downright depressed.

In fact, had my commitment to make television a more positive medium been weaker, I might have been tempted to bang out two letters on my IBM Selectric. The first, addressed to the NFD board, would have announced my resignation. The second, addressed to North Mississippi's United Methodist bishop, would have requested another appointment as a local church pastor.

I was especially frustrated because it had been a long time since we had made any discernible progress with the top "Least Constructive" and "Buzzard" advertisers. One typical example was our stalemate with Heublein Incorporated. This liquor company, which owned Kentucky Fried Chicken, had pledged "to be a good citizen and to be socially responsible in the development of national advertising."[1] Unfortunately our extensive efforts to encourage this Connecticut-based conglomerate to abide by its own standard had fallen on deaf ears. They didn't even acknowledge our thousands of protest letters with a customary public relations department word-processed response.

Even after NFD supporters had simultaneously picketed about 100 KFC restaurants in 27 states, Heublein chairman Stuart D. Watson made his company's intentions very clear. He indicated that we could make all the noise we wanted, but they would continue sponsoring programs like *Anatomy of Seduction, The Woman's Room* and anything else they darn well pleased.[2] Oh, he didn't quite say it that way. But I could see that's what he meant.

I sensed that the only thing that could change Mr. Watson's mind was a hard-hitting economic boycott against his chicken restaurants. However, our tiny army of concerned citizens was far too small to pull that off. Even more discouraging, I couldn't have promoted a KFC boycott even if I had thought it could work. For some reason, NFD financial support had dropped off considerably during that long hot summer. We had not been able to print and mail our *Journal* for an unprecedented three straight months. And it's kind of hard to publicize a boycott campaign when you can't even afford to communicate with your core constituency.

I had so few resources and such big goals that I felt like a mosquito trying to kill an elephant. The task seemed impossible. One afternoon when I was feeling unusually down, I sorted through a pile of almost past due bills totaling $5,000. That depressed me even further. As I left the office, I didn't have any idea how we would cover those expenses.

However, that evening, a successful Mississippi businessman tracked me down on my home phone. He explained that he had recently attended a conference where several well-known Christian leaders discussed America's growing moral malaise. "Since I know your organization is not only talking about our moral decline, but is really trying to do something about it," he said, "I mailed you a check earlier today."

The amount? Five thousand dollars on the nose! I don't think it was a coincidence. I believed it was a confirmation from the God I serve that I was indeed on the right track.

And yet there were still so many problems. Our initial fall 1980 monitoring reports revealed that prime-time network television had taken yet another giant step backwards, not forward as I had hoped. The reason for this development was no secret.

One ratings point was now worth approximately $60 million—almost double what it had been just three years earlier.[3] Consequently top level executives along Network Row had once again turned to "sexploitation" to bolster viewership and garner record profits.

The network media moguls also realized that their days of reaping these windfall profits were numbered. The advent of cable television meant that millions of people would soon be selecting from programming options available on a host of upstart networks. That would mark the end of an era for ABC, CBS and NBC. No longer could they automatically bank on a combined 90 percent audience share and the giant ad revenues that went with it.

So they "were grabbing what they can while they can."[4] At least that's how a number of Wall Street media watchers explained the latest trend toward even more sleaze.

As a result, new programs such as CBS's *Secrets of Midland Heights* cluttered the prime-time schedule. The executive producer of *Secrets* had bragged that the show would be "hot stuff" and make him the "porno king of Hollywood."[5] And who was this new self-proclaimed "porno king"? Why Lee Rich, of course! Needless to say, it made me especially glad that I had refused to apologize for calling him "a leading producer of sex on television" when we had appeared together on the *Tomorrow Show*.

Lee didn't win any award for creativity in developing the first *Secrets of Midland Heights* episode's plot. According to "Sex On TV: Open Season on Smut," a commentary by *Washington Post* TV critic Tom Shales, it revolved around a teenage girl who "embarked on an expedition to lose her virginity on a hay ride." That sounded an awful lot like the premier of ABC's *It's a Living* a month or so earlier in which a young waitress, according to Shales, "embarked on an expedition to lose her virginity at a mountain retreat."

What hurt was knowing we had done our best but were powerless to stop Rich and others from raising the flood waters of TV sex and violence even higher. I had to admit that the networks still regarded us as little more than a nuisance—a minor inconvenience. I realized they would not take our pleas for decency seriously until our efforts had a significant financial impact on programming night in and night out. But to do that we needed numbers. We needed to multiply our ranks many times over. Accomplishing that, however, was easier said than done. I had already gone to the most likely source for those numbers—my church denomination and others like it—and had gotten virtually nowhere.

Simple logic had led me to believe that the organized church would be quick to support our cause. I had assumed that denominational leaders would be gravely concerned about the proliferation of immoral images bombarding their church's members and all Americans.

However, when I approached high-ranking officials in my denomination and numerous others, I found out how wrong I was. Much to my disappointment, most of these church leaders were so focused on building buildings, running programs and attending conferences, they were oblivious to society's loosening moral standards and the corresponding implications. They saw little reason for their churches to address the issue of sex and violence on TV (see chapter 10).

I also discovered that many church leaders believed what the networks and press had been saying about me and the NFD. They figured that since a respected network television official had described us as "crazy, rabid people,"[6] we must be crazy, rabid people. And what respectable person or group wants to identify with a bunch of lunatics?

Teaming Up With Jerry Falwell

With little hope for help from the institutional church, I wasn't sure where to turn next. But in November 1980, I had a brainstorm as I watched and read several national election postmortems. The scope of Ronald Reagan's White House victory, combined with the unusually large Republican gains in Congress, caught many political pundits by surprise. And as these professional Washington watchers groped for an explanation, one name almost always surfaced: Jerry Falwell!

In magazine articles with titles like "Jerry Falwell's Marching Christians" and commentaries by network political reporters, the analysis was pretty much the same: Millions of fundamentalist Christians belonging to and sympathetic with Jerry Falwell's

Moral Majority had come out of hibernation at the Baptist preacher's prompting. They had voted as a block, flexing their muscle at the polls.

End result? A Reagan landslide and a Republican majority in the Senate!

I believed that the press was oversimplifying what had happened. But I could understand how reputable journalists had drawn that conclusion, especially journalists with little understanding of the broad diversity within the Christian community.

Reverend Falwell had seemingly come from nowhere, bursting onto the scene in the late 1970s. His *Old Time Gospel Hour* TV program was aired in practically every media market in the country. And he was continually popping up on nationally syndicated news and talk shows.

He is extremely articulate and fast on his feet in front of cameras and microphones. He also possesses a warm, disarming personality which often mellows hostility. Indeed, Jerry can more than hold his own with any good interviewer in broadcasting—be it Phil Donahue, Ted Koppel or Larry King.

In addition to preaching the gospel message of hope and eternal life, he had strongly encouraged people he called "God-fearing moral Americans" to get involved in the political process. "Campaign and vote for pro-life, pro-family oriented candidates," he told them.

As a result, he was frequently criticized by the press both for his "right wing" views and for "mixing religion and politics." Still, I sensed that Jerry Falwell was well-respected by his journalistic foes. I could also see that the networks and media in general viewed him as an important national figure—a man dedicated to serving Jesus Christ with incredible influence amongst his constituency.

What a revelation! Jerry Falwell had ready media access to call God's people to action. I, in turn, had established communication channels with advertisers, as well as the mechanism to identify the least constructive TV shows and their sponsors. If Jerry and I could launch a *joint* venture advocating constructive television, major advertisers and the networks just might start taking us seriously.

Of course, I realized that our views on every theological, social and political issue didn't entirely mesh. After all, Jerry Falwell is an Independent Baptist and I'm a United Methodist. But we had a common cause in this critical hour. I had frequently heard him voice his disgust with the sad state of network television programming. And on this important, high-priority issue, I knew our views were in perfect harmony.

So I wrote the famous Baptist preacher and suggested that we join forces in a concerted effort to make television better. I explained that the constituencies represented by his Moral Majority, Inc. and my National Federation for Decency would provide a solid foundation for such an undertaking. Then I shared my idea of inviting any and every organized group—be it church-related or secular—that concurred on this one issue to join us. That way we could add much more bite to our bark.

Within a week, Jerry Falwell sent me an "I like your idea, let's proceed" response. A few days later I was in Lynchburg meeting with Moral Majority Vice President Dr. Ronald S. Godwin. Ronald and I hammered out a master plan, including shared leadership responsibilities, for what we would call The Coalition for Better Television. Then we met with Reverend Falwell.

He heartily approved of our strategy, especially its emphasis on teamwork and the pooling of resources. He also pledged to personally contact several organizational leaders, including Phyllis Schlafly of The Eagle Forum, to invite them to join our Coalition. In turn, I promised to get in touch with some of my acquaintances, including Beverly LaHaye of Concerned Women for America and Judie Brown of the American Life Lobby.

By late January, some 150 regional and national organizations, representing approximately four million families, had joined our Coalition and pledged their support. On February 2, 1981, we held a press conference in Washington, D.C. to publicly announce our plans.

Jerry Falwell had a last minute scheduling conflict and couldn't be in Washington that day, so I did most of the talking. As I looked into the bright lights of the ABC, CBS and NBC cameras and addressed reporters from the wire services and America's most prestigious newspapers, I quoted Tony Randall and Lee Rich to illustrate television's sick condition.

Next I quoted the likes of Hubert Humphrey, Bing Crosby, Red Skelton, Lucille Ball, Screen Actors Guild President Kathleen

Nolan and columnist Erma Bombeck to demonstrate that the Coalition was not alone in its concern. And finally, after explaining that our Coalition for Better Television represented the largest number of groups and individuals ever to join hands to promote constructive programming, I said the forceful words that would be featured in the extensive newspaper press coverage we received.[7]

"Starting next month the Coalition will monitor programs for their violent, sexual and profane content," I explained. "This monitoring will continue through the months of March, April and May. Then, sometime in June, the Coalition will select one or more advertisers who rank among the top sponsors in these three categories and ask for a one-year voluntary boycott of all their products.

"We deeply regret that such an action is necessary," I continued. "But until now the networks have responded to our pleas for reason, restraint and responsibility with an arrogance and indifference rarely matched in the history of America."

I concluded by predicting that the networks would respond with the only reply they knew—"by crying censorship." But, as I pointed out, we all have the right to spend our money wherever we so desire. Voluntary selective buying could hardly be construed as censorship.

During the next several weeks, support for our Coalition far exceeded my expectations. Thanks in part to the nationwide press coverage we received, the number of groups and organizations joining our ranks skyrocketed. In a few short months our membership list grew to more than 2,000 groups. This influx of enthusiastic support enabled us to train more than 3,000 new volunteer monitors for the spring 1981 monitoring period.

The press, largely because of Jerry Falwell's participation, continually described the Coalition as more or less an extension of The Moral Majority. But in reality, that was hardly the case.

Just after its inaugural press conference, the Coalition received a strong editorial endorsement from *Our Sunday Visitor,* the largest Roman Catholic weekly publication in America. Soon some 200 Catholic parishes and lay organizations had pledged to support the Coalition's efforts. Thousands of concerned Catholic dads and grandfathers were participating through their Knights of Columbus Chapters, too.

I also was pleased by the support from people belonging to my own denomination. United Methodist local churches and Methodist men's and women's groups by the hundreds promised to stand with us. Lutheran, Presbyterian, Episcopalian, just about every kind of Baptist, Assembly of God, Church of Christ . . . we heard from church-related groups and churches representing the entire spectrum of the Christian community. Some Mormon groups even chose to stand with us.

At the same time, a host of non-religious professional and social organizations also said "count us in." We had nurses' associations, lawyers' associations, right-to-life groups and even Farm Bureaus! As far as I knew, the Coalition for Better Television represented the broadest and most diverse array of organizations ever to unite for one cause. As I reflected on how quickly things had come together, I recognized the intervention of God's sovereign hand.

This solidarity did not go unnoticed by television advertisers. The Coalition's upcoming boycott had gotten their attention like nothing we had ever tried before. Larry Durham and I were soon spending more time than ever interacting with advertisers and ad agency representatives both by phone and face to face.

"Where do we stand in your monitoring?"

"What specific shows seem to be getting us in trouble?"

"Help us better understand your process for determining the least constructive programs?"

We were more than happy to give a detailed answer for each question. With only a few exceptions, we were no longer initiating these discussions. Advertisers, literally by the dozen, were now getting in touch with us.

We heard from companies who normally rated high on our "most constructive advertisers" list. Some simply called to check in, others to let us know they were striving to be even more conscientious in their program selection.

We also heard from other advertisers who had plenty of room for improvement, yet were in no danger of being our boycott target. Many made what I believed were genuine promises to more stringently follow the adequate advertising guidelines they already had in place.

And finally, we heard from several of the companies that had consistently ranked high on our "least constructive advertisers" list. In the past most had brushed aside our frequent pleas to stop sponsoring offensive shows. But now that it looked like they might face economic consequences, they became willing to talk and listen.

During one unusually hectic week, six perennially poorly-rated advertisers—Miles Laboratories; Beecham Products (Aqua Fresh Toothpaste); Esmark (Playtex undergarments); Warner-Lambert; Smith Kline, Inc. (Contac); and Sterling Drug (Bayer Aspirin);—sent representatives to Mississippi. Five of these six companies courteously heard us out and indicated that they would at least try to do better. The one exception was New Jersey-based Warner-Lambert.

Throughout our brief meeting, Warner-Lambert's vice president for public relations, Ron Zier, sarcastically and arrogantly implied: We're out to make as much money as we can . . . and if that means sponsoring The Exorcist, Scruples, SOAP and Three's Company, so be it. Nobody tells us how to run our business.

When our meeting had ended, Larry Durham and I accompanied Zier and his Warner-Lambert colleague outside. Then, just before getting into his car to return to the airport, Zier refused to shake my outstretched hand. Instead, he sucked in his stomach, straightened his shoulders, clicked his heels and raised his right arm 145 degrees.

I glanced at Larry in time to see his jaw drop in disbelief. A few seconds later when their car pulled away, Larry and I had a good laugh. And even today, whenever I see some famous sports personality spell relief R...O...L...A...I...D...S, I usually think of Mr. Zier and chuckle. His "Heil Hitler" salute remains the most unprofessional behavior I've ever seen a high-ranking corporate official exhibit.

At any rate, all totaled, that spring we had detailed discussions with over 50 television advertisers representing yearly television advertising revenues somewhere in the neighborhood of $2 billion. And as I've frequently emphasized, in the television industry, money talks. Seven weeks after our inaugural Coalition press conference, I realized we had made unprecedented headway in our struggle to make this powerful public medium more of a public medium. That's when *Advertising Age,* the most widely read publication in the advertising business, headlined its page one story: "SCRAMBLE UNDER WAY FOR CLEAN TV SHOWS."

"Score one for the Coalition for Better Television," the article began. Then it noted how "the resurgence of group pressure had made TV users more wary of program content." That wariness, *Advertising Age* explained, had suddenly made the "clean shows" very popular with advertisers. The not-so-clean shows, in turn, had become very unpopular.

Indeed, ABC Vice President Alfred Schneider told *Variety*, a Hollywood trade publication, that there had been a big increase, "at a large rate now,"[8] of network advertisers who want out of their prime-time buys.

The immediate impact of this behind-the-scenes maneuvering on television programming far exceeded my expectations. That spring the networks lost money hand over fist on many of the shows we objected to most. They were forced to cancel programs that, under normal circumstances, would have been renewed for the coming season.

The most notable Coalition-related casualty was ABC's filthy situation comedy, *SOAP*. Of course, ABC publicly contended that they had pulled the plug on *SOAP* because the ratings were down. And they were—slightly. But it was still one of the more watched programs on television. The real reason for the show's cancelation, according to the *Los Angeles Herald Examiner*, was because 46 more sponsors had refused to support it.[9]

Naturally, good news like that made me feel like we were finally making significant progress. I was pleased even more when I learned that canceled shows were not being replaced with equally offensive new shows. As the radical change in advertiser buying habits began wreaking havoc with the projected profit margins on sex- and violence-laden programming, the networks sent Hollywood producers a clear two-part directive:

1. Tone down "risqué or violent program elements."
2. Temper the new shows with "more qualitative values."

At least that's what *Advertising Age* reported as it explained that it was no longer business as usual within the television entertainment industry.

But I was most pleased when I learned we had successfully altered the process used to select new programs. Alan Savinson, director of television for NBC Entertainment, told *Variety* that the Coalition had had "noticeable" impact on programming development at all three networks. Then he mentioned that NBC had rejected some "big proposals" due to the recent "backlash against immoral subject matter on prime time."

Throughout the spring, it seemed like every issue of *Broadcasting, The Hollywood Reporter, Variety* and *Advertising Age* included one, two or more stories on the Coalition's stunning influence. And the more I read . . . and the more I listened to advertisers . . . the more amazed I was by what was happening.

I kept thinking about how arduously we had struggled for four years. Each tiny step down the mine-laden path toward constructive television had required a Herculean effort. But now, thanks to a respected Baptist preacher and some teamwork, with God's help, we were influencing a significant portion of the entire prime-time line up.

But here's what amazed me most. The newly-formed Coalition for Better Television hadn't done one single thing. We had merely announced that a voluntary boycott of sponsors was imminent. That's all!

From Small-Time Outlaw to Big-Time Bad Guy

Yet that one simple announcement had America's broadcasting community plenty worried. No, that's too mild a description. Panic-stricken is more like it. In fact, *People* magazine said that the men and women working on New York's Network Row viewed our campaign as "nothing short of apocalypse now."[10]

Almost from the beginning, the entire television industry was up in arms wondering what to do. A few weeks after we launched the Coalition, the National Association of Television Program Executives scheduled a "Sex on Television" panel at their annual convention, which was attended by 4,000 broadcasting professionals.[11]

A few weeks after that, the Academy of Television Arts and Sciences joined the Caucus of Producers, Writers and Directors in a hastily organized special three-day conference. Called "The Proliferation of Pressure Groups in Prime Time," it was designed to "help the industry [television] develop a more thoughtful and coherent means of responding" to outside interests.[12]

The conference took place in Ojai, California, a mountain resort community far from the hustle and bustle of Hollywood. Just about everybody who was anybody in the TV entertainment business was there.

Lee Rich was there. So was Norman Lear, the man who made Archie Bunker America's favorite bigot. Production company president Grant Tinker and *Roots* producer David Wolper were there as well as Director's Guild of America President George Schaffer and Mel Shavelson, president of the Writer's Guild of America.

Naturally, these Hollywood moguls didn't want the nation to know that the Coalition had them on the run. So they distributed a list of some 132 groups that supposedly exerted some influence on TV programming—groups such as The American Psoriasis Society and The American Egg Board, which had no doubt been striking *terror* in their hearts for years.

Of course, the real reason for their get-together was to discuss the fallout generated by an atomic explosion called The Coalition for Better Television. "Wildmon wasn't just a harmless pipsqueak of a preacher anymore," explained Ed Bark of the *Dallas Morning News*.

I wish I had been invited to Ojai. That way I could have eased everyone's anxiety when producer-writer Michael Ross exclaimed, "the era of fear and intimidation is back with us."[13] Of course, Ross had been referring to a turbulent period during the 1950s. At the time, many entertainment industry professionals had been pegged as "communist sympathizers." I also could have responded when Richard Gilbert intimated that our Coalition was comprised of many "fundamentalist leaders . . . who are willing to lie and cheat and do anything they have to in dealing with the enemy."[14]

Instead, I learned about Ojai from news reporters who had attended the proceedings. Then I got the low down from a conference participant who had actually spoken with me on occasion and knew I wasn't Atilla the Hun.

One Grant Tinker statement, quoted in the *Los Angeles Times*, particularly caught my eye. It explained why so many Hollywood big shots had cleared their busy schedules to meet for three days: "It's [the Coalition] getting our attention because it is perhaps unmanageable and has to be dealt with," he said. "The others, you can forgive the term, are manageable."[15]

I suppose some folks might accuse me of reading too much between the lines. But I think Tinker was saying, As long as concerned citizens keep their distance and don't mess with our mastery of the airwaves, we don't mind if they do their thing. But now that a citizen group is significantly impacting programming content, we've got a serious crisis on our hands. Hence, it's time for a war council!

In the eyes of Hollywood producers and network officials, Don Wildmon was no longer just a small-time renegade outlaw taking potshots at programming. I had now graduated, with honors, into the ranks of modern history's big time bad guys.

Newsweek said that TV executives now referred to me as "the Ayatollah of the airwaves." Lee Rich, perhaps taking his cue from Warner-Lambert's Ron Zier, likened me to "Adolf Hitler."[16] Indeed, following my alliance with General Jerry Falwell and his "Fundamentalist" army, most TV industry power brokers envisioned me as the head of an evil empire trying to forcibly take control of their private domain.

Initially our Coalition announcement, combined with its sudden alteration of advertising buying patterns, took the networks by surprise. It seemed to take them a few weeks to assess the damage and regroup. But then, like any powerful army commissioned to protect and defend "threatened" territory, they launched what can aptly be described as a full scale counterattack.

First, all three networks began a letter-writing campaign to advertisers. Essentially, they asked sponsors to join them in resisting what NBC had called "the current resurgence of special interest groups who would force the industry to meet their individual needs."[17] NBC's letter also included an offer to share its "expertise" in working with pressure groups.

CBS carried this basic battle strategy a step further. James Rosenfield began making personal phone calls to a select group of corporation chairmen. Not surprisingly, Rosenfield just so happened to call companies we had listed as either top "least constructive programming sponsors" or top sponsors of sex, violence or profanity.

The second phase of the networks' counteroffensive was

directly linked to dollars and cents. Once the rush to non-offensive programs was on, the networks wasted little time jacking up their ad rates for wholesome shows. They hoped this would discourage sponsors from pulling off or staying off shows with exploitive elements.

In fact, by the time the May "sweeps" period rolled around, the networks had actually set up a two-tier program pricing structure. *Broadcasting Magazine* reported that one level included programs "likely to offend the Coalition." The other, which advertisers told me was about 25 percent more expensive, included shows that *Broadcasting Magazine* said "seem safe from boycott threats."[18]

Though perfectly legal, I viewed this new wrinkle as "free" enterprise at its worst. Of course, the networks argued that their action simply reflected the basic law of supply and demand. But as far as I was concerned, they were guilty of highway robbery.

Remember, advertisers desiring to reach multiplied millions at one shot still had but three alternatives: ABC, CBS and NBC. And since the networks only offered a limited amount of time on a very few quality, constructive programs, conscientious sponsors had little choice except to hand over the extra cash. In anger-inspired press releases I called this new split-level pricing policy a "morality tax" because it penalized advertisers who had decided to take the high road of corporate responsibility.

As you can see, phase one and phase two of the networks' counterattack more or less dealt with damage control. Their strategy was designed to stop the mutiny among sponsors and minimize ad revenue losses.

Phase three, however, was aimed directly at the Coalition for Better Television and its leaders—namely, Jerry Falwell and me. This is the battlefield where the networks, along with their comrades in arms, the Hollywood TV producers, concentrated most of their firepower. I call this the TV industry's war with words.

As I had predicted at our February 2 press conference, their opening salvo of overheated rhetoric sounded the censorship alarm. Then, as their Coalition-related financial losses mounted, their charges became progressively worse. And, as usual, they always seemed to be reported widely in the press.

For instance, Lee Rich's comment linking me with the infamous German führer appeared in *Time* magazine. Unfortunately most *Time* readers didn't know what I believed to be the real reason why Rich called me Hitler. His sex-saturated *Secrets of Midland Heights* had just been canceled; *Flamingo Road*, his frequently adulterous NBC series starring Morgan Fairchild, was in serious trouble; and thanks in part to the Coalition, CBS was even having trouble getting its price for *Dallas* (at that time the highest rated weekly show in network television history).[19]

Unlike Lee Rich, ABC president James E. Duffy didn't try to associate me with any historical bad guy. Instead, he simply described the Coalition as "a band of moral zealots" who were "busy inventing a national problem."[20]

I wondered how many people reading Duffy's claim in *Advertising Age* knew that the *majority* of Americans agreed with us "moral zealots." Indeed, shortly after the ABC president's blast, *Time* magazine commissioned the respected research firm Yankelovich, Skelly and White to find out whether people agreed with Jim Duffy or Don Wildmon. Guess what? Sixty percent of Americans agreed that "television . . . reflects a permissive and immoral set of values which are *bad* for the country."

A short while later, *Advertising Age* conducted a similar poll of advertisers. They surveyed chief executives of the 100 top television sponsors. Eighty-five percent of these industry leaders said that their company was very "concerned" about the amount of sex, violence and profanity on TV. Forty-five percent said their company believed there was "a need for *major changes* in TV programming" (emphasis added). And the vast majority thought that at least some changes were in order. [21]

Nevertheless, the television industry kept describing us as a tiny band of power-hungry neo-Victorians. And they didn't confine their verbal attacks to the print media. Breaking their precedent of virtual silence about our existence, network executives and others within the industry began using television air time, sometimes on their own programming, to bomb the Coalition.

For instance, producer Norman Lear left the Ojai "war council" determined to do everything possible to fight the Coalition. Under the auspices of his newly-formed advocacy organization, People for the American Way, he produced several 30- and 60-second TV ads. These were designed to, in Lear's words, "counter the intolerant messages and anti-democratic actions of the Moral Majoritarians."[22]

Lear and People for the American Way then paid to air the spots locally on more than 300 stations, and nationally on one of the three networks.[23] Slickly done, the ads featured celebrities such as Carol Burnett, Goldie Hawn and Muhammad Ali, and were extremely effective.

Meanwhile, ABC Vice President Alfred Schneider used Ted Koppel's *Nightline* program to tell America that I was directing an "organized conspiracy." Like Lee Rich, who had not bothered to define what he meant by "blackmail" and "threaten" on the *Tomorrow Show*, Schneider completely failed to substantiate his reckless charge.

I appeared on that same show. Unfortunately the moment I began to expose Schneider's ridiculous charge for what it was, Ted Koppel cut me off claiming they were out of time.

This demonstrated just how low the networks were willing to stoop in their efforts to portray us as rabid rowdies involved in some unscrupulous and definitely un-American activity. But just when I thought they couldn't possibly stoop any lower . . . they did!

One mid-April day, NBC, CBS and ABC sent their heavy artillery to a Boca Raton, Florida, hotel. There, the three network presidents blasted away at our Coalition for almost an hour. Their captive audience included hundreds of influential advertising executives. The event was the American Association of Advertising Agencies (Four A's) annual convention.

I didn't even know that the Coalition had been bombed until later that night. And the only reason I found out was because I just happened to have my TV set tuned to the new Cable News Network. So you can imagine my surprise when I heard the news anchor mention my name!

I quickly crossed my den to turn up the sound. When I sat back down, I found myself watching a tape-recorded video image of NBC President Fred Silverman. I had seen the NBC chief executive before on talk shows and in news clips. But I had never seen him look so serious. Of course, the moment I heard him call our Coalition's "boycott threat" a "sneak attack on the foundation of democracy" I knew why he seemed so somber.

"It [The Coalition] is threatening the democratic soul of television," he continued, sounding patriotic. "Ultimately, because television is the central informational medium in our society, it is threatening democracy itself."[24]

I could scarcely believe my ears. Though he didn't mention my name, Fred Silverman was talking about me—a simple Mississippi preacher . . . a proud veteran of the United States Army. Yet, the man from NBC was describing me as though I were the greatest threat to national security since the Cuban Missile crisis.

Gene Jankowski, CBS Broadcast Group president, followed Silverman. He seemed to have simply rehashed his standard Don Wildmon bashing speech. But this time he had replaced the singular subject, "Don Wildmon," with the plural subject, "the Coalition."

"They're [Coalition members] trying to take away your freedom of choice," he warned, just as he had in Jackson two years earlier. Then, as he had before, he called The Coalition's efforts "the disenfranchisement of the real majority by a determined minority."[25]

Last, ABC Television President Fred Pierce took the podium and made what best can be described as a call to arms.

First he appealed to ad agency leaders and their clients to stand "side by side" with broadcasters in this struggle. Then he said, "United we can withstand the pressures of the self-appointed censors who want to stop television from meeting the advertising, entertainment, and information needs of all Americans. . . ."

His words reminded me of the famous opening scene in the movie *Patton*. With a gigantic American flag for a backdrop, George C. Scott, playing the eccentric World War II general, had stood on stage as if he were giving thousands of troops a pre-battle pep talk. Fred Pierce lacked the Oscar-winning actor's dramatic flair. But the message was essentially the same: "We must fight for our honor, our freedom and the American way."

"The viability of free, advertiser-supported television," he concluded, "must not be impaired by decisions based on fears that are induced by coercive tactics."[26]

Soon after the smoke from the networks' big guns had cleared, Turner Broadcasting's Ted Turner tried to organize a three on three face-off featuring Silverman, Jankowski and Pierce versus Jerry

Falwell, Moral Majority Vice President Cal Thomas and me. His neutral Cable News Network would air the discussion so that viewers could determine for themselves whether our democracy was actually in danger.

Not surprisingly, though, all three network presidents refused Turner's invitation. The excuse? Their Florida speeches had covered just about everything there was to say. Hence, in the words of ABC, "a further debate on your [Turner's] network is not necessary."[27]

Silverman, Jankowski and Pierce's refusal to debate confirmed what I had suspected: The men holding perhaps the most important positions in American communications didn't have the guts to publicly defend their incriminating charges against the Coalition for Better Television.

True to their well-established pattern, they had used the Four A's meeting to attack the Coalition, knowing full well that we would have no opportunity to respond. They also knew that explosive statements excerpted from their cleverly-crafted speeches would be reported extensively in the press. That, they hoped, would do even more damage to the Coalition's credibility.

The Network Strategy Backfires

Fortunately this story doesn't end here. I must add that my countenance began to lift a few days later as news stories and columns covering the Boca Raton artillery barrage began arriving in my mailbox. It quickly became evident that the three executives had gone too far with their malicious anti-Coalition imagery. As a result, their cowardly hit and run strategy had backfired.

Journalists all over America, many for the first time, had clearly seen through the networks' smoke screen. And they were having a good time giving the three network field generals a hard time. Bill Carter, *Baltimore Sun* TV critic, best expressed the growing cynicism within his profession.

"When Fred Silverman eloquently denounced interference by the Moral Majority types as a sneak attack on the foundations of democracy . . . the scoffs could be heard all the way down broadcast row in New York," he wrote. He then reminded readers that this "network profit machine" head who had just fervently expressed concern about threatened "democratic principles" was the same man who gave American TV viewers *B.J. and the Bear . . . and The Seven Lady Truckers*. Gene Jankowski, Carter continued, was the guy responsible for *Scruples* and *The Dukes of Hazzard*, while Fred Pierce, Carter reminded his readers, had brought us *Diary of a Teenage Hitchhiker*!

Los Angeles Times columnist Howard Rosenburg had even more fun teasing the men who, he said, had been "wearing out their mouths with self-serving speeches attacking Coalition leaders. . . . If you enjoy seeing grown-ups cry," he mockingly added, "just ask network executives about the Coalition."

I felt even better when the next issue of *Advertising Age* reported that the networks' Four A's call to arms had failed to rally the troops. Describing the three speeches as "lengthy, unimaginative and essentially dull," the respected advertising publication noted that reaction to their appeal "was largely negative."

Summing up the feelings of many, one high-level agency executive had groused, "What partnership? Where were these fellows when we were trying to talk to them about those 16 and 18 percent rate increases?"

Another *Advertising Age* write-up headlined "Four A's Cool to TV Chiefs" indicated that much of the crowd was offended because "all they got was a sales pitch."

"I don't want . . . the Moral Majority, Jerry Falwell or any of them," one disgusted Four A's member told *Ad Age*. "But I don't want *Three's Company* either and that's what I get. The networks program offensive shows, pure trash, and they expect us to defend them."

As I finished the *Ad Age* stories, I realized that our casualties from the Boca Raton blast were minimal. We had withstood everything the networks could fire at us. And not only was our Better TV Coalition still standing, but the backlash against the networks had actually given our cause a little boost.

A few weeks later, I learned that our cause was going to get a much bigger boost. My friend Barry Smyth, a Proctor and Gamble (P & G) public relations executive, told me that P & G Chairman Owen (Brad) Butler was scheduled to speak at an upcoming meeting of the Academy of Television Arts and Sciences in Los Angeles. Butler's address, wrote Barry, would focus on "the need for the television industry to listen to its critics." Barry didn't give me any specifics about Mr. Butler's talk. But he did indicate that I would be very pleased. So I sensed that something big was in the works.

Now let me explain how Barry and I had become acquainted. A year or so earlier the Ohio-based maker of Tide Detergent, Ivory Soap, Crest Toothpaste and Folger's Coffee (to name only a few of their many products), had sponsored a CBS movie called *If Things Were Different*. It starred *Flesh and Blood's* Suzanne Pleshette as a middle-aged wife involved in an affair.

But this was no ordinary affair. According to CBS's full-page *TV Guide* promotional ad, being unfaithful was "the only way to hold her marriage together."

When I complained, Proctor and Gamble didn't ignore me or discredit me as so many other companies had done. Instead, P & G sent Barry Smyth and a colleague, William (Bill) Dobson, to my musty Tupelo office. These two personable men sat on my metal church-style folding chairs and listened while I talked. Then I listened while they talked.

I also visited them in their plush, sixth-floor corporate offices in downtown Cincinnati. Though we didn't agree on everything, we developed a mutual respect and trust which characterizes our relationship to this day. But more importantly, Proctor and Gamble proved (and continues to prove) that they were serious about being a responsible prime-time television advertiser.

At any rate, my good behind-the-scenes relationship with P & G led me to believe that Brad Butler would probably give the Coalition for Better Television a qualified endorsement in his upcoming speech. And that would send shock waves through the television industry.

You see, Proctor and Gamble was the biggest programming sponsor on the planet. In fact, during the previous year (1980), the giant conglomerate had paid the networks and their affiliates $486 million.[28] In return, they got to show America the virtues of everything from Head and Shoulders dandruff shampoo to Mr. Whipple's favorite brand of bathroom tissue.

Consequently when the man representing almost a half billion dollars worth of paychecks, programming budgets, expense accounts and profits talks, TV people listen.

And boy did they ever listen!

Time magazine noted that while the Coalition had given the networks a "severe case of the jitters," Butler's comments had "caused still another run to the Valium." Rick Du Brow, *Los Angeles Herald Examiner* TV writer, said Brad Butler's speech hit Hollywood like a "bombshell." Why? Because it "verified that Don Wildmon had the ear of the nation's top sponsors and they felt he had a point."

When my copy of Brad Butler's address arrived from Barry, I understood why it had sent Hollywood honchos scurrying for cover. Brad Butler had all but taken sides. And the man controlling $486 million in TV ad revenue hadn't sided with the networks. Here's what he said: "Television, as all of you know, not only entertains and informs, but in the process of entertaining and informing, it plays a major role in shaping the future of our society," the influential corporation head began. "And commercial television is too powerful a force in shaping the character of our society to be ignored."

Then Butler made direct reference to the men and women of our Coalition who were ignoring television no longer. "I think the Coalition is expressing some very important and broadly held views about gratuitous sex, violence and profanity," he said. "I can assure you that we are listening very carefully to what they say. And I urge you to do the same.

"I can't help wondering how many of you have personally listened to Rev. Wildmon or Rev. Falwell," he continued. "Certainly they and their constituents have spent a lot of hours watching and listening to what you produce."

Next he asked a question, sounding as if he were a minister with a gossip problem in his church: "Wouldn't you be better served by listening first-hand to what they are saying instead of reacting to a second- or third-hand, and probably false, understanding of these people and their message?"

I can only imagine what the crowd's mood was at that moment. Most likely, more than a few Academy members were squirming uncomfortably in their seats. But the Proctor and Gamble chairman had even more to say about "listening."

"I suspect that you will find, as we have, that careful and thoughtful listening, particularly to your critics, can be a valuable marketing asset," he said. "Complaints and criticism, if looked on as a productive force, can help improve current programs, and identify new opportunities which will assist your industry in its competition with cable, pay cable and other new media.

"Listening to critics isn't going to diminish anyone's First Amendment freedoms," Butler stressed as he went on. "It should stimulate, rather than stifle, creativity."

Then the giant consumer products company chairman indicated that although P & G didn't always agree with the Coalition, due to "offensive program content" they had already decided *not* to sponsor almost all the shows on our top 10 sex-oriented programs list.

"You may be interested to know that during this television year," he also said, "we have withdrawn sponsorship from over 50 programs, including movies, for reasons of taste. In short, the Coalition is not alone in their concern."

But Butler wasn't finished. He quoted several titillating slogans network publicity departments had created to promote certain shows, such as "Sexy Super Ladies Stack Up" (*Women who Rate a 10*); "Blackmail in a Sex Clinic" (*The Misadventures of Sheriff Lobo*); and "What's a Little Love Between Business Partners?" (*One Day at a Time*).

"With headlines like these, is it any wonder that the TV industry is being accused of exploiting sex?" he asked. "Is it any wonder that a large body of our population who continue to adhere to what many of you may think of as an old-fashioned morality are offended and are determined to fight back?

"You can, of course, choose to ignore or to ridicule the Coalition and its leaders," Butler continued, directly alluding to the way the television industry as a whole had reacted to the issues we'd raised. "But you do so, in my opinion, at your peril," he warned.

So that was the speech that shook Hollywood. But Barry had been wrong. I was more than pleased; I was elated. The momentum was back on our side as more and more things seemed to be breaking our way.

And yet I wondered, *With the networks once again in retreat, what would they try next?*

In June 1981 Wildmon squared off for a verbal duel with CBS Vice President Gene "Darth" Mater. Many of the 100 TV critics in the audience agreed with the *Chicago Tribune's* Ron Alridge who said, "Wildmon won the debate—decisively." *Los Angeles Herald-Examiner* photos.

Due in large measure to the efforts of Don Wildmon and his American Family Association, *The Last Temptation of Christ* became the most protested movie in Hollywood history. More than 25,000 Christians participated in this march and rally (which Wildmon co-sponsored) at the Universal Pictures corporate headquarters. *Los Angeles Times* photo.

When CBS cartoon character "Mighty Mouse" was discovered sniffing a powdery substance experts believed to be cocaine, Wildmon alerted the public. "In view of the drug crisis facing this country," fumed Washington

Congressman Rod Chandler, ". . . airing this program was unforgivable."
CBS Vice President George Dessart claimed the substance was "a lucky
chunk of cheese."

Wildmon's first exposure on national television came in this debate with
an angry Lee Rich, producer of *Dallas*, on NBC's *Tomorrow Show* (inset). On
Labor Day, 1985 Wildmon led some 13,000 people who marched to South-
land/7-Eleven's Dallas headquarters to protest their pornographic magazine
sales. Walking with Wildmon are Christian radio show host, Marlin Maddoux (left) and Los Angeles Baptist pastor, E.V. Hill. Six months later
7-Eleven stopped selling porn magazines in 4,500 corporate-owned stores.

During Wildmon's long struggle for decency on network TV, ABC has been a frequent target. In the bottom photo, Wildmon leads a protest at ABC headquarters in New York during a 1978 boycott. (*New York Tribune* photo.) Above, he is interviewed on Ted Koppel's *Nightline*—where he has been a periodic guest.

NEWS ITEM: NATIONAL FEDERATION FOR DECENCY PROTESTS NEW CARTOON SHOW BASED ON VULGAR AND VIOLENT 'GARBAGE PAIL KIDS' CARDS.

CBS-TV PROGRAMMING

"DOESN'T ANYBODY REALIZE THE SHOW WILL HAVE A SOCIALLY REDEEMING VALUE? ...IT'LL MAKE MONEY!"

THE STORY YOU ARE ABOUT TO SEE IS TRUE ...ONLY THE NAMES OF THE SPONSORS HAVE BEEN CHANGED TO PROTECT THEIR PRODUCTS FROM BEING BOYCOTTED!

'BETTER TV' GROUP PLANS SPONSOR BLACKLIST

When the networks overstepped their bounds and clashed with Wildmon, the story often spills over in the nation's editorial cartoons. Wayne Stayskal's cartoons "reprinted by permission: Tribune Media Services."

Wildmon's children take their stand during his first action in 1977—
"Turn the TV Off Week" (from left: Tim, Donna, Angela and Mark). This
family portrait, taken in the early 80s, includes Don's pretty wife, Lynda.

A Duel With
'Darth Mater'

It sounded almost too good to be true. CBS executive Barry Richardson, speaking for his employer, had offered to pay my way to Los Angeles. Once there, he said, I would have ample opportunity to state and defend the position taken by the Coalition for Better Television.

CBS's position would be stated and defended by Gene Mater, their vice president for program policy. This proposed debate between Mater and me, he explained, would occur during the Television Critics Association's annual convention and be witnessed by about 100 journalists who regularly cover the TV beat.

Richardson concluded his invitation by offering to pay Lynda's way to the convention as well. He promised first class airline tickets, ground transportation in a chauffeured limousine and accommodations at the Beverly Hills Wilshire.

As Richardson enthusiastically stressed the V.I.P. treatment, I couldn't help but think, *Why is CBS doing this? I mean, for four years I had begged them for just such an opportunity. Indeed I would have gladly debated any CBS corporate representative at almost any time and place, at my own expense.*

Yet for four years my requests had been ignored. CBS had ridiculed me as if I were some kind of mad man. Now, however, CBS was calling me. Instead of treating me like a maniac, they seemed to be attempting to butter me up with promises of star treatment. It was almost as if Richardson had been given orders to make sure I didn't say no. Before I had a chance to analyze the warning signals my instincts were flashing, Richardson pressed me to accept CBS's invitation. With the debate only seven days away, he explained, numerous arrangements had to be made immediately.

So I made a snap decision and said yes. After all, I figured, it might be four more years before I'd get another chance to verbally duel a real live network official. But as soon as I hung up the phone a rush of second thoughts filled my mind.

Experience had taught me that many CBS executives could not be trusted to tell the truth. Barry Richardson, of course, had assured me that I could expect a fair, honest debate. But I must confess that I had some serious doubts.

Indeed as I turned my memory back four years I had a hard time remembering when, if ever, CBS had been completely honest or fair in their dealings with me, the NFD or the Coalition. So a legitimate debate simply didn't jive with their normal game plan.

CBS's strange eagerness to schedule this face-off didn't make sense either. I knew that a host of television critics had already bought the network line and viewed me as a wild and crazy yahoo from Mississippi. At the very least I believed a fair debate would earn me grudging respect from many writers who previously had been hostile. And I couldn't understand why CBS executives suddenly seemed so willing to give ground in their propaganda war against me.

Finally, basic logic led me to conclude that CBS must have stumbled upon some less than exemplary behavior from my past. That's it, I thought. They intend to lower the boom on me in front of America's most influential and widely-read TV critics.

But what had CBS discovered?

I'm certainly no saint. In fact, the Bible tells me that I'm a sinner just like everyone else—a sinner saved by grace. Yet for the life of me I couldn't think of anything I had done, either personally or professionally, of such a magnitude that CBS could possibly use to discredit and embarrass me. But since I figured there had to be something, I spent the next several hours retracing my entire life.

I thought of the speeding tickets I collected during college while hot-rodding in my dad's '53 Studebaker. But that couldn't be it. I remembered being dismissed from Mrs. Cox's English class at Ripley, Mississippi High. She contended that I had made a few too many smart-aleck remarks. And I suppose she was right. But I knew that couldn't be it either. I even recalled the trouble I had once gotten into when I stole a watermelon from a farmer's patch. I think I was 15.

The more I wondered about the trick I believed CBS was planning to pull, the more I worried. My apprehension mounted. Then when I sized up my competition, that apprehension got worse. A nervous knot would form in my stomach when I remembered the uncanny ability of CBS's top brass to think on their feet and smoothly dance around tough questions.

Along that same vein, Daniel Ruth, TV writer for the *Tampa Tribune* once joked that James Rosenfield and his chums had all graduated from "the Fred Astaire School of Executive Training." That's because, he implied, they were so adept at verbally defending CBS's interest—even when CBS's actions were both irresponsible and inexcusable. Ruth then likened James Rosenfield's public speaking style to that of a "used shark salesman."[1]

However, I wasn't going to be debating "Jaws." I would be dueling the man the CBS rank and file called "Darth Mater."[2] At least that's what the *Washington Post* had reported. Not only was Mater feared by CBS employees for what the *Post* had called his "slashing managerial style," I also knew that he was appropriately recognized throughout the television industry as CBS's "hatchet man"—the guy who usually did their dirty work. Needless to say, I took a big gulp as I wondered if Gene Mater figuratively intended to chop off my head.

Spit and polish as a public speaker has never been my forte. Yet the overwhelming evidence made my case against CBS a whole lot stronger than their case against me. Consequently I figured if the debate stayed strictly within the parameters Barry Richardson had described, I'd do all right.

But I wasn't going to take any chances. If I couldn't hold my own against Mater, the television writers would rip me to pieces, thus dealing a crippling blow to the cause for which I had worked so hard. So I spent the next six days reviewing my facts, figures and arguments time and time again.

I had never flown first class before, but I scarcely noticed the royal treatment on the flight to Los Angeles. My mind was still preoccupied with speculation as to what Gene Mater might have up his sleeve. I didn't really notice all the fancy frills at the Wilshire Hotel either, for the same reason.

However, one unexpected amenity did get my attention, and Lynda's too! A couple of hours before "the big showdown," as one Los Angeles TV critic had dubbed the debate, a delivery man brought a stunningly beautiful floral bouquet to our room. Composed of just about every flower grown in greenhouses, it was huge—like the arrangements I was used to seeing at funerals. Though the card said something like, "Lynda Wildmon: compliments of CBS," I couldn't help but wonder if the flowers weren't really intended to symbolize the death of Don Wildmon later that morning. Lynda absolutely loved the bouquet, so I didn't share my morose thought. My edginess had already made her nervous enough as it was. In fact, I felt it would be a crime to make Lynda helplessly sit and watch if CBS had found a way to polish me off. So I convinced her to take a guided Hollywood tour while I confronted Gene Mater and the TV critics.

For a man used to hauling kids around in a '73 Pontiac Safari station wagon, the limousine CBS sent to take me to the Century Plaza Hotel—the debate sight—made me feel like a Mississippi Catfish out of water. Tinted, one way windows; high-tech quadraphonic stereo system; television; telephone; mini-refrigerator; well-stocked cocktail bar; you name it . . . that Cadillac stretched-limo had it.

However, I wasn't alone. CBS had sent along one of their Hollywood employees who introduced himself as a Christian. At first I was a little leery in case I said the wrong things and it got back to Mater. But then the man offered to pray with me. He also told me he understood how I felt.

Feeling much better as I stepped out of the vehicle, I said, "You stand in the back where I can see you. That way if things get rough I'll know where I can find at least one friendly face."

Once inside I discovered that Mater and I would be speaking from a raised platform in a banquet room. Remembering my experience with Lee Rich on the *Tomorrow Show,* I felt better when I saw that our chairs had a few feet of breathing room between them. While waiting for the program to begin, I joked with a couple of TV critics that CBS had forgotten to place a guillotine over my chair.

Gene Mater had arrived before me and was chatting with several TV critics when I walked in. As I observed him from a distance, he seemed fully relaxed and at ease. His demeanor exuded confidence, as if this debate were no big deal. Once again I couldn't help wondering if he knew something that I didn't.

Mater's stylish but conservative summer-weight designer suit made him look even more professional. In stark contrast, I was wearing my predominantly polyester charcoal brown suit. One of two that I owned, I think I had bought it on sale at J.C. Penney for $59.95. I realized that I'd be in big trouble if this debate were to be judged on the basis of appearance and stage presence.

At any rate, a few minutes later I shook hands with my confident opponent, took my place on stage and before I knew it our verbal duel was underway.

Daniel in the Lion's Den

"I stand here today with mixed emotions and some serious misgivings," I began, trying my best not to sound nervous. "In fact, I kind of feel like a lamb that has been carried up to the altar to be slaughtered."

I hesitated just long enough to look out at the room full of inquisitive faces. Below me several news photographers jockeyed for position.

"Please forgive me if what I say next sounds a bit strange," I continued as cameras clicked and flashes lit up the platform area. "But I see no purpose for CBS to bring me here unless they are 100 percent sure that they can decapitate and ruin me.

"I am here to discuss issues, not personalities," I stressed as I concluded my short opening statement. "And I hope that Mr. Mater will do likewise."

At that point, the game show host hired by CBS to be a neutral moderator, asked the small entourage of photo journalists to finish their business as quickly as possible. Then he cued Mater for his opening statement.

"I'm not sure what Mr. Wildmon's comment about separating issues from personalities means," Mater commenced, sounding a little puzzled. "But I will say that I have no intention of decapitating him, literally or figuratively."

Mater paused a moment while the chuckles coming from the audience faded out. Then he said, "I understand that Mr. Wildmon told Rona Barrett the other day that he feels like Daniel in the lion's den."

"AMEN," I shouted, prompting another chorus of snickers.

"Well, I promise you I will not say 'Amen' this morning," Mater responded with a slightly sarcastic air. "But I certainly can sympathize with what Mr. Wildmon feels. You see, last year Mr. Wildmon and I were guests on Pat Robertson's *700 Club* program. And at that time some of my colleagues joked that I had been thrown to the Christians."

I've got to hand it to the CBS veep. He had wasted no time demonstrating his quick wit and skill as a public speaker. His "thrown to the Christians" line had elicited raucous laughter and seemed to break some of the tension in the air. It was so clever, even I cracked a smile.

Still, I wasn't sure I could believe Mater's "no intention of decapitating him" statement. The acid churning in my stomach made me feel like he was just about to unveil his mysterious revelation and start swinging his sharp figurative hatchet.

I'm happy to report, however, that I was wrong. Instead, once the room quieted down, Mater said, "Let me say that I have no personal qualms with Mr. Wildmon. I also have no problem with his vocal objections to certain TV broadcasts. But I am concerned about what he and his supporters are trying to accomplish.

"We at CBS see Mr. Wildmon's Coalition as perhaps the greatest assault on intellectual freedom that we have witnessed in this country in many years," he went on, slowing his delivery so the journalists could record the quote. "I say that not to be dramatic," he emphasized. "I say it because I believe that the essence of the Coalition is only a half step away from book burning."

Mater, who said he was speaking as a "broadcaster, journalist and concerned citizen," then went on to blast the Coalition for attempting to, in his words, serve as a national arbiter of taste and a filter for national TV programming.

"Mr. Wildmon recognizes that viewing recommendations alone will not work," he explained. "He also knows that the democratic system of choice will not serve the Coalition's purposes.

"Therefore," Mater claimed, "Mr. Wildmon seeks to eliminate

everyone's freedom of choice. And there is something decidedly immoral in that approach."

Though Mater wasn't flinging his axe at my personal life, he wasn't mincing his words either. I had erroneously assumed that the backlash to the Boca Raton speeches would teach Mater and CBS a lesson or two. But no.

Like Fred Silverman, Fred Pierce and Gene Jankowski had done two months before, Mater was once again categorizing the Coalition as an unpatriotic, dangerous organization which posed a major threat to the well being of American society. At the time, I had thought the three presidents were bluffing. However, the more I listened to Mater huff and puff about our jeopardized freedoms, the more I realized he wasn't kidding. He really felt that way! Mater and his colleagues actually believed their own overheated rhetoric. And I didn't quite know what to make of that.

Nevertheless, it disturbed me to think that Mater found my efforts to improve television content, based upon my personal moral convictions, to be "immoral." That's because I doubted that he would call Jesse Jackson's boycott of the Coca-Cola Company—Jackson wanted Coke to put more blacks in mid and upper management positions—"immoral." And I didn't think he'd object to the United Farm Workers' boycott campaign against California lettuce growers.

Since the only boycott effort he opposed was the Coalition's, it seemed almost as though Mater defined morality, as well as right and wrong, on the basis of what he perceived to be in his or his employer's best interest. In his way of thinking, our taking issue with the adultery, fornication, dishonesty and profanity constantly airing on his network is wrong. That concerned me because that was precisely the opposite of the way I, as a Christian, viewed morality.

At any rate, as Mater droned on far past the allotted three minutes for his opening statement, I realized that he didn't have some secret weapon to use against me. This really was a *legitimate* debate. And though Mater was trying to paint the Coalition for Better Television as a horrible, sinister consortium, he hadn't really said anything that I couldn't easily or logically refute. Consequently I relaxed and actually looked forward to my first opportunity for rebuttal.

When he finally finished, I decided not to launch into a long discourse defending my right as a U.S. citizen to practice and promote selective buying. Instead, I thought I'd ask Mr. Mater some questions and try and make him do that for me.

"I believe you recently told *Ad Media* magazine that the Coalition's efforts, no matter how well-intentioned, amount to censorship," I said looking him in the eyes. "Did you say that?"

"I probably did," Mater shrugged.

"Would you agree to that?"

"Yes."

"Okay, let me ask two more questions then," I continued, preparing to shoot holes in CBS's censorship claim. "Do I as a citizen have a right to boycott?

"Yes you do," Mater responded.

"Is boycotting censorship?"

Mater hesitated a moment because he knew I was trying to back him into a corner. Then he answered: "No, boycotting per se is not censorship."

"Then why have CBS officials gone all over the country accusing us of censorship?" I asked him.

"A boycott per se is not censorship," Mater repeated somewhat defensively, slowly and carefully choosing his words. "However, I think your efforts are tantamount to censorship because you are attempting to determine what the American people will or will not be able to see on TV," he added. "That is the ultimate goal for your particular movement."

"Hey wait a minute," I shot back. "First you said that I had a right to boycott. Then you said that boycotting is not censorship. If that's the case," I continued, "I see a great disharmony when you accuse us of censorship."

I then reminded the TV critics that the real censors are the handful of network executives who determine, in Mater's own words, what the American people will or will not be able to see.

Naturally, Mater objected. First he argued that programming decisions are based upon the "broad general interest" of the viewing audience. Second, though I knew better, he adamantly testified that CBS executives "do not inflict their personal views" upon the public.

By this time I had been able to keep Mater on the defensive for a good 10 to 15 minutes, and I could tell that he was anxious to go back on the offensive. So when the moderator gave him his opportunity, he reached inside his suit pocket and grabbed a letter I had sent to NFD friends and financial supporters.

Here we go again, I thought, as visions of Lee Rich's tirade danced in my head. But Mater remained calm and collected as he read a paragraph which ended, ". . . today with shows like *Anatomy of Seduction, A Killing Affair, Gay Power/Gay Politics* and *Scruples,* you can hardly watch TV with your family anymore."

"Mr. Wildmon," he coolly questioned as he put my letter back into his suit pocket, "what was your objection to the CBS news program, *Gay Power/Gay Politics?*"

"I don't really know . . . what did I say?" I hesitantly replied as I rifled through my briefcase looking for that particular letter.

"That is all you said about it," Mater answered.

"Well," I stammered, desperately trying to remember the program's context, "it seemed to be just a little bit distorted."

"In which direction?" he pressed.

"Well, I would say probably that it was in the direction of the homosexuals. . . ."

"To this group I quite frankly rest my case," Mater concluded. "This was quite possibly one of the more controversial programs put on by CBS news. But as far as I know no one said that it portrayed the gay community in a favorable light. Nonetheless, you objected."

Of course, Mater was too smart to try and defend *Scruples* or *Anatomy of a Seduction.* Still, I had to admit, he had tallied some points in his effort to portray me as someone with a credibility problem who shouldn't be taken seriously.[3] Consequently, I wasn't surprised when Mater grabbed a file folder and started talking about another CBS made-for-TV movie called *Fallen Angel.*

Airing the previous February, *Fallen Angel* focused on America's tragic child pornography and child prostitution problem (see chapter 8). Though a few TV journalists in the audience had written negative reviews (i.e. Monica Collins of the *Boston Herald American* called *Fallen Angel* ". . . a manipulative tool, an exploitive masquerade"), most TV Critics Association members felt that CBS had dealt with this painful, delicate subject with sensitivity and taste.

Mater was well aware of that fact. And since I had articulated some objections to what turned out to be the highest rated program of the 1980/1981 season, I sensed that Mater thought he could make me look bad again. But little did he realize as he prefaced his comments on the well-watched movie, that I was ready for him.

"Not only was *Fallen Angel* praised by most TV critics," Mater boasted as he held his file high, "but it was also widely praised by groups like The American Society for the Prevention of Cruelty to Children. This file also contains letters of praise from individuals all over the country as well as press clippings crediting the movie with some arrests of child pornographers," he proudly continued.

"So I'm saying that the movie served a definite useful purpose," Mater went on. "And yet you thought it was a terrible program," he exasperatedly added, as if I simply had to be off my rocker.

"Mr. Wildmon, since you did not like *Fallen Angel,* may I ask you where this topic should be discussed?" he sarcastically interrupted just as I was beginning to respond. "Or should it never be discussed at all on television? Would you prefer to read about it in a newspaper?"

"First, let me emphasize that I've never said that there are topics which should not be dealt with on television," I replied after Mater concluded his patronizing questions. Then, making sure all the critics heard me I added, "Let me also make it clear that I've never criticized *Fallen Angel* on the basis of its content.

"My problem stemmed from the fact that CBS chose to feature this subject matter in drama rather than news documentary form," I explained. "I also found it interesting that CBS chose to air *Fallen Angel* during the February "sweeps." Consequently I was very suspect of the true motives of the network executives.

"Let me ask you something," I went on, knowing that the time had come to show everyone the evidence I had placed in my briefcase. "Would you consider *Fallen Angel* to be a serious look at a serious problem?"

"Oh, very much so," Mater asserted. "I think it was an eye-opener. In fact, some of these positive letters from state officials indicate that there may be as many as 100,000 children involved in child pornography."

"Then let me ask you one more question before we move on,"

I said. "Did CBS advertise and promote *Fallen Angel* as a serious look at a serious social problem?"

"Well . . . ah . . . I really have no idea how we looked at it," Mater answered.

At that point I held up the full-page ad CBS had placed in *TV Guide* the day the program aired. "New! First time on television!" I read. "Howard lured innocent girls to star in his movies. He didn't count on Jennifer's mom—who'll fight to save the daughter she loves."

"Now I want y'all to notice," I added as I made sure everyone in the room got a good look at the magazine ad, "the focal point of the CBS promo is a seductive, airbrushed picture of an 11-year-old girl unbuttoning her blouse."

Bill Kelley of the *Ft. Lauderdale News* later described the audience's reaction: "The critics," Kelley wrote, "most of whom had recommended *Fallen Angel,* were visibly and audibly surprised when Mater professed a lack of background knowledge about the film's promotional campaign, and when Mater virtually backed out of Wildmon's charge on the basis of ignorance."

Score one for Wildmon!

Beating Mater at His Own Game

As the debate waged on, I continued to score points against Mater, sometimes in bunches. When it was all over, the consensus among the critics seemed to indicate that I had beaten Gene Mater at his own game. In fact, headlines such as "Television Executive Loses a Round to TV Foe" (the *Cleveland Press*) and "Southern Preacher Rattles Network TV" (the *Boston Globe*) peppered America's major newspapers during the next several days.

At the same time, many critics had a field day chastising CBS for the ridiculous way they had heretofore stereotyped me. Numerous astonished audience members echoed the sentiments of the *Milwaukee Journal's* Mike Drew, who wrote, "Imagine my surprise to find out that Wildmon—the blue-nosed book burner we'd all been warned about in speeches by network leaders—didn't seem much like a wild man."

No doubt such embarrassing publicity was a bitter pill for Mater and his colleagues to swallow. I came to the same conclusion reached by many critics: CBS executives had listened much too much to their own propaganda designed to discredit Don Wildmon.

I suspected that the top CBS money men were betting that Gene "Darth" Mater would figuratively slice me up and eat me for lunch. Members of the TV Critics Association, CBS assumed, would in turn write the obituary for Don Wildmon and the Coalition for Better Television. Then CBS could get back to the business of making money just about any way they darn well pleased.

Dennis Washburn of the *Birmingham News* labeled this failed CBS battle strategy "a major tactical error." Meanwhile, the *Chicago Tribune's* Ron Alridge called this "media manipulation ploy" a "failure and disaster" for CBS.

"The folks at CBS seem to think Wildmon is so hickish . . . so wrong . . . so ignorant . . . that mere exposure will cause him to dry up and blow away," Alridge concluded. "What Wildmon's opponents fail to grasp is that he is surviving, thriving and gaining influence because he is (a) sincere, (b) smart, (c) more than a little bit right!"

As I savored the sweetness of all the positive press, I realized I had much to be thankful for. The scenario that I believed CBS had meant for ill, God had turned into a great triumph. Indeed in 90 short minutes, with the Lord's help, I had reclaimed much of the territory that CBS had unfairly captured in their propaganda war against me and my cause.

However, most of my thoughts relating to our duel focused on some comments Gene Mater made during our concluding question and answer session with audience members. In fact, I had a hard time getting what he said off my mind.

It all started when Marilyn Preston of the *Chicago Tribune Press Service* brought up the subject of *values*.

"Mr. Mater, Mr. Wildmon has shown the courage to sit here and spell out his values for us," she said as she prefaced her question. "Would you do the same and tell us what your values are and how they affect programming?"

Mater twiddled with his microphone cord for a moment before he answered without answering: "I didn't know this was going to be a quiz about my personal value system."

After Preston rephrased the question, Mater said something to the affect that his personal likes or dislikes have nothing to do with programming selection. "The question," he said, "is whether the audience likes the program."

Since he was still beating around the bush, Preston tried once more to pin him down. Finally, he said, "Mr. Wildmon is a minister and has a stated set of values. I am a broadcaster, and I don't."

The comment drew raucous laughter from the critics. Mater flushed beet red with embarrassment as he realized how silly he had sounded. His entire case against me and the Coalition had been based upon a deeply engrained set of values—values which, on the surface, seemed to be strongly motivated by the pursuit of the almighty dollar. Yet, despite his earlier claim to the contrary, I could sense there was something about me that really bothered Mater besides the fact that I was costing him money. But what?

Mater indirectly answered that question minutes later. I had asked him, "Why is it all right for homosexuals to boycott and use their clout to try and influence TV programming, but not us?"

"The difference—I think what sets you apart—your organization apart," Mater said, "is the fact that you are cloaked in this self-assumed aura of religious respectability."

"You mean if I was not a Christian it would be okay to complain?" I noted.

"I didn't say that at all," he replied defensively.

"Well, in essence that's what you said."

"No, I did not say that," he replied again.

"Well, tell me what you did say," I pressed.

"I'm sure that people in other organizations like Action For Children's Television, are also Christian," Mater finally said. "I think it's the church relationship that's involved."

"Oh, if I wasn't a minister I'd be okay?" I responded.

"I didn't say that either," Mater shot back.

When I asked Mater to explain what he really meant, he did his Fred Astaire imitation and verbally danced around my inquiry. And that made it quite clear that the fact that I am a Christian was quite disturbing to him. The fact that I acted on what I believed seemed to bug him even more.

In the weeks to come, as I mulled Mater's response over in my mind, I felt like I was much closer to fully grasping what was behind it all. . . .

7

I Discover What's Behind It All

My view through the tiny airplane window made me marvel at God's creative majesty. Jagged snow-covered mountain peaks stretched to the horizon in almost every direction. Several thousand feet below I could see the sky blue waters of Lake Dillon. And with a little help from the flight attendant, I spotted the grass covered slopes at the famous Breckenridge, Keystone and Copper Mountain ski areas.

A few minutes later the noisy Rocky Mountain Airways propeller plane began its descent toward Vail, Colorado. Another look through my window revealed that we would be touching down in a long narrow valley between two mountains.

One was covered with wide snake-like trails which I supposed would soon be topped with snow and teaming with skiers. I also had a bird's-eye view of countless condominiums, hotels and fancy homes built on the level area at the mountain's base.

But I wasn't flying into Colorado's most famous resort community for a vacation. In fact, Vail, Colorado, was just about the last place I wanted to be on that late September 1981 day. That's because my briefcase contained a speech that I wished for the life of me I didn't have to deliver.

After all, people connected with and sympathetic to the networks were already calling me practically every name imaginable simply because I was trying to do something about televised sex and violence. Now that I was about to charge the big three networks with "religious discrimination," I figured many Don Wildmon haters would assume I had gone off the deep end.

However, I knew beyond any shadow of a doubt that I was right. Gene Mater's antagonism toward my Christian faith the previous June had convinced me of that. And now the time had come to publicly tell the truth—the truth I had first seen, yet didn't want to believe, two and a half years earlier.

At that time I discerned there was something else wrong with network television besides exploitive sex, violence and profanity. But for several months I couldn't pinpoint the problem.

Then one evening in March 1979 I watched an NBC movie called *The Cracker Factory* and wondered, "*Is this it? Is this the problem?*" Set in a mental institution, the lead character is a severely depressed, alcoholic housewife in need of psychiatric treatment. Interestingly, the movie implicates her husband's Christian faith as a prime reason for her drinking and depression.

Meanwhile not even a hint of compassion, love or understanding emanates from her Roman Catholic priest. Instead, he is presented as obnoxiously cruel and uncaring. In other words, the only two characters identified as Christian were portrayed in a highly derogatory manner.

After that night I paid special attention to the way Christianity and individual Christians were depicted in TV programming. And as the months rolled by I began to spot three trends.

One: Christianity and/or faith in God, as well as characters identified as Christian, were primarily confined to programming set long ago.

Two: Christianity and/or the religious dimension of life were conspicuously absent from shows set in modern settings.

Three: When present-day characters *were* identified as Christian, they tended to be stereotyped as closed-minded, ignorant fools. They also tended to be portrayed as liars, cheaters and/or adulterers. I especially noticed that fictional TV ministers and evangelists usually seemed to have a "habit of breaking one or two of the more conspicuous commandments,"[1] as Tom Shales of the *Washington Post* described the one who appeared regularly on NBC's salacious 1980 serial *Number 96*.

Hoping that my observations would be proved wrong, I developed a new monitoring study in the spring of 1980. It specifically charted how Christians and Christian values were depicted on prime time. Five hundred volunteer monitors did the job. And 12 weeks and 742 hours of programming later, the verdict was in.

Sadly the study revealed that prime-time network television was the "unrecognized foe of the Christian faith and its values," as I told NFD supporters and friends after tabulating and analyzing the results. Indeed I found that present-day "Christian" characters were portrayed "unfavorably" and "very unfavorably" far more often than they were depicted in a "favorable" light.

However, with the exception of occasional comments to my core constituency, I said virtually nothing about this dis-criminatory phenomenon for more than a year. One reason for my silence was because I knew of no one else who was talking about this problem. Hence I wanted to take plenty of time to observe even more programming and collect additional data.

I also knew that any statement charging the networks with an anti-religious and specifically an anti-Christian bias would be viewed as radical. I sensed that this charge would bring on yet another round of vicious criticism. Quite frankly, I did not relish that thought.

But when Gene Mater condescendingly called my selective buying efforts "immoral" and said my faith-inspired actions were "cloaked in a self-assumed aura of religious respectability," I realized that somebody had to speak out. Someone had to confront the television industry with truth. And if that somebody happened to be Don Wildmon, then so be it.

Consequently when I received a surprising invitation to "ad-dress my concerns" to television professionals attending the Na-tional Broadcasters' Association for Community Affairs (NBACA) convention, I decided I would indeed candidly address my concerns. NBACA members, who are primarily responsible for community-oriented programming on network affiliate stations, would be the first to hear my discomforting conclusions. And that's why I was flying into Vail carrying a speech entitled, "Religious Discrimination on Network Television."

Telling It Like It Is

In contrast to my limousine ride prior to the Gene Mater debate, I didn't feel like Daniel on his way to the lion's den. That's because I didn't expect any surprises. I already knew everything I was going to say, as unpleasant as some of it was. Though I normally speak from an outline and rough notes, I had decided to type my speech and read it because I was breaking new ground. After the speech I supposed I'd answer a few questions and then leave.

Nevertheless, I felt a few butterflies dancing in my stomach as I arrived at the convention center. I was scheduled to speak right after dinner, which I barely touched. Those butterflies had turned into a kind of queasy, sinking feeling that left me a bit light-headed. And I began to wonder if I might be getting myself into more trouble than I had bargained for.

As I stepped up to the podium I heard the hollow sound of scattered, noticeably unenthusiastic applause. I glanced at the 300 or so mostly expressionless faces pointed in my direction, took a deep breath and looked down through my bifocals.

"Years ago we decided that discrimination based upon skin color, national origin or religious preference was unacceptable in this country," I began. "Of course, everyone knows that the struggle to eradicate this ugly and unfair discrimination—much of it deeply rooted in society—has been difficult.

"However, to our credit," I continued, trying not to sound like I was reading, "our society has come a long way in helping to correct prejudice-driven behavior." Then, after briefly describing gradual yet marked improvements in the treatment of minorities, I noted that significant strides had been made toward eliminating religious discrimination, too.

"But one very important institution in our society still practices religious discrimination," I stressed, getting right to the point. "And that institution," I added, after a short dramatic pause, "is network television!"

"G-- d---," swore one gentleman at a front table, loud enough so I could hear him.

"That's bull sh--," exclaimed another man near the back, loud enough so everyone in the room could hear. "Pure bull sh--!"

"Aw . . . p--- off," voiced someone else, again clearly discernible to all.

I could not believe my ears. I realized that my research and observation-based conclusion would not be popular with this predominantly pro-network audience. But I never dreamed it would be greeted by an outpouring of profanity. Somewhat startled, I took a moment to collect my wits before moving on.

"It takes no genius to notice that religion, religious people and religious values are generally excluded on network television," I continued, trying not to sound rattled. "And when religion, religious people and religious values *are* depicted on network television, it is usually in a negative connotation."

Once again my statement was met by an onslaught of gutter-level jargon. The distraction made me temporarily lose my place and I groped to get back on track.

Once I found my spot, I began explaining my discovery that network television tends to depict religion as something that had meaning in the past but is not relevant in today's society. To illustrate my point, I referred to two of the most-watched programs in the Wildmon household—NBC's *Little House on the Prairie* and CBS's *The Waltons*.

"*Little House*," I said, "set in the 19th century, consistently depicts religion as a significant part of the character's lives. *The Waltons*, set in the early 20th century, portrays religion in a much more cursory manner. And the closer you get to a modern day setting, the less relevant religion becomes to everyday life.

"For example," I continued, "*M.A.S.H.* basically depicts religion as funny and harmless, primarily suited for the naive."

Then I said, "To my knowledge there is not a single continuing series on network television which shows anyone who has a continuing meaningful relationship to a religious body which is set in a modern day setting. Nor has there been such a series in some time."

As I continued to speak, so did many of the audience members. You name it, they said it! And as you might expect, their taunting made it harder and harder to concentrate.

As I struggled on, my mind flashed back to other candid speeches I had made before essentially unfriendly audiences. Without exception, they had politely and courteously listened to what I had to say, and I had expected the same from this group.

Hence, their reaction just didn't make sense. Especially perplexing was the fact that the rude behavior wasn't limited to just a few. It seemed like several dozen public affairs directors had gotten into the act. But I didn't have much opportunity to analyze the bizarre scenario. I needed all my faculties just to keep reading.

"More than 80 million Americans go to church regularly," I pointed out as the audience grew even more restless. "But rarely on television.

"People make decisions based upon Christian principles . . . but rarely on television.

"People pray . . . but rarely on television.

"Every community in America has churches and synagogues which contribute to their local communities and this country . . . but they hardly even exist on television.

"About the only time one hears the name of God on network television," I said, "is when his name is used in a profane manner.

"And all too often," I went on, "when individuals are identified as Christians in programs which air on the networks, they are characters only to scorn, prompt revulsion and to ridicule.

"In fact," I added, "I cannot remember seeing a program on network television set in a modern setting which depicted a Christian as a warm, compassionate, intelligent or gifted human being."

The blatant animosity and back-room language directed toward me seemed to increase with each point. Indeed, the air in the room literally felt laden with anger. I say that because there seemed to be some kind of eerie, invisible force pressing down on my shoulders.

Though I didn't sense that I was in any physical danger, I took a quick glance around the room just in case. It was not comforting to discover that there was only one way out—right through the middle of the hostile crowd!

About that time my mouth became so dry I was having difficulty pronouncing some words. So I stopped long enough to take a swig of water. That also gave me a moment to regain my composure.

When I did, I described how network television has taken many Judeo-Christian religious values (i.e., marital and pre-marital fidelity, honesty and integrity in dealing with others, a helpful or service-minded attitude, stewardship, forgiveness, etc.) and ridiculed, belittled or basically ignored them. However, as I spoke I no longer cared about the supporting material I had included to back my statements. I just wanted to finish my speech and get out of there.

"No one denies that any and all Christians have their faults and failures," I said as I thumbed through the rest of my manuscript trying to decide what to cut. "But to continually present Christians, their values and culture in a negative light is a gross injustice.

"Christian people are a patient people," I added after skipping several pages. "I believe that this patience, born of *agape* love, has been misunderstood by those calling the shots at the networks. It seems to have been interpreted as a sign of weakness.

"Our patience is exhausted," I went on as the gutter language coming from the audience continued. "No longer will those of us who cherish our religious heritage and values accept being treated as non-people or continually portrayed in a negative light.

"Christians provide more than $3 billion a year to network television," I pointed out, preparing to wrap things up. "And what do we get in return? Precious little other than exclusion, scorn and ridicule. This ugly, intentional and patent discrimination must end!"

On that note, I breathed a sigh of relief and quickly grabbed my papers, which were now spread out all over the podium. A few people clapped while I hurried off the platform. Several others continued the taunting. Most of the audience just sat there.

But I didn't care. I was just glad to get back to my seat and have the unusual ordeal over with.

I soon began feeling better after the meeting was dismissed. That's because I was immediately surrounded by a small cluster of friends, not foes. They all had been embarrassed and outraged by the crude behavior exhibited by their peers.

I was especially encouraged by a young black woman representing a large TV station in my home state. After apologizing profusely, she told me she essentially agreed with me. Then she thanked me for having the courage to tell it like it is.

Still, it was the most bizarre experience I've ever had. And I might add, I was not sorry to leave Vail.

During the next several weeks I frequently asked myself, *Why did my speech trigger an avalanche of profanity-laced hostility from this group of well-educated, cultured and, under most circumstances, dignified broadcasting professionals?*

I eventually concluded that I had struck a sensitive nerve with a fiery dart of truth—a truth that these television industry insiders found extremely threatening. I believed that I had exposed something significant that a whole host of people, for some inexplicable reason, didn't want exposed.

Convinced more than ever that I had hit the nail on the head, I directly confronted the big boys on Network Row in mid-November 1981. In personal letters to Thornton Bradshaw, chairman of RCA (which at the time owned NBC), CBS Chairman William Paley and ABC Chairman Leonard Goldenson, I repeated all the key points I had made in Vail.

I also reminded them of the standard line executives from their network use to justify sex, violence and profanity in programming: "We're only depicting life as it is." With that claim in mind, I asked that they insert Christian characters, culture and values into their entertainment programming to make it more commensurate with life as it really is. I then gave them until February 1, 1982, to take concrete steps to stop what I called "this ugly anti-Christian bigotry." (I used strong, forceful language to get their attention and make sure they knew exactly what I was talking about.)

As it turned out, I didn't have to wait more than two weeks for their answer. Within a matter of days executives from each network apparently put their heads together for a "how-do-we-deal-with-Wildmon-this-time?" pow wow.

I'm guessing that's what happened because all three responses arrived in my Tupelo mailbox during Thanksgiving weekend and all three replies read like they were written by the same person.

Gene Mater, responding for CBS, called my letter "intemperate and extreme." Then he added, "We categorically reject your unfounded accusations."

ABC President John C. Severino, answering for his boss, entirely rejected my "blanket allegations of religious discrimination." And not surprisingly, new NBC President Raymond J. Timothy rejected my "intemperate and groundless charges" as well. "You offer no example to back these allegations," he scolded.

I could only smile at the irony of Timothy's reply. That's because I knew that the very day my letter had arrived at NBC's New York headquarters, his network had insulted the Christian faith and had figuratively slapped millions of Christians in the face.

It happened during *The George Burns Early, Early, Early Christmas Special* when five scantily-clad *Playboy* Playmate "carolers"[2] serenaded the octogenarian comic. But instead of singing Christmas-related numbers, they offered a rousing rendition of the song *My Body Keeps Changing My Mind*. Naturally (no pun intended), these former centerfolds all appeared nude in that month's *Playboy* magazine.

In other words, NBC had used the occasion to promote a magazine which propagates hedonistic values diametrically opposed to the teaching of the One whom the special was named for.

A few weeks later NBC once again demonstrated contempt for the Christian faith on *Saturday Night Live*. During one blasphemous skit, an actor hyped a mock "born-again rock and roll collection" called "Jesus in Blue Jeans." With cynical evangelistic fervor, he promised that the music will "deliver your children from evil." "Send for the record today," he impassionately added, "or burn in hell-fire eternal."

The offensive spoof also included recorded parodies of several popular songs. For example, "Help Me Rhonda" by the Beach Boys became "Help me Jesus, help, help me Jesus." Meanwhile, as the chorus sang, "Yummy, yummy, yummy I've got God in my tummy," a painting of The Last Supper flashed on the screen. Other not so humorous titles included "Hound God," "Why Don't We Get Drunk and Pray" and "Holy Ghost Writers in the Sky."

As the weeks rolled by, blatant examples such as "Jesus in Blue Jeans," which NBC's Ray Timothy claimed did not exist, continued to appear on television. It seemed like every issue of my journal included descriptions of two, three and sometimes more instances of anti-Christian programming on Timothy's network alone.

Though at first I stood virtually alone in my criticism, soon other concerned Christian leaders began to join me in taking the networks to task. For example, the Rev. Dr. Miltiades B. Efthimiou, a top-level official with the Greek Orthodox Church in America, wrote me asking for help in protesting what he called the "religious bigotry" exhibited by NBC's "derogatory, sacrilegious, false and misleading" portrayal of an Orthodox Christian priest.

Dr. Efthimiou had been outraged by a 1982 episode of *Taxi*. (A staple at ABC for four years, *Taxi* had been picked up by NBC for its fifth and final season.) Latka, played by Andy Kaufman, had just had an adulterous fling with a co-worker, which had caused a rift in his marriage to Simka. So the two paid a visit to their priest, Rev. Gorky.

"Since Latka sinned with someone he worked with," Rev. Gorky tells the couple, "Simka must sin with someone Latka works with."

"Latka, we are religious people," Simka proclaimed after Rev. Gorky exits. "We are Orthodox. Our church has told us what we must do. And we must obey if we are to remain married."

"You mean to tell me you are going to sleep with one of my friends?" Latka responds. Then, as Simka nods affirmatively, he adds, "Baby, you're the greatest."

That scene prompted these words from Dr. Efthimiou to NBC: "The suggestion that any priest, especially an Orthodox priest, would desecrate the sacrament of confession by counseling a parishioner to commit adultery is blasphemous."

I agreed. Yet NBC seemed oblivious to the concerns expressed by a steadily growing number of Christians. It also became apparent that NBC officials had no intention of complying with their own Broadcast Standards for Television manual.

Their manual specifically states, "In general, programs should . . . endeavor to depict men, women and children in a positive manner."[3] It also says every effort should be made to avoid airing material which "incites prejudice" or "offends legitimate sensitivities."[4] Regarding religion or religious characters, NBC's written guidelines specifically call for "special sensitivity . . . to avoid contributing to damaging or demeaning stereotypes."[5]

Still, NBC continued to regularly air programs such as *Sister, Sister* and *Celebrity*. *Sister, Sister's* primary character was a hypocritical, married minister who stole money from the church treasury and went to bed with women in his congregation.

The miniseries *Celebrity* featured the exploits of a fictitious faith healer and evangelist named Thomas Jeremiah Luther. In addition to being an unrepentant liar, swindler, fraud, thief, extortioner, rapist and murderer, he also headed a pro-life, pro-family, pro-church and pro-morality movement called The Right Side. The implications were obvious.

The Coalition Calls a Boycott

Needless to say, in spring 1982 when the Coalition for Better Television board held a strategy planning session, NBC and its parent company, RCA, were not held in high esteem. The previous summer, our coalition had made a last-minute decision to call off its threatened boycott. At the time, as explained in chapter 5, all three networks had significantly cleaned up their act. Many of the advertisers who consistently sponsored offensive programs showed signs of improvement, too. So we had hoped that our action would be viewed as a good faith measure—kind of a reward for good behavior. In turn, we trusted the networks to follow the Proctor and Gamble chairman's wise counsel and start listening to their critics.

Unfortunately the networks interpreted our good faith gesture as a sign of weakness. Instead of opening the door for consultation and fair compromise, after we aborted the boycott they resumed operating as if the Coalition for Better Television didn't exist. And by late fall 1981 and winter 1982, gratuitous sex and violence in programming reached pre-Coalition levels.

Left with no alternative but to make good on our earlier boycott pledge, the Coalition board quickly zeroed in on RCA as the obvious choice. My colleagues were especially eager to target the giant electronics maker when I explained that RCA/NBC had recently announced plans to air a miniseries based on the salacious novel *Princess Daisy*.

Written by *Scruples* author Judith Krantz, the book makes *Flesh and Blood* seem tame. *Princess Daisy* subplots include: (1) sex between a young man in his 20s and his 15-year-old sister (incest); (2) the seduction of a 14-year-old boy by his mother's best female friend (adult/child sex); and (3) a sexual affair between a married woman and a female friend (lesbianism/bisexuality). Of course, these subplots are written as though these are just normal, everyday behaviors.

By putting *Princess Daisy* into production, it almost seemed like executives at RCA and NBC were daring us to go after them. And go after them we did.

Some 150 reporters and photographers representing most of America's major news magazines, newspapers, wire services, radio news syndicates and television networks jammed into a conference room at the Washington, D.C., Hyatt Regency for our boycott-launching press conference.

As I explained our plan to ask millions of Americans not to buy RCA products, a dozen microphones must have been taped to the podium directly in front of my face. Meanwhile blinding television lights made it almost impossible for me to see the throng of journalists busily scratching notes.

I concluded my short speech by listing the conditions on which the boycott would end—conditions that NBC could easily meet by simply following their own guidelines.

For the record, here's what the *NBC Broadcast Standards for Television* manual says about "Sexual Themes":

> Explicit, graphic or excessive presentations of sexual matters and activities will be avoided. Sexual themes may not be gratuitously injected into story lines. When such themes contribute to plot or chacterization [sic], they must be presented with intelligent regard for commonly accepted standards of taste and propriety and not in a manner that would appeal to prurient interests.[6]

Of course, RCA and NBC officials reacted to the Coalition's boycott announcement the way I had expected. They went into hiding, refusing virtually all interview requests. Instead of communicating in a forum in which they could be challenged, they issued a terse press statement promising to "fully resist . . . this obvious attempt at intimidation." Then, every once in a while, some highly-placed official would come out of hiding long enough to figuratively equate the Coalition's selective buying promotion with criminal activity. For example, NBC Entertainment President Brandon Tartikoff called the Coalition's campaign "the first step toward a police state." Sound familiar?

But despite RCA/NBC's incriminating rhetoric, it quickly became evident that millions of Americans did not feel much sympathy for the electronics and broadcasting conglomerate. For instance, the *Los Angeles Herald Examiner* conducted a telephone poll of 4,000 readers which found that 42 percent of those polled supported ". . . the Rev. Wildmon's TV boycott." A similar survey by the *Ft. Worth Star Telegram* found that six out of ten readers stood behind us—60 percent!

That's why I wasn't surprised when the *Wall Street Journal* reported that RCA showed a "steep drop in electronic earnings" during the summer quarter of 1982. We certainly couldn't take all the credit. But I believed that our boycott played a major role in RCA's sudden sales slump.

Besides hurting the NBC owner in the pocketbook, the national publicity our boycott announcement generated significantly bolstered the membership of The Coalition for Better Television as well. Several hundred new groups and organizations signed on shortly after I appeared on ABC's *Nightline*, PBS's *The Mc-Neil/Lehrer Report* and several nationally syndicated call-in interview/talk shows.

At the same time, the supporting constituency of my own National Federation for Decency grew to the point where we were mailing to more than 200,000 friends each month. That gave us the back up support to make NBC's *Princess Daisy* perhaps the most vigorously protested program in television history.

Thanks in part to the "several hundred thousand"[7] anti-*Princess Daisy* letters and calls which NBC admitted receiving, the adult/child sex scene was cut from the script. The homosexual and bisexual affairs also got the axe. And according to *TV Week* magazine, the NFD's efforts played a big role in the heavy editing and reduction of "the incidents of incest."

It's a good thing those scenes were toned down. That's because an NBC spokesman had bragged during production that one of the incest scenes would be "incredibly revealing . . . and . . . steam your glasses."[8] He had also boasted that he and his NBC colleagues were "proud" to have this "trend-setting" miniseries in their programming line up.

As usual, I had difficulty seeing how anyone could be "proud" of a production riddled with fornication, adultery and incestuous promiscuity, no matter how "tastefully" they claimed it was done. Yet by this time I had heard executives from ABC, CBS and NBC make similar statements dozens of times. So I had to believe that NBC officials weren't kidding when they crowed about "breaking new ground"[9] with *Princess Daisy*.

Of course, I had always assumed that money, and money alone, was the driving force behind the networks' constant portrayal of illicit sexual activity. However, as I contemplated the strange pride exhibited by many network officials when introducing a new form of deviant behavior, I wasn't so sure. It almost seemed like some other less tangible yet powerful force was motivating network programming decisions.

But what?

Unmasking a 'Bogeyman'

Several prominent Christian leaders whose paths had crossed with mine claimed to know the answer to my question. "It's all related to humanism," they said. Or sometimes they'd use the term "secular humanism."

I listened to their remarkably similar explanations with much skepticism. These people were trying to make things too pat . . . too simple, I reasoned. They were trying to define and make visible what to me seemed an undefinable and invisible phenomena.

At the same time the national media was severely criticizing my colleagues for attributing much of America's moral malaise to secular humanism. For instance, *Newsweek*, in an article titled, "The Rights' New Bogeyman," likened statements made by Jerry Falwell, Pat Robertson and Tim LaHaye (head of the American Coalition for Traditional Values) to the "virulent . . . anti-communist crusade of the 1950's."[10] Claiming that Falwell and others had "created a conspiracy where none actually exists," *Newsweek* chalked up all the humanism "labeling" to ignorance and the "essentially bellicose" fundamentalist mindset.

Needless to say, with negative coverage like that, I was not anxious to join my friends and acquaintances in the media's meat grinder. Besides, I considered "secular humanism" a confusing, nebulous term. In fact, the term made me so uncomfortable, I scrupulously avoided using it entirely.

Still, I believed Jerry wouldn't say that "secular humanism has become the religion of America" unless he knew what he was talking about. So I decided I had better do some homework and learn everything I could about this "new bogeyman."

My research quickly led me to two documents several friends had guaranteed would be real eye-openers. They were called *The Humanist Manifesto* and *The Humanist Manifesto II*.

As I scanned the long list of influential people who had signed their names to either the original 1933 declaration or its 1973 sequel, I realized that what I was about to read had already left its indelible mark on American education, government and culture. John Dewey, often called the father of modern education, had signed the document. So had R. Lester Mondale, brother of former Vice President Walter Mondale. Other Manifesto signees included Joseph Fletcher, America's best known proponent of "situation ethics;" B.F. Skinner, Harvard's famous behavioral psychologist; Nobel Prize-winning physicist Andrei Sakharov and science fiction author Isaac Asimov. I was intrigued to see that National Organization for Women (NOW) founder Betty Friedan and former Planned Parenthood president Allen F. Guttmacher had signed their John Hancocks as well.

As I began reading what these well-known educators, scientists, authors and social activists had called their "vision of hope, a direction for satisfying survival . . . for the future of mankind," I was impressed by the clear and unapologetic manner in which they spelled out their beliefs and goals. In fact, in some ways the two Humanist Manifestos reminded me of The Declaration of Independence. However, these men and women weren't declaring their independence from another nation, but from God and the rules of order he gives us through Scripture.

For instance, they explained that "humanists regard the universe as self-existing and not created." Since the universe is not created, that can only mean that "man is a part of nature and has emerged as a result of a continuing process."

Of course, I had read and heard evolutionary theory articulated perhaps a hundred times. Therefore I already knew that many people do not believe man is created in God's image, possessing infinite worth, meaning, purpose and value. Instead they view man as an educated animal—basically a piece of meat wrapped around bones, functioning among other pieces of meat in a social and cultural context which just happened. Nothing new there.

Then I read on. And when I reached the section describing how humanists view what I, as a Christian, believe, I almost fell out of my chair.

"Humanists believe that traditional theism, especially faith in a prayer hearing God, assumed to love and care for all persons, can hear and understand their prayers, and is able to do something about them—is an unproved and outmoded faith," the Manifesto authors said. "We find insufficient evidence for belief in the existence of a supernatural," they added. "It is either meaningless or irrelevant to the question of the survival and fulfillment of the human race. As non-theists we begin with humans, not God—nature, not deity."

There it was in plain simple English. These humanists were saying that Christianity is "irrelevant" and "meaningless" for today. They contended that we now live in an enlightened age in which man, through his own reason and intelligence, combined with knowledge provided by science and technology, has everything, is everything and is therefore fulfilled by being self-sufficient. Anyone who still believes in "messianic ideologies" and "false theologies of hope" is not only out of touch with reality, but is actually a menace to society. That especially became evident when the Manifesto writers said, "Promises of immortal salvation or fear of eternal damnation are both illusory and harmful."

To put it more succinctly, anyone who proclaims biblical truth damages the well-being of others.

Indeed as I read statement after statement pointing to Christians as "the enemy," my thoughts drifted to my abbreviated Vail speech, the one that elicited an outpouring of profanity. I had simply noted the anti-Christian bias that anyone who watches television could easily observe. But I didn't know *why* programs set in the 1980s excluded Christian characters and references to Christianity. I also didn't understand why the few Christian characters who did appear tended to be portrayed as bimbos, kooks and hypocrites. Now, however, the obvious anti-Christian bias on network television was beginning to make sense. Apparently, it had something to do with this "bogeyman" called secular humanism.

After the Manifesto authors completed their vindictive assault on Christianity, they turned to the subject of morals and values. And once again, I was startled by the implications of what I found myself reading.

"We affirm that moral values derive their source from human experience," the Manifesto writers declared. "Ethics is autonomous and situational, needing no theological or ideological sanction. Ethics stems from human need and interest . . . "

In other words, these people were saying that it's up to each individual to determine right and wrong. That scared me because they had rejected the Lord's teachings as "irrelevant." With his absolutes and behavioral guidelines out of the way, the door is opened to interpret right and wrong almost any way one pleases. In fact, since ethics are "situational" and stem from "human need and interest," I could see how people in general agreement with the doctrine of humanism could honestly view behavior such as lying and abortion as both justifiable and good.

Next the Manifesto authors articulated their views on sexuality. Again, I read that people like me who view sex inside marriage as a beautiful gift from God are the bad guys. "We believe that intolerant attitudes often cultivated by orthodox religion and puritanical cultures unduly repress sexual conduct," they said. Then, after denying any sexual taboos, they gave the green light to every type of "sexual behavior between consenting adults."

Adultery, fornicatious promiscuity, homosexuality, bestiality, even incest—they're all quite acceptable and "should not in themselves be considered evil," the Manifesto adherents noted. The Manifesto writers also emphasized that "the right to abortion should be recognized."

Whew! Again, I couldn't help but notice that the humanist view of sexuality closely paralleled what the networks broadcast over the public airwaves virtually every night. In fact, as I read on I realized network programming consistently propagated the philosophy espoused in *The Humanist Manifesto* and *The Humanist Manifesto II*. Consequently, I reasoned that the majority of those who call the shots in the TV industry must embrace the Manifesto's teachings. At least, the products of their labor sure seemed to indicate that they did. Yet other than my observing television programming along with hearing and reading occasional random statements, I had no objective way to pinpoint the actual personal value system adhered to by Gene Mater, Lee Rich and most of their powerful peers.

Hollywood and America: The Odd Couple

Then one morning in February 1983 I heard a familiar voice shout, "Don . . . Don Wildmon" from across a hotel lobby. As I do almost every year, I was attending the National Religious Broadcasters Convention in Washington, D.C. So I wasn't surprised to see my friend Forrest Boyd weaving his way through a crowd of people to greet me.

Forrest had been a correspondent with NBC News before beginning his own television news service. A committed Christian, he frequently gave me his insider's perspective on how network broadcast journalists tend to stereotype us "Jesus freaks."

"Have you seen the latest edition of *Public Opinion* magazine?" Forrest asked as he shook my hand.

"Uh, no I haven't," I replied. "I've never even heard of *Public Opinion.*"

"Well you ought to get it," he said rather emphatically. "It contains incredibly revealing research data outlining how the most influential people in the TV industry view religion, morality and social issues. There's even a brief reference to you in the article."

Later that day Forrest handed me a photocopy of the *Public Opinion* story. And as soon as I glanced at the title, "Hollywood and America: The Odd Couple," I understood why he had gone out of his way to get my attention.

The piece was written by three of America's most respected researchers, professors Linda and Robert Lichter of George Washington University and Stanley Rothman of Smith College. As part of a study for Columbia University's Research Institute on International Change, the Lichter-Rothman trio had conducted in-depth personal interviews with 104 executives representing what they called "the cream of television's creative community."[11] Their sample included 15 independent production company presidents, 18 executive producers, 43 producers—26 of whom are also well-known for their script writing, and 10 network vice presidents responsible for program development and selection.

I was extremely interested in what Lichter and Rothman had to say because I had only seen one other piece of literature which directly focused on the beliefs and values of those who shape the shows. A few years earlier, Ben Stein, a former *Wall Street Journal* TV and film critic, had written a book called *The View from Sunset Boulevard.* Like Lichter and Rothman, Stein had personally interviewed several dozen production company heads, producers and network vice presidents.

His conclusion? "The super-medium of television is spewing

out the messages of a few writers and producers (literally in the low hundreds), almost all of whom live in Los Angeles. Television," said Stein, "is not necessarily a mirror of anything besides what these few people think."[12]

Unfortunately Stein did not include scientifically sound statistics to back up his claims. Consequently every time I'd quote Stein, TV industry big shots would discredit my statement by saying, "Stein is full of baloney" or something to that effect. This time, however, I knew there was no way Lee Rich or whoever could deny the validity of the Lichter-Rothman research team's conclusions.

At any rate, after garnering some basic demographic data (e.g., 63 percent earned more than $200,000 in 1981; 25 percent earned more than $500,000), the questioning focused on religion. Though 93 percent claimed to have had a religious upbringing (59 percent were Jewish, 25 percent were Protestant, 12 percent were Catholic) the research team found that 45 percent no longer claimed to have any "religious affiliation whatsoever." But even more illuminating was the fact that 93 percent confessed that they "seldom or never attend religious services."

In other words, the statistics indicated that for most of these individuals, faith in God had become meaningless and irrelevant, just as the Humanist Manifestos had said "faith in a prayer hearing God" was. This reality emerged again later in the study. Each interviewee was asked to rank 10 leadership groups (Intellectuals, Feminists, Consumer groups, Business, Media, etc.) in terms of the influence they believed that group should have in American life. Just as I had expected, religion placed next to last. Only the military fared worse.

Though Lichter and Rothman did not ask these television big wigs *why* they had rejected religion, Ben Stein did in his book I mentioned earlier. Not surprisingly, Lee Rich's views on religion, said Stein, "embraced most of the comments made by others and summed them up."[13]

"The church has been narrow-minded and hasn't grown with the times," said Rich, sounding as if he could have written "The Humanist Manifesto" statement on religion himself. "It's been lumbering along and hasn't taken cognizance of what's going on in the world.

"The church brought us up to believe that things were the way they made them out to be," Rich continued. *"But as we've become wiser and more educated* we've started to challenge these implanted beliefs" (emphasis mine).[14]

Lee Rich's statement gave me a chuckle when I learned that he hadn't been to church since he was a teenager. Not only that, he told Ben Stein that he didn't even "know anyone who goes to church." Yet he was talking as if he were an ecclesiastical expert.

Lee Rich's representative comments, combined with the Lichter-Rothman data, were the final pieces in the puzzle. I finally fully comprehended why Christians and Christianity almost never get a fair shake on network television.

After Lichter and Rothman finished asking their religion-related questions, they moved on to politics. And once again I was intrigued by how little these top TV decision makers have in common with the general population. For example, in 1972, while President Richard Nixon was racking up 62 percent of the national popular vote, he could attract the support of only 15 percent of the TV elite. Eighty-two percent cast their ballots for the liberal Democratic candidate George McGovern. Indeed on most political issues the 75 percent of the TV leaders who described their views as "left of center" took the liberal and sometimes socialist position which most consistently jibed with the politics preached in *The Humanist Manifestos.*

"This contrasts sharply with the national picture," said the researchers as they referred to a 1982 national poll showing that only 27 percent of the general public classified themselves as liberal. According to Lichter and Rothman, 32 percent had labeled themselves conservatives with the rest being self-described moderates.

Next, Lichter and Rothman moved on to sex and morality. Or, rather, sex and immorality. Incredibly, 97 percent of these top TV executives stated that a woman has a right to decide for herself whether to murder her unborn baby via abortion. Even more astounding, 91 percent strongly agreed with what is euphemistically called the "pro-choice" position. Their pro-death view is definitely out of kilter with the general population and made it easy to understand why I had never seen a television program posturing abortion as immoral.

Next came homosexuality. After seeing the pro-abortion statistics, I was ready for anything. Sure enough, four out of five—80 percent—did not regard homosexual relations as wrong. Meanwhile, only five percent agreed with the biblical view that homosexual behavior is immoral.

These figures helped me understand why homosexuals have literally been welcomed with open arms into the TV industry's top echelon. According to *TV Guide*, many of the men who qualified for the Lichter-Rothman study (subjects had to have been associated with the development, production or selection of at least two successful prime time series) are homosexual.[15] At the same time, I could comprehend why the Gay Media Task Force was recognized by TV insiders as the most powerful lobby in Hollywood.[16] The statistics also revealed why more and more TV programming had been depicting homosexuality as a normal, healthy lifestyle and a viable alternative to heterosexual relations.

And speaking of heterosexual relations, only 16 percent of the study's participants strongly agreed that extramarital affairs are wrong, while the majority, according to the research team, "refuse to condemn adultery as wrong."

"From this evidence," they continued, "it would be difficult to overestimate the clash of values when television's creative community confronts . . . Christian critics like the Moral Majority or the Coalition for Better Television."

Indeed, as I finished reading the article I realized that Lichter and Rothman were absolutely right. For most of the previous six years I had erroneously assumed that those who decide what we can watch on TV, despite their obvious animosity toward Christianity, still viewed the Ten Commandments and Judeo-Christian values as the ultimate measure of right and wrong.

Now, however, the truth had become clear.

To most of them, the killing of unborn babies or participation in various forms of illicit sex is A-OK. Why? Because they have adopted a completely different value system—a value system which has replaced God with man, who in turn has become the center of all things and the measure of all things. Just as *The Humanist Manifesto* declared, they believe right or wrong behavior is determined by how it fulfills the needs and interests of each enlightened person, not by some pre-existing God-ordained standard which, they reason, frequently limits human "freedom."

I also fully comprehended that the constant departure from
God's morality on network television programming is much more
than money-related. It is by design. As a matter of fact, I came to
believe that the powerful individuals who create and control network programs (Lichter and Rothman said there are about 350 of
them) see television as a mechanism to justify their rebellion
against God's sovereignty over their lives.

For instance, by featuring sex outside of marriage more than
eight times out of every ten, they reinforce to themselves the notion
that such behavior is an acceptable and approved lifestyle. In the
process they are endeavoring to make this belief, which is rooted
in *The Humanist Manifesto* and runs contrary to God's way, the
accepted norm throughout society.

Contrary to my conclusion, however, I had heard TV executives deny they had a method to their madness time and time again.
Gene Mater, when he had appeared with me on Pat Robertson's
700 Club show, emphatically insisted that TV's two purposes are
merely to entertain and inform. "Commercial TV is nothing more
and nothing less," he said. "We don't need society changed."

Norman Lear, known in Hollywood as "King Lear" because of
his string of smash TV hits such as *All In The Family, Maude* and
The Jeffersons, took the same "entertainment only" tact when *USA
Today* had asked him about the social messages frequently found
in his programming. "Nothing was ever done to send a message,"
he claimed. "We use Western Union for that purpose."

Of course, I now understood that Mater and Lear were probably operating on the humanistic situational ethic that makes distorting truth perfectly acceptable when it's in one's best interest. So
they had purposely spoken somewhat mendaciously to mask their
true feelings from the American public. How can I assume that
these two gentlemen weren't being completely honest? Because
Lichter and Rothman strongly indicated that they weren't.

TV Programmers: 'Rebels With Causes'

"The television elites believe they have a role to play in
reforming American society"[emphasis mine], the three researchers noted in a section they had not coincidentally subtitled
Rebels With Causes. Then, after stating that these people who
"have a major role in shaping the shows whose themes and stars

have become staples of our popular culture . . . would like to alter society in *profound* ways," [emphasis mine], Lichter and Rothman added, "Two out of three believe that TV entertainment should be a *major force* for social reform[emphasis mine].

"This is perhaps the single most striking finding in our study," the scholarly trio concluded. "According to television's creators, they are not in it just for the money. They also seek to move their audience toward their own vision of the good society." [17]

Though Lichter and Rothman kept their list of 104 names confidential, I had a hunch that one of the two women (only a handful of women met the research team's strict qualifying requirements) they interviewed was Virginia Carter, vice president of creative affairs for Tandem/TAT Productions. Described by *Esquire Magazine* as "a fervent feminist and passionate liberal," she had originally been hired by the head man at Tandem/TAT for one specific purpose: to incorporate humanist values and leftist philosophies into his programs, thereby propagating his vision of the "good society." In fact, *Esquire* did not hesitate to call Virginia Carter what she is—a "propagandist."

"I consider it a duty to serve as an advocate," Carter told *Esquire.* "To waste that valuable air space I'd have to be a crazy lady."[18]

I specifically mention Carter's "advocacy" because the head man at Tandem/TAT who hired her is the same man who told *USA Today* that "nothing was ever done to send a message" in his shows. Indeed, after reading the aforementioned *Esquire* article featuring Ms. Carter's boss, Norman Lear, I realized that the world's most influential evangelist at that time was not Billy Graham, Jerry Falwell or some other famous TV preacher. Throughout most of the 1970s and early 1980s the world's most influential evangelist was this man who "talks" via television "to more people each week than any person in history." At least that's how a National Association of Broadcasters brochure referred to Norman Lear when several of his shows were consistently in the top 10.

And what do Lear and his team of ideological clones such as Virginia Carter say to their huge audiences through characters such as Archie Bunker, George Jefferson, Maude Findley, Fred Sanford and Mary Hartman? Well, one message preached happened to be that abortion is no big deal. In fact, through dialogue in one *Maude* episode, Lear and his accomplices told millions of viewers that granting life to an unborn little one would actually be the "wrong" thing to do.

In the scene, the thrice divorced, middle-aged lead character discusses her unexpected pregnancy with Walter, her fourth husband. After Walter confesses that becoming a father was never one of his life's ambitions, Maude's entire perspective on the baby changes:

> Walter: Maude, I want you to have whatever it is you want. Does that include the baby?
>
> Maude: Well, it did when I thought you wanted it.
>
> Walter: Maude, I think it would be wrong to have a child at our age.
>
> Maude: Oh, so do I, Walter. Oh, Walter, so do I. For other people it might be fine, but for us I don't think it would be fair to anybody. Oh, Walter, hold me close [emotion-charged pause while they embrace].
>
> Walter: Frightened, Maude? About the operation, I mean.
>
> Maude: Oh, don't be ridiculous. Why should I be frightened?

These few lines of dialogue are brimming with the humanistic doctrine of situational ethics. Right and wrong is literally determined on the basis of selfish convenience and what the two TV characters perceive to be "fair." What's "fair" for the soon-to-be-slaughtered unborn child is never considered.

" . . . Just tell me that I'm doing the right thing not having the baby," Maude whimpers a few moments later, as if she's made a brave and courageous decision.

"For you, Maude, for me, in the privacy of our lives, you're doing the right thing," Walter replies, reinforcing to both Maude and millions of Americans that abortion is frequently a just and moral "operation." The scene ends with Maude praising her husband for his enlightened wisdom. "I love you, Walter Findley," she croons.[19]

In addition to readily-available abortion services for any woman who views the life within her as an unfair inconvenience, Norman Lear's "good society" also condones illicit sex as proper, sophisticated adult behavior. Indeed he and Virginia Carter had fervently preached this message just three weeks before Forrest Boyd handed me the Lichter and Rothman "Odd Couple" article. That's when an episode of Tandem/TAT Productions' *Diff'rent Strokes* saw young Arnold accidentally discover that his single stepfather, Mr. Drummond, had been sleeping with his lady friend, Miss Saunders.

Dad, as he is called, proceeded to sit Arnold down and tell him about "adult relationships." His explanation? Just because two adults are good enough friends to sleep together doesn't necessarily mean they desire to get married. Later, when Miss Saunders is invited to stay for another night, she asks the boy, "Are you sure you don't mind?"

"Yea, we understand," Arnold replies, with his new, enlightened understanding shining through for millions of American young people to see and hear. "We're all adults here."[20]

That these two evangelistic messages I've just described were unwelcome in most American homes was evidenced in part by *The Connecticut Mutual Life Report on American Values in the 80s*. According to Research and Forecasts, Inc., the market research firm Connecticut Mutual commissioned in 1981 to conduct their study, 85 percent of the American public considers adultery to be morally wrong. *Eighty-five percent!* An overwhelming majority—two out of every three Americans—also believe that abortion is morally wrong.[21]

When I juxtaposed these creditable Connecticut Mutual statistics with the detailed data in the "Odd Couple" article, I realized that a statement made by NBC President Fred Silverman just before he was fired in 1981 was utterly ridiculous. "This industry and this company . . . ride in the mainstream of American values," he had told a group of NBC affiliate managers. "The Coalition for Better Television and the Moral Majority, with their narrow and narrowing views, do not."[22]

But just as the Lichter-Rothman study had proved Fred Silverman to be dead wrong, it also made something else very clear. When it comes to the subject of "values," Norman Lear, Virginia Carter and their powerful peers have almost no intention of respecting the wishes of the great majority who disagree with them. "The TV elites," reported the research trio, "reject the criticism that television is too critical of traditional values by an eight-to-one margin."[23]

Instead, as I've noted earlier, they intend to continue using television to propagate what they believe is best for America and its people. That way, they hope, sometime in the near future Fred Silverman's "we ride in the mainstream of American values" fantasy will become reality.

As I pondered the ultimate goal of what Ben Stein had called "this tiny community in Hollywood which has been given the fulcrum [television] that can move the world,"[24] I realized all the cards were finally on the table. It almost embarrassed me to think that when I left my Southhaven church in 1977, I had thought I would be fighting sex and violence on TV; nothing more, nothing less.

Now I understood that for six years I had actually been on the front lines of a great war. Not a war fought with bullets and bombs, but a spiritual war being fought with images and ideas.

Those fighting on the front lines on the other side have essentially cast their lot with the revolutionaries who declared their independence from God by adopting the humanist view of man; the view that believes enlightened individuals ought to be allowed to set their own, as well as society's, standards of right and wrong conduct. I now comprehended that much televised violence, as well as gratuitous and illicit sex, was simply a natural manifestation of this man-centered and man-measured value system.

Most of those on my side, still as old-fashioned as *The Humanist Manifestos* make us out to be, believed in a prayer-hearing God. We also were convinced that God, in his love for us, had laid down certain basic parameters for living (e.g. The Sermon on the Mount, the Ten Commandments). These standards, we believe, are designed both for our individual benefit and for the good of society as a whole.

At stake in this spiritual war are the hearts and minds of mankind. This struggle will help determine whether or not the Christian view of man will continue to serve as the foundation of both our society and western civilization.

If you don't think Norman Lear, Virginia Carter and many of their powerful TV contemporaries know what's at stake in this war, you're only kidding yourself. And you'd better believe they know who their enemy is!

It's no coincidence that Lear describes the bulletin for his social activism organization *People for the American Way* as "a monthly report on the activities of the Radical Religious Right."[25] Indeed, read almost any of Lear's "American Way" literature and you'll see that he considers almost any Christian who speaks up for and acts on his or her faith to be "dangerous."[26]

Why are Christians so dangerous? Two reasons. First, on the basic human fundamentals of who we are, where we come from and where we are going, our views are diametrically opposed. Second, in the eyes of many of the TV elitists like Lear, Christians are the only major obstacle in the creation of their "good society."

At any rate, one thing I knew for sure: I didn't want any part of Norman Lear's "good society." But I also knew that Lear's godless human utopia would not be long in coming if God's army here on earth, those who are serious about their Christian faith, did not enlist and join the fight.

Don't Thank Heaven for 7-Eleven

"That was the last time I saw Linda alive!" The voice on the other end of the telephone line sounded remarkably steady, considering that it belonged to Dixie Gallery, a Denver woman whose 22-year-old daughter had been kidnapped, drugged, gang raped and murdered only a few months before.

"Linda had been home for Christmas, and we had a marvelous time together," Mrs. Gallery told me. "But she was also anxious to get back to Albuquerque. She had a wonderful boyfriend there and wanted to spend quality time with him and other friends before classes started again at the University of New Mexico.

"I will always remember seeing her in line at the airport waiting to get on the plane," Mrs. Gallery continued. "She was happy . . . smiling . . . everything was great."

Mrs. Gallery hesitated a moment as she somehow mustered the courage to tell me the grisly details of her daughter's final two days on earth—details which had surfaced during the just-completed trial of the four men responsible for her death.

It all began when 44-year-old Johnny Zinn decided to make a pornographic movie. However, he didn't have a "product" (his derogatory jargon for a woman) to play the starring role. So he promised three young men $1,500 if they could find him a "product."

For several days and nights Randy Pierce, Thomas Sliger and James Scartacinni (ages 24, 21 and 17, respectively) scoured the streets of Albuquerque in an unsuccessful attempt to locate a willing participant. But their failure didn't discourage Zinn, who was still determined to make his movie. Finally he told the three, "Okay, you will just have to grab someone off the street."

And that's exactly what they did!

Mrs. Gallery's daughter, Linda, an attractive 5'2" blue-eyed blonde with long, flowing hair, had the misfortune of being in the wrong place at the wrong time. Zinn's henchmen spotted her early one evening while she was shopping for a few grocery items.

Knowing that "the boss" had a kinky affinity for blondes, they proceeded to follow Linda to her next stop—her boyfriend's parents' home. There, two of the three accosted Linda in the driveway, forcibly threw her into their vehicle and sped away to a motel.

Bravely, Mrs. Gallery went on to describe how her daughter was tied up, drugged and repeatedly raped throughout the night. Of course, much of this sexual terrorism was captured on film.

The next morning the Albuquerque media reported that Linda was missing, posing a problem for this band of rapists and kidnappers. Since "the boss" knew that Linda could identify them, he ordered his three partners to "get rid of her."

So they drove to a secluded spot in the mountains. And while Linda begged and pleaded for her life, Randy Pierce loaded his gun and blew her head off.[1]

"Why did this happen?" Mrs. Gallery asked rhetorically. "Because one perverted, sick man wanted a 'product' for a pornographic movie."

She then explained that she had always thought something like this could never happen in her family. "I had erroneously believed that pornography and drugs and the frequent crime that accompanies it only happens to the 'low-lifers,'" she confessed. "People who ask for it by the way they live. You know, drug users . . . prostitutes . . . alcoholics." But she'd learned the hard way that this isn't the case at all.

"Since Linda's death, I've become aware that there are a lot of innocent victims out there," she went on. "And a lot of those innocent victims, like Linda, are dead."

Then Mrs. Gallery told me a little bit about her "all-American girl." Linda had been a cheerleader, an honors student and was close to finishing a college degree in anthropology.

"Linda really had something to offer society," Mrs. Gallery said as her anger and pain became more evident. "And yet her life was taken by animals that roam day and night looking for victims—kind of like the devil who roams the earth 'seeking those whom he can devour.'"

What could I say to this hurting mother whose pride and joy was literally yanked off the street, mercilessly violated, shamelessly photographed and then destroyed? I said the only thing I could say.

I pledged to pour even more resources into the war against America's pornography plague. I also promised to communicate her sad story and let people know, as she requested, that a similar tragedy could happen to anyone.

Sadly, I had a similar conversation with another heartbroken mother just a few weeks later. Sandra Hunter (not her real name) introduced herself to me right after I addressed a group of NFD supporters and friends in Dallas, Texas. Though her tragic tale did not end in murder, the circumstances surrounding it were just as horrifying.

Mrs. Hunter explained that her five-year-old daughter, Susie (not her real name), had been playing in the front yard when the brand new neighbor across the street called her over. The man then struck up a conversation designed to entice her into his house. When Susie hesitated, saying she'd have to get her mom's permission, he grabbed her arm and dragged her inside.

But Susie wasn't shown the child's fantasy movie he had promised. Instead, she was forced to watch a XXX-rated "adult" fantasy.

"When the neighbor had been sufficiently aroused by the pornographic film, he raped and sodomized my daughter," Mrs. Hunter said as she described the gut-wrenching details. "Not once, but twice.

"Susie was chased through the house, screamed at, slammed against a wall and held down on a cold bathroom floor," Mrs. Hunter went on. "And when it was over, much of her body was bruised and swollen."

Mrs. Hunter then told me that much of Susie's ordeal, including her assailant's penetration, was chronicled by another man with a camera. Since the photos disappeared before a search warrant could be issued, Mrs. Hunter and I could only speculate where they went.

But we had a fairly good idea. Chances are they were sold to one of the many illegally-produced and distributed magazines featuring child pornography—magazines with names like *Torrid Tots, Lolita, Children Love* and *Night Boys*.

It's also likely that the photographer made multiple copies of each print. That way he could trade photos of Susie's sexual assault with other "kiddie porn" collectors—much the same way Topps baseball cards are traded.

Knowing that Mrs. Hunter was fortunate to have gotten Susie back (Experts estimate that more than 20,000 children are abducted for sexual purposes each year and are never seen again), I asked how Susie had been doing since the attack.

"The bruises on her body have now faded," Mrs. Hunter responded soberly. "But the emotional bruises remain, and the healing process is painfully slow.

"The happy, gregarious, open child that we used to know became a withdrawn, mistrusting, angry child overnight," she added. "All because a young man took pleasure in causing her pain.

"Since her rape 10 months ago, Susie has had only nine nights without nightmares," Mrs. Hunter shared with an anguished expression on her face. "We're thankful for those. But we know that most of the time there will be screams in the dark as her private monster attacks her over and over again."[2]

As Sandra Hunter talked on about her tormented child, I thought of the countless times people have told me, "Pornography is a victimless crime. It doesn't hurt anybody." When Barry Lynn of The American Civil Liberties Union and porn industry spokespersons such as *Playboy's* Christie Hefner appeared with me on national news programs, they would repeatedly describe pornography (now an $8 billion a year industry in the U.S.) as harmless entertainment.

But my conversation with Mrs. Hunter strengthened my conviction that Hefner, Lynn and all those who perpetuate and believe the *pornography is harmless* fairy tale have seared consciences and scales over their eyes which have blinded them to reality.

I'm convinced that's the case because Sandra Hunter and Dixie Gallery aren't the only people who have shared their real life pornography-related horror stories with me. During the past few years I've talked by phone or face to face with scores of Dixie Gallerys and Sandra Hunters. I've also received personal correspondence from hundreds more. And virtually each of these depressing "Dear Don" letters is a variation on the same theme: Pornography breeds destruction.

Pornography Breeds Destruction

The testimonials which stand out most vividly in my mind are those penned by murderers and convicted sex offenders who are serving time behind bars. Here's just a small sampling from the dozens of letters I've received from prisoners:

• "Pornography's influence on my personality was awesome. While I am personally responsible for the crimes I committed, pornography helped bring me to the point where I didn't care any more . . . ."

—Convicted murderer, Pennsylvania

• "I am writing to let you know just how wrong these people are who believe pornography has no effect on people. Every crime I committed was planned while reading some pornographic book or magazine. Pornography provided the stimulus for my mind."

—Convicted child rapist, New York

• "Pornography nearly destroyed my life. I was so overcome, obsessed and possessed by the lure of this material that it virtually controlled me and my actions."

—Convicted rapist, Iowa

• " . . . In addition to arousing and stimulating myself, I found that *Playboy, Penthouse* and *Hustler* worked very well for my devious seductions of young children."

—Convicted child molester, Oregon

After hearing quotes from some of these sex crime perpetrators, "blinded" pro-pornography propagandists have often tried to write off every single statement as invalid. "Jailed sex offenders can't be trusted to tell the truth," they say. "These men are just trying to earn brownie points for parole." Or " . . . Pornography is just a convenient scapegoat."

Barry Lynn, appearing on ABC's *Nightline* program, used this line of reasoning to discredit the plethora of scholarly studies which clearly show that these testimonials are indeed valid. "What I deny," he said, "is that no study now nor ever will demonstrate that sex abusers are caused to be the kind of people they are because they look at pornography."

However, this denial of the obvious is utterly ridiculous. I can say that confidently because I have read several hundred newspaper articles linking pornography to specific crimes such as the murder of Dixie Gallery's daughter.

As a matter of fact, my morning mail almost always brings porn-related sex crime stories that have been clipped from magazines and newspapers and sent to me by supporters of my organization. And yet, these stories are only the tip of the iceberg of what's really happening across America. As I read these stories, I can't help but wonder how many similar sad scenarios never get reported.

Still skeptical? Ask any detective. He or she will tell you that virtually all rapists and practicing pedophiles possess hefty pornography collections, and that pornography often triggers the abusive and criminal impulses that shatter their victims' lives.

This whole disgusting problem was best summarized by a jailed child rapist who recently told me, "Certainly other factors played a role in my crimes. But just as it can be said for the car that won't run without gas, it won't run without all the other parts either. But all the other parts are useless without the gas.

"Pornography," he said, "was my gas."

Though this person and the other criminals I've mentioned are victimizers who have left a trail of pain and emotional turmoil in their wake, in many ways, they themselves are also victims. Each told a somewhat similar story of how, over a period of time, they became enslaved to pornography's perverted lure. Eventually their insatiable lust for more, more, more drove them to the point where they began to act out their deviant fantasies.

"When I could get material [pornographic] that dealt with kids," explained the pedophile who penned the gas analogy, "I would imagine what it would be like to have sex with them.

"What's unfortunate," he added, "is that I was not content to let it go at that. I wanted it in real life."

Still, as much as I've seen how pornography fuels the flame of notorious sex crimes, my listening and reading has shown me that pornography's destructive impact goes far beyond what newspapers report. For example, I've learned that pornography often is the primary tool the Evil One uses to destroy marriages and tear families apart. Indeed, most of my porn-related correspondence documents this great American tragedy.

A pastor once told me about a man in his church who was having marital difficulties. During counseling, the man, who frequently travels on business, revealed that he had watched a pornographic movie at a Holiday Inn.

That, said the pastor, "ignited a spark within him that he could not extinguish." He was hooked with one look. During every business trip his compulsion for pornography grew until he confessed it had become a "serious, uncontrollable problem."

According to the pastor, who was shocked by the reality of pornography's adverse impact on many of his parishioners, the man had spoken of a "growing sexual dissatisfaction" with his wife. "Normal sex no longer interests me," he explained, since he now wanted to act out many of the bizarre sexual scenarios he had seen in the movies.

The concerned pastor concluded, "He was frustrated, his wife was confused, and the whole house seemed disrupted."

In many ways this businessman was very fortunate. (1) His family was still together. (2) He was able to admit he had a problem and was actively seeking help. (3) We were able to refer his pastor to an organization which helps in releasing porn addicts from bondage.[3]

Unfortunately, in the vast majority of cases I hear about, the damage has already been done. So it was with June Olsen (not her real name) who told me her sad story.

June said she had married a "seemingly well-adjusted, loving" older man who was viewed by others as a community leader (he was a United Way president and little league coach, etc.). A few months later, she explained, her husband had rented some X-rated movies and invited his daughter and son-in-law over for a VCR porn party.

Shocked, June confronted him with her displeasure only to be told, "Don't be a drag. Everybody does this." After that, she said, the X-rated movie watching became a regular part of her new husband's routine. And it wasn't long before he also began bringing home books and magazines featuring sex with animals (bestiality) and sex with family members (incest).

"At first I felt ashamed, embarrassed and cheap," she confessed. "But I tolerated it [the pornography] to fit into my new family. I even convinced myself that it wasn't going to hurt anything."

As the material got progressively more perverse, she tried to shut what he was doing out of her mind. But she couldn't. "It was always with me," she explained, "kind of like a bad cloud hanging over my head."

To make a long story short, while all this was going on, June gave birth to a beautiful baby girl. Then, two weeks after her daughter's first birthday, her worst fear came true.

"I discovered my husband naked in the family room with my daughter's little hands wrapped around his genitals," she told me in a matter of fact manner. "I felt angry . . . betrayed . . . confused . . . sick. And when I begged him to go for help, he laid there and said, 'You're so stupid. I'm not hurting the baby. In fact, it's fun and exciting, just like in the movies.'"

June explained that the incestuous scenario was repeated again the next day. But this time, when she tried to stop it, her husband became violent, slapping her across the face and growling, "Maybe you're into pain? After all, the girl in the movie I watched yesterday was into pain, too."

"Yes, there were other problems in the marriage," June concluded after she told me about the traumatic divorce proceedings. "But I feel that the pornographic materials that he frequently looked at contributed greatly to his attitude and actions."

Unfortunately this is not an isolated example. I could write about several dozen other June Olsens I've heard from who are living proof that pornography destroys marriages and victimizes entire families.

When I left the parish ministry in 1977 to battle indecency on television, I never dreamed that I would one day expand my focus to fight the scourge of pornography. To tell you the truth, in 1977 I hardly knew anything about it. I essentially equated pornography with fancy photographs of nude women in *Playboy*. And I didn't even know child pornography existed.

However, as pornography-related horror stories like those I've described began to come to my attention, I decided I'd better follow my usual procedure and do my homework. Finding, as was the case with television, that a mountain of studies on pornography's cause and effect was already in print, I quickly learned that:

• Pornography is addictive and can lead to sexual deviancy for disturbed and normal people alike.

• Pornography is the literature of sexual deviants.

• Users of pornography frequently lose faith in the viability of marriage.

• Pornography fuels child sexual abuse.

• Pornography victimizes . . . and victimizes . . . and victimizes.

In fact the evidence proving pornography's destructive impact was so overwhelming, I even wrote a book a few years ago called *The Case Against Pornography* (published by Victor Books). Since then, many people have asked me which type of pornography—hard-core or soft-core—has done the most damage to society.

Of course, they usually think I'm going to say hard-core pornography. That's the material which features graphic presentations of vaginal intercourse, anal intercourse, homosexual anal intercourse, oral sex such as fellatio and cunnilingus, rape (both vaginal and anal), gang rape, sadomasochism and/or bondage (often includes leather whips, rope, chains, handcuffs, etc.) bestiality and just about every sexual perversion imaginable.

But they're wrong. As I've studied pornography, I've become convinced that soft-core porn (i.e., some television programs, many R-rated movies, *Playboy, Penthouse,* etc.) has been far more destructive to society.

My rationale?

1. The only essential difference between *Playboy* and *Penthouse* and the hard-core pornography is in the explicitness of the pictures. The underlying philosophy and message is the same: Women are sex objects designed primarily for the self-gratification of men.

2. *Playboy* and *Penthouse*, especially *Playboy* with its high quality, glossy photos, "award winning" articles and anniversary specials on network television, have played a key role in making

pornography acceptable, respectable and even fashionable. Hugh Hefner, his specious magazine and his cable network are sort of like ravenous wolves disguised in sheep's clothing. Why? Because . . .

3. Soft-core pornography is the entry point into the bizarre world of sexual perversity. I can't tell you how many letters I've received from convicted sex offenders, admitted perpetrators of incest and other porn addicts who've said, "It all started years ago [usually about age 12 or 13] when I found a *Playboy* magazine . . ."

Please don't misunderstand! I'm glad more and more citizens all over America are fighting the tidal wave of hard-core pornography that has flooded into their communities. My organization gives much assistance to groups of concerned citizens who want national, state and local obscenity laws to be enforced. I'm simply saying that much more emphasis should be placed on battling soft-core pornography. After all, the less pervasive soft-core porn is in society, the less of a problem hard-core porn is going to be.

At any rate, while I was becoming educated about one of America's greatest tragedies, I discovered that most of the pornography business—"adult bookstores" as well as hard-core movies and magazines—is controlled by about a dozen or so Mafia families. That didn't startle me a bit.

7-Eleven: Your Friendly, Neighborhood Porn Pusher

But one day I stumbled across another pornography-related fact that nearly made me drop my teeth. According to *Everybody's Business*, an almanac published by Harper and Row, the world's largest retailer of pornographic literature was the Dallas-based Southland Corporation.[4] That's the company that owned and franchised more than 7,500 friendly, neighborhood 7-Eleven convenience stores.

This was particularly galling because I had seen print advertising and letters written by 7-Eleven officials calling their stores "family-oriented" establishments. And yet they were the biggest seller of magazines that attack virtually everything the family stands for.

Right then (January 1983) I decided that 7-Eleven needed to be encouraged to live up to its claim. And I figured we were the ones to do it. So I asked NFD friends to hit 7-Eleven officials with a round of courteous communication, both by phone and letter. Our message? *Please stop selling pornographic magazines!*

Thousands of NFD supporters rallied to the cause. Consequently I wasn't surprised to hear from Allen Liles, Southland's vice president for public relations. When he asked if we could get together I figured he had smelled smoke and wanted to snuff it out before our initial low-key protest effort spread into a full-scale fire.

Of course I knew that meant I'd get to hear Liles tell me what a wonderful company Southland/7-Eleven is. Here's a condensed version of the usual public relations spiel: Rev. Wildmon, you must be mistaken. You can't possibly have a problem with us. We're a responsible corporate citizen with a heartfelt concern for the well-being of the communities we serve. We're the good guys!

And sure enough, that's exactly how the personable 7-Eleven P.R. man commenced our meeting. "Since 1976, as a national corporate sponsor of The Muscular Dystrophy Association, 7-Eleven has raised more than $25 million for research and patient care," Liles bragged. "We also raised more than $1 million last year for the March of Dimes' fight against birth defects."

And while he was extolling 7-Eleven's good deeds, he made it a point to let me know they had "voluntarily" stopped selling cigarette paper because they had learned many customers were using it to roll marijuana joints.

I responded the way I always do after a corporate representative tries to impress me by tooting his employer's horn. I expressed appreciation for 7-Eleven's philanthropic generosity on behalf of some fine causes. I also said that I was glad to know of 7-Eleven's concern about America's growing drug use problem. But then I reminded him of the reason he had come to Tupelo.

"Aren't you kind of robbing Peter to pay Paul?" I asked. "I mean, with one hand you're helping Jerry's kids. And that's great for the company image.

"Yet, with the other hand," I continued, "in the name of corporate profits, you're a major contributor to America's huge child sexual abuse problem. I find that markedly hypocritical."

I don't remember exactly how Mr. Liles responded. But I do remember that my comments didn't stop him from trying to convince me that I should leave 7-Eleven alone. He felt that if I was going to insist on making pornography sales an issue, I should pick on some of the other, "less responsible" convenience store chains.

"We have a very restrictive policy for selling adult magazines," Liles said as he made his case. "In fact, our policy is usually much more stringent than local ordinances and serves as a model for the convenience store industry."

He then went on to explain that in company-operated stores (approximately two-thirds of all 7-Elevens nationwide), only *Playboy, Penthouse* and *Penthouse Forum* are available and approved for sale.

"They're kept behind the sales counter in a special rack that obstructs the covers from view," he emphasized. "We also prohibit their sale to minors under 18."

Of course, Liles' wanted to convince me that they had "voluntarily" taken all of these responsible measures in their effort to be, as one 7-Eleven newspaper ad said, "good neighbors."

But I wasn't convinced. Though Liles defended his company's enforcement procedures, I told him that I knew their "18" rule was frequently ignored in many parts of the country. Then I said, "I find it a bit unusual that a 'family store,' as you call it, sells items that can only be purchased by certain members of the family."

As our conversation continued, I checked my watch to see how much time was left before church started. Though I thought his requested meeting time was a bit strange, Mr. Liles had explained that Sunday morning was the only time Southland's corporate jet was available. So I had said I'd be happy to oblige as long as he met me early before Sunday school and worship.

With time running short, I mentioned one final reason why I felt 7-Eleven had no business pushing porno magazines. Early in my research of the sickening, perverted world of pornography, I discovered that *Playboy, Penthouse* and the more explicit publications frequently attack Christianity with a vengeance. So I showed Mr. Liles an eight-page section from a recent *Playboy* which happened to be titled, "PRAYBOY: Entertainment for Far Righteous Men."

Designed to look like a miniature issue of *Playboy*, the section is one of the most belittling, demeaning mockeries of Christians and the Christian faith I've ever seen. For example, *PRAYBOY's* cover features a photo of a nude Eve under an apple tree. Bold, tasteless cover-blurbs such as "Girls of the Moral Majority: A Sensational Fully Clothed Pictorial" and "Christ Played Hurt: A Reverent Interview with Tom Landry" hype the contents inside.

The "Praymate of the Month" centerfold, "Mrs. December," is clad in a nightgown and pictured in her kitchen. One arm cradles a baby while the other holds up a scrub brush. Conspicuously visible behind her are a "Ten Commandments" plaque, a "Stand By Your Man" needlepoint sampler, an American flag and four books—*The Bible, Bible Stories, More Bible Stories* and *Still More Bible Stories*.

Also appearing with "Mrs. December" are her four older children. One of the girls carries an angel's harp. Indeed the picture's entire theme is one of ridicule and scorn for the home, the family, the country and Christianity.

And that's only the beginning. Among a rather irreverent interview with "God" and a full-page advertisement for a "sin surveillance system" (a high-tech chastity belt) are plenty of blasphemous barbs making fun of Christ's words promising eternal life and his references to heaven.

After I finished reading some of the condescending copy from *PRAYBOY*, including a ridiculous letter that was not so subtly attributed to "J.C. II of Tupelo, Mississippi," I told Liles, "Your company sold more copies of this blasphemous mockery of heaven than anyone. Yet, your national advertising slogan is 'Thank Heaven for 7-Eleven.' Don't you find that a bit ironic?

"I want no part of thanking heaven for 7-Eleven," I continued before he had a chance to answer. Then, intimating that the thought of a boycott had crossed my mind, I concluded, "I betcha there are millions more, who, just like me, might not want any part of it either."

When I finished, Mr. Liles replied by noting that he was on a first name basis with both Hugh Hefner of *Playboy* and Bob Guccione, publisher of *Penthouse*. He even mentioned that he had been a guest at Hefner's famous mansion in Beverly Hills. Since "Hugh" and "Bob" did millions of dollars worth of business with 7-Eleven, Liles promised that he would use his influence and "personally" see if he could get them to stop their constant Christian bashing.

As Liles did his name dropping, I smiled to myself. I knew he would only be wasting his time. Still, I figured it was about time Guccione and Hefner knew that their days of unchallenged rosy relations with America's retail community were numbered.

If our Sunday morning meeting had been a debate, I would have beaten the easy going 7-Eleven P.R. professional hands down. But I wasn't interested in demonstrating who had the better case. I was interested in getting porno magazines out of some 7,500 7-Elevens. So when Mr. Liles called two months later and asked if I could meet him and the director of The National Convenience Store Association in Washington, D.C., I was more than happy to oblige.

Thinking that a breakthrough with 7-Eleven was imminent, I flew to the nation's capital with a sense of expectancy. However, as the meeting began, I discovered that 7-Eleven was holding fast to their position. In fact, as Allen Liles talked it seemed that nothing I had said during our previous Sunday morning rendezvous had registered.

Still operating on the principle that 7-Eleven stores are the good guys, Liles proposed a plan to get the entire convenience store industry to adopt 7-Eleven's "strict adult magazine" sales policy. Of course, Liles thought I'd be pleased. After all, he said, his plan would make the more sexually explicit magazines (*Hustler, Chic, Swank, High Society*, etc.) being sold by many other major convenience store chains less readily available.

"If you'll back our plan," Liles told me, "we'll use our influence to help make our policy the industry-wide standard."

I listened intently until Liles finished. Then I once again made my position very clear. I told him that I had no intention of supporting any plan enabling 7-Eleven to remain the world's number one porno pusher. "My intention," I emphasized, "is to get 7-Eleven to pull the magazines."

As I spoke, I could tell that Liles was flustered by my no-compromise attitude. In the corporate world, compromise is a way of life. Indeed, it's how most business deals are made. Most likely, when he learned that his superiors at Southland had no intention of discontinuing *Playboy* and *Penthouse* sales, he worked overtime coming up with a deal that he figured would get me off 7-Eleven's back. But now he had played his hand, and we were still locked in a stalemate.

At that point I knew, and I think Liles did too, that it was useless to try to work out our differences behind the scenes. Still, a couple of months later on a hot July afternoon I once again found myself seated across from Allen Liles. This time it was on his turf in the office of Southland's president, Joe Thompson.

A friend and NFD supporter who knew Joe personally had scheduled the appointment. He was certain that if we could present our case face to face, Joe would "see the light" and pull the magazines. I had serious doubts but went along anyway to see what the Southland president had to say.

Joe Thompson, who I guessed was about 50, was friendly and politely listened while our mutual acquaintance quoted Scripture and appealed to our host's moral conscience—an approach I've found rarely works with most bottom-line oriented corporate CEOs. I hardly said a word. When the plea was over, Joe Thompson responded exactly the way I thought he would.

"Our market research tells us that customers who buy these magazines also tend to buy soda, potato chips, cigarettes . . . stuff like that," he said. "Pulling the magazines would cost us tens of millions of dollars."

Then he explained that if 7-Eleven stopped selling porn and their competition didn't, they'd be handing business over to the other guys on a silver platter. "I appreciate your perspective," Joe Thompson concluded as he ushered us to the door. "But the magazines stay."

Joe Thompson no doubt regretted his "our competitors all carry the magazines" argument a month or so later. That's when I learned that the Chief Auto Parts chain, which is owned by Southland, stocked and sold the anti-Christian porn magazines. Some simple research revealed that Chief was the only major auto parts chain in the country to do so.

My subsequent front page *NFD Journal* article pointing out this hypocrisy apparently embarrassed someone in Southland's corporate cathedral. Two weeks later all porn magazines were removed from Chief stores. Still, as fall 1983 arrived the magazines were still being sold in 7-Eleven stores. Nevertheless I hadn't yet called for an official nationwide boycott against 7-Eleven. That's because, much to my disappointment, I had discovered that most Christians and church leaders were oblivious both to pornography's destructiveness and its prevalence. And since I had never promoted a non-television-related boycott, I had some reservations about whether we could be successful.

I also had dragged my feet because, quite frankly, promoting consumer boycotts is not one of my favorite pastimes. Believe me, I can think of a thousand things I'd rather be doing instead of encouraging people not to buy "Brand X" or patronize "Store Y." If I could be faithful to my Lord by way of another calling I'd walk out of my office in a minute and never come back. But, to be responsible, I must press on. After all, how could I sleep at night if I didn't do something?

Putting the Pressure on 7-Eleven

At any rate, on October 25, 1983, while I was still pondering whether or not to boycott 7-Eleven, I found myself standing on the stage at the Dallas Convention Center. People in the Dallas area had always been highly supportive of NFD's efforts to improve television. So we had organized a "Rally for Decency" there to generate additional enthusiasm.

Five thousand friendly folks had turned out for the rally. And after I showed several examples of anti-Christian programming on some giant screen TVs, I started talking about pornography. During my presentation, I pointed out that the world's largest retailer of porn magazines was headquartered "right here in Dallas."

With countless pornography victims in mind, I continued, "It's about time those of us who are sick and tired of what this trash is doing to America send 7-Eleven a message. I, for one, have not patronized a 7-Eleven since last January."

My comment was greeted by a loud crescendo of "Amens" and "Right Ons" mixed in with spontaneous applause. And that surprised me. But it was a good surprise. In fact, the approval coming from the audience seemed to trigger goose bumps from the top of my balding head to the tip of my toes.

Completely disregarding my notes, I excitedly continued. "Will you join me by not going into a 7-Eleven?" I asked the crowd.

As if on cue, the entire audience rose as one and their voices echoed in a chorus of agreement. Since it was obvious they shared the deepest desire of my heart, I added, "Will you ask your friends not to buy from 7-Eleven?" And with that the emotion reverberated with an ear-splitting roar. It sounded like the Cowboys had just scored the winning touchdown in the Super Bowl.

I could hardly believe my ears and eyes. Here we were in downtown Dallas, only a stone's throw from the Southland/7-Eleven Corporate Center. Southland is one of the biggest employers in the city and respected as a pillar of the community. Yet, here were 5,000 Dallas area residents telling me they weren't going to spend one more dime at 7-Eleven until it pulled the porn.

At that moment, I realized I had heard the answer to my question. Yes, we were supposed to boycott 7-Eleven.

7-Eleven reacted to my subsequent official boycott announcement the same way the networks often do. They responded by not responding. Citizen complaints were almost completely ignored by Mr. Liles' staff. And with the exception of a few memos designed to help individual store managers articulate the company line, 7-Eleven's national office tried to pretend the boycott didn't exist.

The handful of 7-Eleven executives (mostly at regional offices) who did respond couldn't seem to understand what the fuss was all about. For instance, Bob Schiers, the 7-Eleven public relations director for New Jersey and Delaware, noted, "We don't think we're really doing anything wrong."[5]

John Pearman, South Florida division manager, seemed to be exasperated as to why Don Wildmon or anyone else would possibly have a beef with his fine employer. In his replies to complaint letters he proudly told how 7-Eleven President Jere W. Thompson (Joe Thompson's younger brother) had "personally seen to . . . " the removal of cigarette papers from 7-Eleven stores.

"This did affect the profit of the Southland Corporation," he explained. "But it was a conscientious decision that we made because of the detriment it was having on the young people of our country." Then he added, "Thompson made this [decision] not only as a president of a large corporation, but also as a father of seven children."[6]

I suppose some would commend Mr. Pearman for his corporate loyalty. But in light of my July meeting at 7-Eleven headquarters, I must say his letter elicited a good laugh. And about that time I needed a good laugh because I sensed our battle with 7-Eleven was going to be a lengthy campaign.

Still, I wasn't discouraged because plenty of good news was coming from other fronts in the porn magazine war. Throughout the fall of 1983 I had been writing and calling top officials at many of the nation's smaller convenience store chains to explain our concerns. Most regional and national food and drug store chains had been contacted as well.

At the same time, I was strongly encouraging concerned citizens all over America to let their voices be heard. And soon our efforts, combined with the work of some other anti-pornography organizations, began to bear fruit.

Fifty stores here. A hundred stores there. During the winter of 1984 I got word of a minor victory almost every week. I was especially pleased in late January when I learned that 190 Eckerd Drug Stores in their Dallas division pulled all their porn.

The seeds of that triumph were planted when a Ft. Worth woman who had attended our Dallas rally showed some best-selling porn magazines to some friends. One of those friends happened to be the wife of a Dallas-area Eckerd Drug supervisor. She was shocked by the material's perversity and couldn't believe her husband's company was pandering it.

Eventually, the "magazine issue" made its way through corporate bureaucratic channels. And in April it reached Eckerd Drug's founder and chairman, Jack Eckerd. Mr. Eckerd, who had recently made a serious Christian commitment (thanks in part to the witness of Chuck Colson), didn't even hesitate. He ordered the pornographic magazines out of all 1,000 of his stores.

I mention Eckerd because they were the first major player in the porn retailing scene to take an anti-porn stand. And I believed Eckerd's action might help influence some other large national chains to stop selling porn.

As soon as I heard of Eckerd's decision, I called Allen Liles and asked if 7-Eleven planned to follow suit. When he said no, I decided that it was time to increase our pressure. So I scheduled our first nationwide picketing of 7-Eleven stores for August 6.

I was convinced we needed to get tougher with 7-Eleven when I learned that an eight-month-old St. Petersburg, Florida, girl had died while she was being sexually assaulted by two boys, ages seven and nine. According to testimony at the trial, while the babysitter was in another room, the two boys looked at some of their mother's sex magazines (not all porn addicts are men). Using a coat hanger (chains), pencil (dildo) and a belt (whip) the boys mimicked what they had seen.

But that didn't kill the baby. According to the medical examiner, she died from "trauma to the chest and stomach" when one of the boys, imitating what he had seen, climbed on top of her to perform oral sex.

And speaking of oral sex, the May 1984 issue of *Penthouse* had graphically featured oral sex between a man and his teenage niece. In this same *Penthouse* "Erotic Encounters" letter, "Uncle Ted" also tells how he administered several forms of violent sexual punishment, including spanking ("My hand was stinging so badly I couldn't continue") and a sadistic form of buttocks pinching, during "doggy style" intercourse.

"I could sense Gayle [the niece] was enjoying her punishment and that her defiance and pleading were only an act," Uncle Ted wrote. " . . . She was moaning and crying with the intense feeling of pleasure and pain."[7]

As I read what 7-Eleven had sold, I couldn't help but wonder just how many men would be motivated to act out "Uncle Ted's erotic encounter" with their own niece or daughter. I also wondered how many of these men would convince themselves that the cries of their victims were "only an act."

When August 6 arrived, I'm pleased to say that faithful friends jointly walked the picket lines at 560 7-Eleven stores in 168 cities (according to figures based upon written reports mailed in by our volunteer picketing coordinator in each city). We also picketed scores of other porn-selling stores in cities without a 7-Eleven. To our knowledge, it was the most massive picketing of its kind in history.

Yet, true to their strategy of pretending we boycotters didn't exist, 7-Eleven officials did all they could to deny our impact. For instance, Doug Reed, 7-Eleven's media relations director, told the press "his office had received spotty reports of protesting in a few areas of the country, but nothing substantial."

"We put it in the category of not being a big deal," added 7-Eleven regional manager, Fred Davis.

But contrary to their no-big-deal public facade, I knew that our effort was "an issue of great concern to Southland." That's a direct quote from a memo written by Kent Young of Southland's Dallas Corporate Office. He then warned the approximately 40 managers who received the memo that things "will become more heated as Rev. Wildmon tries to put more pressure on the company."

A copy of this memo arrived in my mail the same way just about every other 7-Eleven in-house directive detailing the company's boycott battling plans did. It was sent by one of the thousands of Southland 7-Eleven employees who were on our side. Since they couldn't officially support the boycott, many realized they could help by unofficially supplying "the enemy" with inside information.

Therefore, I knew just about every countermove 7-Eleven was going to make before they made it. These inside sources let me know we were "putting a dent in the wall of 7-Eleven's pornography sales," as one high-level supervisor, who requested anonymity, wrote. "These responses [memos] from our Division merchandizing department let me know that the scuttle in the air is working," he added shortly after our August 6 picket. "I would not continue to work here if I didn't see some light in this issue."

Since I knew we were having an impact, I scheduled and announced three more national 7-Eleven pickets for October, January and April. I figured if we could keep turning the screw, sooner or later Joe Thompson would wise up and say, "Hey, the best thing to do is to get out of this mess because it's just going to keep getting bigger and bigger."

In October sign-carrying friends demonstrated at more than 600 stores. And in January, our numbers were remarkably good considering the circumstances. Being a warm-blooded Southerner, I had forgotten how cold it sometimes gets in the Dakotas, Minnesota, Michigan and upstate New York.

And wouldn't you know it, on the day of our picket, temperatures throughout the Midwest plunged far below zero. Wind chills, which ranged anywhere from -50 to -90, only made things worse.

Brrrrrr!

Nevertheless, thousands of hearty, faithful souls braved the elements to let the Southland Corporation know that their porn-pushing outlets did not "enhance and improve the quality of life" as the 7-Eleven promotional brochure "Your Neighborhood Store" claimed.

Larry Johnson, our volunteer picketing coordinator in Cedar Rapids, Iowa, told me that despite a -80 degree windchill, they had 125 people picketing nine 7-Elevens. Then he proudly said, "We only had one case of slight frost bite."

"We'll help whenever you say go," added George DeLong of Beaver Crossing, Nebraska, as he indicated how "pleased" he was with their turnout. The "16 below zero" temperature reading, he said, only seemed to make it more of an adventure for everyone— an adventure that included plenty of steaming hot chocolate.

As I poured over the January picketing reports, one non-weather related comment in particular caught my eye. I read how our protestors in Lincoln Park, Michigan, had been pleasantly surprised when the 7-Eleven manager, at the risk of being fired, removed the magazines. Then he put on his jacket and joined them. He even carried a sign for awhile.

Similar occurrences had happened several times before, but this incident had special meaning. This manager had witnessed firsthand the destruction caused by sexual deviancy. You see, the previous spring I received a letter describing a brutal rape and beating in the back room of a Lincoln Park, Michigan, 7-Eleven. The rapist was none other than the 7-Eleven clerk. The teenage victim had simply stopped at the store for a soda on her way home from work.

Thinking the girl was dead, the attacker put her in a garbage bag and threw her in the back of his pickup. But she revived and escaped while he finished working his shift.

The letter, which was also sent to 7-Eleven officials in Dallas, was written by a Lincoln Park man who had spoken with police and the girl's mother at the hospital.[8]

Three months later, in April, we picketed almost 1,000 stores—700 of them owned or franchised by the Southland Corporation. Still, the Thompson brothers (Joe's older brother, John, serves as Southland's chairman) weren't giving in. This was despite the fact that some 7,000 stores (600 SUPERx drug stores, 400 Super America gas stations, 450 Albertson's food stores, etc.), including hundreds of independently owned, franchised 7-Elevens, had stopped selling porn magazines during the past year.

Then, during the summer of 1985, two things happened that made me realize that I just might have to try to embarrass the Thompson brothers into pulling the porn.

First, I learned that the Southland Corporation had given a $250,000 grant for child abuse awareness and prevention. To add insult to injury, Southland bragged that this was the largest corporately-funded effort of its kind ever undertaken in this country.

Second, at the same time, the music star Madonna appeared in various stages of undress in both *Playboy* and *Penthouse*. Referring to Madonna's porn magazine debut, Dr. Judith Reisman, who was just finishing an in-depth study on "Images of Children, Crime and Violence in *Playboy, Penthouse* and *Hustler* magazines," concluded that many children would now be more easily victimized by child pornographers since the youngsters would be urged to simply do what their idol Madonna had done.

Dr. Reisman's study, prepared for the office of Juvenile Justice and Delinquency Prevention at the U.S. Justice Department, discussed how the photographs, illustrations and cartoons depicting children in these magazines (*Playboy,* 8.2 times per issue; *Penthouse,* 6.4 times per issue) make "children more acceptable as objects of abuse, neglect and mistreatment, especially sexual abuse and exploitation."[9]

With Southland's ridiculous double standard in mind, I decided to hold a March Against Pornography in Dallas, Texas, on Labor Day morning, 1985. Labor Day, of course, is when Jerry Lewis holds his annual Telethon for Muscular Dystrophy.

Some 13,000 concerned citizens (by official police estimate) turned out for our rally in Cole Park which featured short speeches by Jerry Falwell, Tim and Beverly LaHaye, and several other nationally known evangelists, pastors and Christian leaders who had flown in for the occasion. Then, all 13,000 "porn busters," as some of the press called us, made the three-quarter-mile trek through the streets of Dallas to the Southland/7-Eleven Corporate headquarters.

Indeed at the very moment Jerry Lewis was trumpeting 7-Eleven's corporate generosity, we were holding hands, singing hymns and chorusing "Don't Thank Heaven for 7-Eleven." To our knowledge, it was the largest anti-pornography event ever held—anywhere!

Though virtually ignored nationally, our Dallas rally and march was covered extensively by the local media. And as I found out later from our strategically-placed friends, the Thompsons were plenty embarrassed. I also learned, again from my well-positioned inside sources, that 7-Eleven was really starting to feel our boycott where it counts—in the pocketbook.

That fall, *Advertising Age* reported that porn sales were worth about "\$30 million" a year to 7-Eleven. Yet, enough people had taken their business elsewhere to more than offset 7-Eleven's profits from porn peddling. The problem was, 7-Eleven knew if they pulled the magazines right away it would look like they had knuckled under to Wildmon and his, to quote Hugh Hefner, "evangelical terrorists."[10] They needed a reason, any reason, that would allow them to get out of the porn business while saving their corporate pride.

That "reason" finally came in April 1986 in the form of The Meese Commission Report on Pornography. After announcing that 7-Eleven would no longer sell adult magazines in their 4,500 corporately-owned and run stores, 7-Eleven president, Jere W. Thompson explained, "The testimony [of the Meese Commission] indicates a growing public awareness of a possible connection between adult magazines and crime, violence and child abuse." [11]

7-Eleven's action started a chain reaction. During the next few weeks, 5,000 more stores pulled their porn, including 2,000 Revco drug stores and 1,400 Rite Aid "family" drug stores. I was especially thrilled with Rite Aid's wise decision. Rite Aid's chairman, Alex Grass, had once called us "rabble rousers" [12] as he defended films like *Daddy's Little Girls*, *The Younger the Better*, *Bodies in Heat* and *Desires Within Young Girls* which appeared in his company's video catalog. I wonder if my "you're next" letter had anything to do with his change of heart?

At any rate, thanks in large measure to 7-Eleven's action, the two-year total of porn-pulling stores passed 20,000. As I contemplated this, I knew that much of the credit needed to go to the 18,000 folks who attended our two Dallas rallies and the 100,000 people who directly contacted 7-Eleven by phone or letter.

I also knew I owed a special word of thanks to each faithful friend who had carried a picket sign in scorching heat and bone-chilling cold—the folks Hugh Hefner had angrily called "literary death squads."[13] Of course, I could certainly understand why Mr. Hefner was so agitated. In the months immediately following 7-Eleven's action, *Playboy's* circulation dropped 26 percent—an average of 674,000 copies per month.[14]

Most of all, I realized that the praise for this victory needed to go to God himself, whose Holy Spirit, through us, was actively waging the war against pornography. Still, there wasn't much time to feel good about what had been accomplished.

Ma Bell Listens to Some 'Sweet Reason'

Perhaps you have heard of AT&T's "Dial-It" 900 service? It's like the 800 long distance telephone service where callers can reach businesses free of charge. The 900 numbers are used by businesses as well, except the tab is paid by the caller. AT&T has made tens of millions of dollars because the charges are usually much bigger than rates for normal long distance numbers. Many businesses offering such information as sports scores, state lottery results and stock market information, have also made good money from the kickbacks AT&T has given them for each call.

Unfortunately many pornographers had discovered AT&T's 900 service was a great way to make a buck. All they had to do was create a tape recording of seductive sounding females (or males for homosexual callers) who graphically describe various sex acts, advertise their numbers with names like "Fantasy Phone," and people from all over America would call.

By 1987 "Dial-A-Porn," as it's called, got to be so big, it was accounting for almost half of AT&T's 900 service revenue.

It was bad enough that "Ma Bell" had become one of America's biggest porn profiteers. But it bugged me even more when I learned that many children were dialing these numbers like there was no tomorrow. Rare was the day when I didn't hear from outraged parents who were having to foot the bill for their child's porn fetish. Some of the bills were astronomical. In March 1987 I learned of one California 15-year-old who had run up phone sex charges of $5,313.[15] Though in that instance AT&T was not the beneficiary, I decided it was time to ask America's largest phone company to get out of the pornography business.

AT&T chairman, James Olson, responded to my phone calls and letters by claiming that the FCC required them to "carry the communications of all customers upon request, regardless of content."[16] I knew that was not necessarily the case because MCI, U.S. Sprint and Allnet had already dropped Dial-A-Porn. The 11th U.S. Circuit Court of Appeals had also upheld Southern Bell's decision not to do business with phone sex firms stating that this was not a public utility or First Amendment issue, but rather a business issue.

After months of receiving the run around from chairman Olson, I realized that the whole issue boiled down to dollars and cents. AT&T simply didn't want to kiss all those millions goodbye. So I wrote Mr. Olson again in December 1987. I gave him until January 15, 1988, to disassociate AT&T from the porn industry. "If no action is taken by then," I said, "I'm going to mail 600,000 letters encouraging people to switch to another long-distance carrier."

Surprise, surprise! A few days before my deadline AT&T announced that it would no longer give businesses with 900 numbers a financial kickback on their calls. AT&T also announced that they would no longer provide direct to the caller billing services for "Dial-A-Porn" firms.

This action meant that the 900 service was no longer profitable for the porn merchants. It also reduced the epidemic of child callers since "Dial-A-Porn" could now only be accessed on regular numbers by people owning credit cards.

Though AT&T lost, according to one "Ma Bell" official, about $40 million, it's amazing how effective sweet reason can be when a company knows that hundreds of thousands, if not millions of concerned citizens, will make them pay an even heavier price for their corporate greed and moral irresponsibility!

Mighty Mouse Snorts Coke and Other Horrors

Dear Ann Landers:

In February you printed a letter about a toddler in Boston who was stabbed seventeen times by a five-year-old. You said the child probably got the idea from watching TV. Well, let me suggest another possibility. I shall do my best to tone my letter down because the words to describe this filth cannot be printed in a family newspaper.

This trash is called Garbage Pail Kids, published by Topps Chewing Gum Company. These cards are obtained when the kids buy gum. They are traded back and forth and the idea is to get a big collection.

I shall try to describe some of the cards I'm looking at. One is a colored drawing of a child who has been stabbed in the back and his head has been split open with an axe. The blood is gushing out. Another card shows a child who has been run over and crushed by a car. Still another pictures a little boy with fourteen spikes going through his body.

The most disturbing card pictures a child grinning after he shoots a little girl. The dead child is lying on the ground with three bullet holes in her body. The boy is laughing.

Our eight-year-old neighbor boy has a Garbage Pail poster that shows an infant stabbed with knives, hypodermic needles and swords. The infant is wearing a target. The caption on the poster says, "Have a Nice Day."

At a time when so many children are being abused we do not need this kind of trash that pictures children as garbage. Please use the power of your column to alert parents to this monstrous thing.

—Ellen H. in Houston, Texas

Dear Ellen:

I wrote about Garbage Pail Kids a few years ago and was under the impression that we had gotten rid of them. Apparently we haven't.

I urge all parents to refuse to patronize drugstores, grocery stores, candy stores or novelty shops where these cards are offered. Tell the manager why you won't be coming in any more.

If your child has these cards, take them away and explain why they are bad to have. Make it plain that hurting and killing people is not funny and that nobody should joke about violence and murder.

—Ann Landers[1]

Garbage In: Garbage Out!

America's favorite advice columnist is right! *Garbage Pail Kids* cards, produced and marketed by Topps, the company famous for its baseball cards, truly are a "monstrous thing," as Houston's Ellen H. asserts. But, the shocking children's trading cards she described in her letter to Ann Landers only scratches the surface of the *Garbage Pail Kids* nightmare.

Other cards depict "Busted Bob," a baby boy whose severed arms and legs are scattered across the floor and "Well Done Sheldon," who has been roasted to order at the stake. Toddler "Nerdy Norm" smokes four cigarettes at once. "Boozin' Bruce" is an infant wino clutching a liquor-filled baby bottle. And these are only a few of the revolting characters available.

Within days after these bizarre collectibles featuring murder, brutality, self abuse, sadistic torture, rebellion, anarchy, cannibalism and even child suicide first hit store shelves in 1985, I began getting phone calls and letters from exasperated parents. "What's this world coming to?" many asked. Then they'd tell me how their children, just like many of their friends, had blown their entire allowance on the grotesque cards.

Indeed, the cards were tremendously popular. For a couple of years, *Garbage Pail Kids* collecting obsessed millions of young people. In 1986, Topps spokesman Norman Liss revealed that "the demand is incredible—more than we can keep up with." And that's what broke the hearts of the parents who contacted me.

Since children are only beginning to learn how to differentiate between right and wrong, good and evil, these parents believed that frequent exposure to these diabolical images couldn't be anything but harmful. Simple logic told them that children who see deranged behavior portrayed as humorous and cute will be more likely to accept abnormal behavior as normal. Realizing that an entire generation was being weaned on this appropriately named "Garbage," these parents were furious.

Many state PTA organizations, such as New Jersey's, called the cards "psychologically harmful" and begged Topps to stop making them and stores to stop selling them.[2] Scores of psychologists who feared that some children would act out what they had seen joined the crusade as well.[3]

Unfortunately Topps Chairman Arthur T. Shorin apparently determined right and wrong on the basis of profits. His public relations people pointed out the "enormous popularity" of his torrid card series, as if that somehow justified its existence. Then, inferring that *Garbage Pail Kids* critics didn't know what they were talking about, Topps officials repeatedly stated, "We wouldn't put them out if we thought they were wrong." They also had vowed with recalcitrance to keep "marketing them as long as *parents* keep buying them" (emphasis added).[4]

I countered Topps' self-serving rationalization by urging everyone to do what Ann Landers recommended: Boycott stores that sell *Garbage Pail Kids*. I also reproduced some actual cards in our monthly journal so people could see for themselves how blatantly abusive they are.

But, with so many of my organization's resources tied up in pressuring pornography pushers, I didn't make battling *Garbage Pail Kids* a top priority. However, that policy changed instantaneously one sweltering July day in 1987.

I had been browsing through one of the entertainment industry trade journals when I stumbled across some shocking, but not surprising, news. I learned Judy Price, CBS vice president of children's programming, had purchased the television rights for these abominable characters that promote demonically based behavioral change. CBS planned to headline its new fall Saturday morning line-up with *Garbage Pail Kids*, the cartoon show.

That's right! Come September 19, millions of little ones would get to see creepy, make-believe characters such as "Bustin' Dustin" (a baby boxer with a perpetual nosebleed) and "Basket Casey" (a boy who dribbles his own severed head like a basketball) magically come to animated life. Through various sources I learned that the animated children on the *Garbage Pail Kids* show would first appear as if they were normal. But by uttering the mantra "Trash Out," they could magically assume the identity of a grotesque *Garbage Pail Kids* character.

Of course, Judy Price claimed that the program would be harmless. She promised that no television character would cut off his own head, poke her own eyes out, set off firecrackers in his mouth or stuff herself into a trash compactor, as some of the card characters do.

But as far as I was concerned, CBS had stooped lower than they ever had before to make a dollar. I agreed with my friend, Dr. Thomas Radecki of The National Coalition on Television Violence, when he said, "By using anything related to the cards, they're saying it's okay to get a laugh out of brutal sadism."

Time was short. Still, I was determined to mobilize a large protest against CBS. In the process, I hoped that hard-hearted CBS officials would be so overwhelmed with anti-*Garbage Pail Kids* sentiment that, for once, they'd sit up and take notice.

As I thought of the sick, slick message a *Garbage Pail Kids* cartoon show would send to young ones all across the land, I was mighty glad I could count on more concerned friends than ever before to stand with me. Direct support for my organization (now called The American Family Association) had multiplied many times during the 1980s. That enabled me to challenge and inform 325,000 individuals, couples, pastors and churches through the monthly *American Family Association (AFA) Journal*. In fact, almost half the pastors and churches in America received timely updates.

The days when people had kidded me about being the Lone Ranger from Tupelo were ancient history. Now I had plenty of highly-skilled riders in the storm. This increased support also helped the American Family Association significantly expand its overall outreach.

For instance, we were able to hire a national director for our 400 AFA Chapters located in almost all 50 states. Made up of citizen volunteers, these groups primarily focus on ridding their communities of pornography and porn-related businesses.

To better support our AFA Chapters, we also added a legal department. Believe me, when you do battle with the well financed and highly-organized pornographers you need all the legal expertise you can get.

Four thousand volunteer monitors now helped us keep close tabs on prime-time network programming and sponsors each fall and spring. Someone else had taken over responsibility for coordinating that effort. Another AFA staff member helped with the extensive research and preparation necessary for my daily Don Wildmon Report radio broadcast aired on some 200 stations nationwide.

At any rate, in addition to publicizing my *Garbage Pail Kids* protest in the *AFA Journal* and on my radio show, I mailed out 620,000 individual letters to people I believed would take action. The response was incredible. During late August and early September, CBS was bombarded with cards, letters and phone calls from flabbergasted adults. Their message? *Trash the show.*

But it wasn't only grown-ups who let CBS know their feelings. Some kids were disgusted too. After signing and sending a protest card to CBS, nine-year-old Chad Birdwell of Kingsville, Texas, sent me part of his allowance to assist our effort. He explained that he thought the cards "were sickening and a very bad influence," especially the ones that "suggest suicide."

"After Dad told me what your letter was about, I was happy to know that there are some adults out there willing to help us kids," Chad wrote. "Thanks for trying to clean up America for us kids."

Needless to say, touching testimonials like Chad's gave me plenty of incentive to personally contact every potential *Garbage Pail Kids* advertiser I could think of. My request was very simple: Please don't help pay for CBS's "Garbage." Then, after warning them of probable economic repercussions if they sponsored the show, I explained why so many people did not want to see the *Garbage Pail Kids* on TV.

Normally when I write or call about a yet-to-be-aired program, only a handful of sponsors will take the time to send a "we agree with you, we won't be on the show" response. However, I knew CBS's *Garbage Pail Kids* plans had shocked officials at many of America's major corporations that advertise on children's programs when what seemed like almost every company on my list responded. Not only did they tell me they wouldn't be buying *Garbage Pail Kids* commercial time, but also most said they wouldn't appear on the show even if CBS gave the time away.

As a result, on September 15, four days before the scheduled *Garbage Pail Kids Show* premier, CBS quietly announced that they were canceling the show. The dearth of willing advertisers, combined with the intense public protest, had forced CBS executives to eat their $3 million *Garbage Pail Kids* investment (almost a dozen episodes were already completed).[5]

The next day *Variety* reported that "nobody at CBS wanted to comment on the abrupt tossing out of its 'Garbage'; however," *Variety* went on, "insiders admitted the move was due to demands by various pressure groups not to air the series."[6]

Since the American Family Association was the only group the article specifically mentioned, I recognized that I was reading about a great victory—a victory that ultimately belonged to both the children of America and the Lord of heaven whose love for little ones is immeasurable. Faithful friends like young Chad Birdwell had helped make television history. To my knowledge, this was the first time a network had ever announced a decision to air a series and then canceled that series because of public outrage.

As I reflected on CBS's historic action, I chuckled as I recalled some defiant words spoken by CBS Broadcast Group President Gene Jankowski. "CBS will never cave into Wildmon's demands," he had promised after my duel with Gene Mater six years earlier. "To do so would be tantamount to betraying our own principles.

"We are clearly dealing with principles here, not money," Jankowski had proudly continued. "No show will be canceled from CBS because of pressure of this type, regardless of sponsorship or no sponsorship."[7]

I hope I'm not guilty of the same stubborn pride when I admit it felt kind of good to see my longtime network nemesis "betray his principles." Still, I had learned enough about CBS to know that sooner or later some high level executive would look at the $3 million and try and resurrect the show. I was especially concerned when I discovered that Judy Price was lobbying hard behind the scenes to get Jankowski and her other bosses to reverse their decision. "It ain't over until the fat lady sings," she told the *Los Angeles Times*.[8]

A few months later I got a tip that CBS was considering sneaking *Garbage Pail Kids* into the schedule before another protest could be mounted. So I was left with no choice but to ask AFA friends to hit CBS with another round of cards, letters and phone calls. I also had people implore CBS not to sell the completed episodes to a cable network or a children's programming syndication service.

Unfortunately that's exactly what CBS finally did. CBS dumped the video version of this trash, no doubt at a fire-sale price, on The Movie Channel (TMC), a pay cable network. As I write this, TMC has not aired any of the episodes. But it's quite possible that the smelly *Garbage Pail Kids* saga is not yet over.

At any rate, even though CBS ultimately did not air *Garbage Pail Kids*, Judy Price's children's division was still tossing plenty of junk onto the trash heap of mind-polluting television programming. Let me elaborate . . .

CBS Deals Dope on Saturday Morning

One May 1988 morning I found myself standing next to several American Family Association staff members in our video recording room. That's where we keep about a half-dozen donated video cassette recorders and televisions.

Since 1983 AFA has videotaped virtually all evening prime-time programming (365 days a year) aired on ABC, CBS and NBC. That way, when the networks ridicule Christianity or present uncalled for violence or gratuitous sex, we have the evidence in living color. However, on this particular occasion, we weren't watching a program we had taped ourselves. Instead we were all watching a Saturday morning cartoon show a Kentucky mother had recorded while she was out shopping with her kids.

This woman had phoned our office a few days earlier. And to be honest, I had thought she was just another crank caller trying to play a practical joke on us. The incredible charge she made against

CBS was so ludicrous, I found it impossible to believe. Sensing I thought she was off base, she offered to send me her video tape so I could see for myself.

As the tape she sent rolled I focused my eyes on a furry little mouse with big ears and a cape. The animated rodent, who was depressed because the lady mouse he loved had not been responding to his affection, was reclining next to a campfire at the end of a long day. A few moments later the melancholy mouse reached under his cape and pulled out a powdery looking substance. Then I noticed that the powder suddenly disappeared right up the creature's nose.

"Please tell me I didn't actually see what I think I just saw," I said to my co-workers, who appeared to be in a state of shock. "Let's see that again."

When the tape rewound, we again watched the TV screen in incredulous wonder as the scenario repeated itself. Into the cape went the cartoon character's hand. Out came a powdery substance. Up his nose it went.

"Our Kentucky friend wasn't kidding," I finally said, breaking the sober silence in the room. "It's as plain as day. They've really got Mighty Mouse snorting cocaine."

I was especially outraged because in the next scene Mighty Mouse's depression had lifted and he was his usual, heroic self. Though I doubted if any children watching the Saturday morning show were cognizant of the subliminal message, I sure didn't miss it: Need a lift? Just take some cocaine. It's the perfect pick-me-up.

Later that day, to make absolutely certain our eyes weren't playing tricks on us, we invited an agent from The Mississippi Bureau of Narcotics to our Tupelo office. Without telling him what to watch for, we showed him the taped episode. His response? "There's no question. Mighty Mouse is snorting coke."

During the next several days I tried to figure out how and why CBS could have allowed the unthinkable on a cartoon show viewed by millions of children. And the more I thought, the more I realized my questions weren't all that difficult to answer.

First, I remembered a two-part series about cocaine use in Hollywood that appeared in *TV Guide* magazine back in the early 80s. "Cocaine is so popular in the world of Hollywood television studios, it sometimes is used to pay producers, performers and writers," the nation's most-read TV publication had reported. The previous year (1987), The Associated Press had quoted Tom Kenny, director of a Hollywood substance abuse counseling center called Studio 12. Drugs in the movie and television business are "out of control," said Kenny. "Cocaine is the prime culprit."

Second, I turned my attention specifically to *Mighty Mouse: The New Adventures*, which the latest issue of *TV Guide* had ironically called "sly, hip and unpredictable." *TV Guide's* message to parents continued, "If you're not joining the kids on the couch Saturday mornings, you're missing something." *That's for sure*, I thought to myself.

But when *TV Guide* said that the new "refashioned" CBS cartoon hero was produced and animated by none other than Ralph Bakshi of *Fritz the Cat* fame, all kinds of red flags went up inside my mind. You see, when I had of necessity familiarized myself with the pornography business I'd learned that *Fritz the Cat*, bankrolled in part by Hugh Hefner, made history as the first X-rated animated feature film. Knowing that CBS had hired a notorious pornographer to create a new children's hero, I decided I'd better check out the man behind the mouse. And it didn't take long to find out that Ralph Bakshi is no Walt Disney.

To my dismay, I discovered that sex, violence and drugs are major subthemes in most of Bakshi's X- and R-rated feature films such as *Heavy Traffic, American Pop* and *Coonskin*. *Fritz the Cat*, for example, features a marijuana-smoking orgy. Bakshi's imagery becomes more understandable when one learns that he grew up in a New York City ghetto where the neighborhood gang called themselves "The Hell-Bent Rapists."[9] Referring in part to his claim to have been "accidently splattered by blood from a Mafioso hit" at age eight,[10] the *New York Times* once concluded, "At bottom, Bakshi is well aware that his scarring upbringing will underlie everything he does in films."[11]

"I work in a stream of consciousness, recalling events from my whole life," Bakshi told the *Times*. "I go all out to express my hostilities."[12] That comment especially made sense when I learned that the National Coalition on Television Violence had ranked *Mighty Mouse: The New Adventures* the most violent program aired on Saturday mornings, featuring some 60 violent acts per hour.

After I had studied Bakshi's revealing bio, the third and final piece of the Mighty Mouse cocaine-snorting puzzle fell into place. I remembered some comments made one year earlier by CBS vice president for children's programming, Judy "Garbage Pail Kids" Price. In a *Los Angeles Times* interview, Price explained the surprising reason why she had entered the field of children's programming. "I could get away with more, which is strange, isn't it?" she bragged. Noting that she could get more "controversial subject matter" past the network censors, she continued, "I think we've broken a lot of ground where people would not have dared to go in prime time."[13]

In the midst of the *Garbage Pail* stink I had indirectly asked Price if that series was what she meant by "breaking new ground" and "getting away with more." Now I wondered if Mighty Mouse epitomized what she had been talking about.

Of course, Price never answered my question relating to her "breaking new ground" and "getting away with more" statements. Instead she repeatedly denied making them. I got a kick out of her mendacious response, however, because the *L.A. Times* interviewer confirmed that Price had actually reviewed and approved the completed article before it went to press.

I decided that there was absolutely no way I was going to let Judy Price and her employer "get away" with sending a pro-drug message to America's children. So I had several hundred black and white still photographs reproduced from the actual video. Then on Saturday, June 4, 1988, with the pictured evidence enclosed (see photo section), I mailed an exposé-type press release to newspapers and magazines all over America.

Anatomy of a CBS Cover-up

On Monday, June 6, pandemonium broke out at CBS headquarters. Journalists bombarded CBS with Mighty Mouse-related inquiries. And panic-stricken CBS officials, caught completely by surprise, didn't have the foggiest idea of how to respond. Finally, by mid-afternoon, CBS had changed their "no comment" to "we'll release a prepared statement tomorrow [Tuesday] afternoon."

Hurriedly, CBS vice president for program practices, George Dessart, prepared a response indicating that "CBS categorically denies that Mighty Mouse or any other character was shown sniffing cocaine." It included a bizarre explanation that Mighty Mouse was, in reality, "enjoying the smell of his 'lucky chunk of cheese.'"[14]

How it's possible to grate a "lucky chunk of cheese" into a fine powder and then snort it, I'll never know. But apparently, at first, that's what CBS wanted me and millions of Americans to believe. I say "at first" because I wasn't supposed to receive Dessart's "lucky chunk of cheese" letter, dated June 7, 1988.

You see, CBS had remained silent much too long. So when Tuesday afternoon arrived, several reporters were begging them to make good on their promise to issue a prepared statement. Consequently George Dessart foolishly faxed a few copies to a handful of anxious reporters as soon as it was ready. Of course, he had no way of knowing that one of those reporters happened to be a friend of mine. And that meant I had his letter in my hands within minutes.

Later that day, prior to final mail call, CBS discovered they had a problem. Though they weren't talking to reporters, Ralph Bakshi was. Naturally, he was absolutely livid, calling my charges "lunacy." Then, sounding a lot like Lee Rich, Gene Mater and other Don Wildmon bashers, he said the whole affair "smacks of burning books and the Third Reich." However, CBS's trouble stemmed from the fact that Bakshi never mentioned any "lucky chunk of cheese." Instead, he claimed the substance disappearing up Mighty Mouse's nose was a handful of—get this—"crushed flowers."

Imagine my surprise when I discovered that George Dessart had quickly changed his story to match Bakshi's. In my "official" letter, dated June 8, Dessart told me that I had actually seen Mighty Mouse sniffing the "aroma" from a "mass of crushed stems, tomatoes and flowers."[15]

Dessart's letter, which was also released to the media at large, is the most deceptive letter I've ever seen written by a major network official. He called my "flight of fancy" an "irresponsible misrepresentation" which takes "three seconds of airtime [actually, it's about six seconds] out of context."

Sadly, much of the media around the nation believed Dessart's lies. Not knowing the truth, officials at the *Texarkana Gazette* wrote an editorial representative of many. Labeling me a "zealot reactionary trying to make a name for himself," they said, "Frankly, we think Wildmon is full of himself. If the Mouse's creator,

Ralph Bakshi, or CBS, committed any sins, it was in having the dignity to respond to such lame attacks."

I guess I can't really blame the editorial staff at the *Texarkana Gazette* for blindly siding with CBS. I myself had found the thought of Mighty Mouse snorting coke difficult to believe at first. At the same time, most of the good folks on America's Main Streets did not know that CBS, proving that they indeed had something to hide, was not honoring requests for the video footage. Most major television advertisers, radio stations, newspapers and even ABC and NBC television stations had to get their copies of the actual coke-snorting scene from me.

Shortly after the initial Mighty Mouse media furor died down, I was startled to learn I had not been the first concerned individual to alert CBS to this travesty. That dubious honor went to Dino Corbin, general manager of the CBS television affiliate, KHSL, in Chico, California.

Like me, Mr. Corbin had been highly skeptical when a viewer said that her 6- and 10-year-old children had seen "Mighty Mouse snort coke." But when Mr. Corbin reviewed the tape, like me, he became a believer. Before he contacted Judy Price, he showed the episode, called "The Littlest Tramp," to eight station employees. To a person they all said, "Mighty Mouse is doing a line"—slang for snorting cocaine.

But most startling of all, Dino Corbin had alerted CBS to Mighty Mouse's drug habit the previous December. That's right! The videotape I saw was not made the first time the cartoon had aired, but the third.

Even more startling was the fact that CBS officials had assured Corbin in December that the scene would be cut. Yet they did nothing. It made me wonder if some high ranking CBS executive were deliberately trying to poison the minds of our young people by teaching them that it's okay to use drugs.

By late June I was sick and tired of CBS's obvious conspiracy to cover up the truth about their cartoon mouse. Not only had they deceived the American public with a whole series of distorted lies, they had done it so craftily that most people believed that Don Wildmon was the villain. As I prayed about additional ways to bring the truth to light, I remembered an offer George Dessart made in his deceitful June 8 letter.

"We would be happy to show you or your associates the episode of *Mighty Mouse: The New Adventures* which was broadcast over the CBS Television Network on April 23, 1988," he had written. "It would appear that you have not had that opportunity since what is described in your press release bears no relation to anything CBS has broadcast or would consider broadcasting."[16]

Of course, George Dessart knew darn well I had seen the episode. He had cunningly made and worded his offer so the nation's journalists would think Don Wildmon had completely lost touch with reality. I don't think he ever for a moment thought I'd actually take him up on it. But that's what I felt led to do.

Since Tupelo doesn't have a CBS affiliate station, I called Dessart and asked if I could see the episode while I was in Washington, D.C., on some other business. He couldn't very well renege his offer. So once the arrangements were made, I invited all 535 U.S. congresspersons and senators to the special screening. I also invited several members of the national press corps.

When showtime arrived, so did more than two dozen congressional staff members, including aides to Senator Helms of North Carolina and Representatives Bliley of Virginia, Chandler of Washington and Dannemeyer of California. When reporters such as Bill Anderson of United Press International began appearing, the CBS employee in charge excused herself, I assumed, so she could call New York. The moment she returned she told the members of the press to leave. However, when I pointed out that that would appear to be an obvious admission of guilt, she eventually let everyone enter the screening room.

When it was over, I could tell that everyone was horrified that Mighty Mouse had taken drugs and angered that CBS had so brazenly lied to the American people.

The next day Congressman Rod Chandler expressed his "utter outrage" to CBS president Laurence Tisch. After describing his skepticism at what "simply had to be a crazy accusation," Chandler told Tisch he had dispatched two attorneys from his staff to the screening.

"They both concluded, after viewing the entire program once and the scene in question several times, that the only conclusion that could be reached is that Mighty Mouse indeed had snorted cocaine," Congressman Chandler wrote. "Frankly the response of

CBS has been completely inadequate. That the powder in question was a 'mass of crushed stems, tomatoes and flowers which the character was smelling in typical cartoon fashion,' *is unbelievable to anyone who has seen the program* (emphasis mine).

"In view of the drug crisis facing this country and the need to educate our children on the dangers of drugs," Chandler continued, "airing this program was unforgivable. The fact that CBS has refused to admit its mistake or to act to prevent this kind of mistake in the future, is equally unforgivable."[17]

So outraged was the Washington congressman, and rightfully so, that he sent a copy of his letter, along with still pictures of the coke-snorting scene, to every one of his colleagues on Capitol Hill.

But it wasn't just public servants who got good and mad at CBS. So did many big-time advertisers, including Ralston Purina and Mars, Incorporated who both had unsuspectingly pushed products on the infamous coke-snorting show.

Ralston chose to take a low key approach and simply told CBS that they, "in all candor, share the concerns of the critics." Mars, on the other hand, wrote the most condemnatory letter I've ever seen a sponsor address to a network. CBS certainly didn't help their cause by making Mars beg, time and time again, for a copy of the episode.

After he finally had seen it, Mars vice president Edward J. Stegemann told Laurence Tisch that he had been directed by Mars stockholders to "express their outrage." "This appears to be one of the most irresponsible and unprofessional examples of network programming we have ever heard about," Stegemann said. Then he explained that Mars first learned about "this outrageous episode" when they were "deluged" by consumer complaints.

"We're dumbfounded that something like this could have taken place," Stegemann continued, "and once taken place, to be so terribly mishandled by one of the country's major communication companies. We believe that CBS owes the public an apology for airing so reprehensible an episode.

"The fact that it appeared during 'children's time' on Saturday morning," he added, "just magnifies the misconduct."[18]

Still, despite the justifiable clamor for a public apology from individuals the *Texarkana Gazette* could hardly label "zealot reactionaries," CBS never once even intimated wrongdoing on their part. As usual, they arrogantly abrogated all responsibility, confident the whole matter would quietly fade away.

Oh sure, CBS finally did cut the coke snorting sequence from the episode. It took Congressman Chandler's forceful letter to get them to do that. Laurence Tisch also fired George Dessart soon after he received the letter from Mars, Incorporated. Though I hoped Tisch would fire Dessart for being deceptive, I'm afraid he was fired for not being deceptive enough (i.e, the "lucky chunk of cheese" escapade and allowing the Washington, D.C., screening).

I say that because CBS never disciplined the real culprits behind *Mighty Mouse*. As I write this, Judy Price is still "getting away with more" as head of children's programming. Ralph Bakshi in turn, was allowed to "express his hostilities" via *Mighty Mouse* for one more year before CBS finally canceled the show. Meanwhile the innocent, highly impressionable minds of American children continue to be influenced by people who have demonstrated that they have no business molding and shaping young minds.

Still, as crucial as exposing *Mighty Mouse* was, virtually all of my time during the summer of 1988 was consumed by even a more critical issue.

An Offensive
Movie Awakens
a Sleeping Giant?

"I'm not Michael Jackson or Lionel Ritchie. I'm a common person just like all of you. And just like you, I have dreams."

These were the opening remarks of Steve Gooden, a handsome young black singer who stood no more than four feet in front of me at the rally. Beyond Steve, more than 25,000 peaceful protestors tried to make themselves comfortable underneath the hot Southern California sun. As Steve described some of his dreams, I could tell that the enormous crowd was hanging on every word.

"I dreamed that one day I could buy my mom a beautiful home, have plenty of money in the bank and do the work of the Lord," Steve said as powerful loudspeakers amplified his words. Then he explained how he had signed a multi-year recording contract a few months earlier with MCA Records. This legal agreement, which gave MCA the go ahead to release as many as nine Steve Gooden albums, represented a giant step toward the fulfillment of his dreams. Indeed plans for his first single and album had been moving along right on schedule.

But then Steve learned that Universal Pictures, which is owned and operated by MCA, planned to release a movie called *The Last Temptation of Christ*. And that had placed this gifted young man in a very awkward position.

"When I came to understand that this film depicts Jesus in a very defaming and blasphemous way," Steve told the crowd as his voice began to crack with emotion, "I faced a great struggle within myself." Though he didn't have enough microphone time to share all the details of his struggle, I fully understood why he was having difficulty retaining his composure. That's because privately he had already told me the reasons for the bold action he was about to take.

It had all started when he had seen another Universal movie called *Cry Freedom*. Intensely moved by this cinematic portrayal of South African apartheid, Steve immediately went to his church, sat down at a piano and with God's help composed a song which expressed his feelings about injustice. One thing led to another, and Steve dropped off a demo tape at MCA Records, the largest label in the music business.

"I realized that it was a one in a million chance," Steve had told me. "But since my inspiration to write music and ability to sing comes from God, I simply left things in his hands and waited for MCA's reply."

MCA executives were highly impressed. And when the contract came through, Steve signed on the dotted line. Of course, Steve knew that most MCA musical artists and high-level officials could care less about the Lord he loved. But Steve believed that his Christian testimony could serve as a light in what is generally considered to be a spiritually dark business.

"When I learned that *The Last Temptation of Christ* makes a mockery of my Lord," Steve had candidly revealed during our face to face chat, "I agonized over what I should do. In fact, I could hardly sleep for almost two weeks because a part of me, my flesh, didn't want to let go of my dream.

"But in the end, I knew I really didn't have a choice," Steve concluded. "There was no way I could use my talents to make money for a company which has displayed such reckless disregard for the personal faith of millions of Christians."

So now Steve Gooden's moment of truth had arrived. . . .

"This contract is my righteous stand for a righteous cause—the only cause that is worthy of what I'm about to do," Steve told the 25,000 onlookers while he held up what appeared to be a rather lengthy document.

Next, as both police and news helicopters rumbled high overhead, Steve challenged others to put their "conscience and convictions ahead of their personal gain."

"I pray that God will raise up a generation in these last days that will not compromise . . . that will not bow to the things of this world," Steve cried as his voice began to break. "And I will not compromise!"

Finally, with tears streaming off his cheeks onto his shirt, the MCA artist dramatically concluded, "I tear up this contract in the name of my Lord and Savior Jesus Christ."

As Steve tossed the pieces of his MCA agreement in the air like confetti, those who had found a place to sit stood and joined the rest of the multitude in an ear-splitting ovation. Naturally I cheered and clapped just as loud as everyone else. But I also found myself wiping away tears when former pro football star turned actor Roosevelt Grier, who, like me, was waiting to say a few words to the crowd, proceeded to smother young Mr. Gooden in a giant bear hug of love.

All in all, Steve's action was one of the most courageous things I've ever witnessed. I mean, this young man had put his Lord first and had laid a *secure* and perhaps fame and fortune-filled future on the line. I realized what he had done could really cost him. I knew MCA could refuse to release him from his contract, effectively destroying his career. MCA still held the upper hand, and out of spite they could prohibit Steve from signing with another record company, be it religious or secular.[1]

The date was Thursday, August 11, 1988. The place was a park adjacent to Universal Studios and the MCA/Universal corporate headquarters in Universal City, California.

Though my American Family Association had helped organize this rally, with lots of help from others, including three Los Angeles area radio and television stations, after Steve spoke I made just a few quick comments. That's because I knew that these 25,000 friendly faces (official police helicopter estimate)[2] weren't there to hear speeches. They were there because MCA/Universal planned, the very next day, to release a movie which portrays the Lord Jesus Christ as a liar, a fornicator and a weak, confused, fearful individual unsure of who he is. They were appalled that MCA/Universal executives would so brazenly, to quote Rosey Grier, "make fun of the Creator of the universe," and they wanted to peaceably demonstrate their outrage.

And demonstrate they did! Our protest march route took each

participant, walking in rows 10 to 15 abreast, within a few dozen feet of the 15 story black tower where MCA/Universal executives do business. Though we couldn't see through the dark-tinted windows, I knew that Universal Pictures President Tom Pollack had the perfect vantage point to watch our procession—a procession airborne news reporters said stretched on for several blocks. From their executive suites high above, I figured Pollack and his co-conspirators in this modern day betrayal could hear the crowd's call to "Boycott MCA . . . Boycott MCA" loud and clear.

What Paramount Rejects, MCA/Universal Accepts . . . Judas Then, MCA/Universal Now . . . Don't Change HisStory . . . The Lie Costs $6.50, The Truth Is Free . . . The Greatest Story Ever Distorted . . . Jesus Christ: Fact, Not Fiction . . . Jesus Christ Is Lord: Please Show Respect for My God . . . Literally thousands of homemade, hand-printed protest signs like these also got our point across.

Who were these people who made this event what many authorities called "the largest of its kind in Hollywood history?" Well, before and after the march I had a chance to mingle with several hundred protestors. I discovered they didn't fit any demonstrator stereotype. Almost everyone told me it was the first time they had "ever done anything like this."

Grandmothers, grandfathers, mothers pushing baby strollers, men in business suits who had taken time off from work, mechanics wearing grease-stained uniforms, teenagers in shorts and shirt sleeves, Catholic and Episcopal priests wearing clerical collars, blacks, whites, Hispanics, Asian Americans . . . There were even a couple dozen burly fellas wearing leather jackets mixing with the crowd. They were members of "Christ's Sons"—a Christian motorcycle gang from Orange County that gets high on Jesus instead of drugs.

Minor theological differences and denominational labels such as United Methodist, Lutheran, Roman Catholic, Assembly of God, Church of Christ, Southern Baptist or Evangelical Free mattered not at all. We were a family, united in a bond of love for the Lord of all. Our common desire was to see the name of Jesus honored and glorified, not desecrated and defiled.

This bond of unity was especially evident when 25,000 voices joined together to sing "Amazing Grace" and "God Bless

America." I still get goose bumps when I think of one special moment. As I marched underneath the foreboding MCA/Universal tower, thousands of voices behind me chorused the words " . . . His truth is marching on" from "The Battle Hymn of the Republic." Somehow I knew that no matter how hard men try to ridicule those who believe in Christ's deity and resurrection, and no matter how hard they try to deface and disguise the historical, biblical Jesus, his truth will always keep marching right along. There will always be a core of believers who will stand firmly on the promises of Christ their Lord no matter what the cost.

Many thousands more would have joined our "glory, glory hallelujah" chorus that day had they been able to get there. Police reports stated that the Hollywood freeway had backed up for miles prior to and during the demonstration. Surface streets in and around Universal City were so jammed that the California Highway Patrol had to close freeway off ramps.

Unfortunately if you happen to live outside of the Los Angeles area, you never would have known what really took place that day at the base of the MCA/Universal shrine to the god of this world. Dan Rather, on the CBS Evening News, put the crowd at "about 5,000." ABC radio said—get this—only "hundreds" were there. So much for network claims of "unbiased" and "accurate" news reporting!

But it wasn't just Southern Californians who took the time to personally express their heartache over MCA/Universal's celluloid desecration of Jesus. People from every state in the union got in on the act as well.

Reliable inside reports indicate that for more than a month the MCA/Universal switchboard was jammed with some 10,000 protest calls per day. And that's just the folks who were able to get through.[3] Letters addressed to MCA Chairman Louis Wasserman, MCA President Sidney Sheinberg, Tom Pollack or simply addressed "Dear Universal" arrived by the hundreds of thousands. In fact, our Christian friends inside the MCA/Universal black tower told us that on one early August day, 122,000 protest letters and cards arrived in the MCA/Universal mail room.[4] You read that correctly . . . 122,000 in one day!

Quite simply, there has never been anything like it!

The Making of a Counterfeit Jesus

For me, the saga surrounding this movie began several years earlier—1983 to be exact. That's when I learned that Paramount Studios intended to make a film based on the 1955 novel, *The Last Temptation of Christ*, by Greek author Nikos Kazantzakis.

I knew Kazantzakis had been excommunicated by his Orthodox church because of the novel's blasphemous portrayal of Christ. And when I picked up a copy in the library, I could see why his church had taken such harsh measures. Kazantzakis' Jesus is a weak and highly unstable man whose life is gripped with sin and lust. The novel has almost nothing in common with biblical and historical accounts of Jesus' life and teachings.

One typical scene finds Jesus telling an old Rabbi that he has fallen "into every conceivable sin." Jesus also indicates that all the serpents of sin are "hissing and dancing" in his breast. "But ever since my childhood, Rabbi," Kazantzakis' Jesus confesses, "I have not only kept the devil of fornication hidden deeply within me, but also the devil of arrogance . . . . "[5]

A bit later Jesus adds, "I haven't been in my right mind. I am Lucifer!"[6] In other words, Kazantzakis' Jesus actually believes he's the devil. Skeptical? You'll find this dialogue on page 146 of Simon and Schuster's *The Last Temptation of Christ* hardbound edition.

I've never written a screenplay. But I didn't see how anyone could write a movie script based upon this book that did not insult the hundreds of millions of people around the world who lift up Jesus Christ as both the Son of God and their personal Savior.

I became especially concerned when I learned that Paramount's *Last Temptation* was to be directed by Martin Scorsese. Some quick homework had revealed that this director of *American Gigolo, Raging Bull* and *Mean Streets* "views his films as personal therapy—a way to vent what he [Scorsese] calls his 'anger and rage and craziness.'"[7] At least that's what *Los Angeles Times* movie critic Dale Pollack had written after a lengthy in-depth interview.

"To make a film," Pollack continued, "Scorsese says he finds it necessary to burrow into his own psyche and rip out the elements that give his characters their tortured on-screen personae. Perhaps that is why, as one critic said, 'Martin Scorsese makes movies about people you don't want to know.'"

Of one thing I was certain. I already *knew* the real Jesus—the Jesus who said, "I am the way, the truth and the life; No one comes to the Father but through Me."[8] The more I read about this man whom Dale Pollack said uses the film medium to try and "find himself," the more I believed Scorsese's Jesus, adapted from the twisted imagination of Nikos Kazantzakis, would be a cheap counterfeit that could lead viewers who don't know the one and only original astray.

Hence I organized a massive outcry of protest—phone calls, postcards, letters and more—from Christians across the country. Thankfully this flood of communication convinced Paramount, which had already spent $2 million on the *Last Temptation* project, to cancel its plans.

But sadly, four years later Martin Scorsese convinced Universal Pictures to pick up where Paramount left off. Apparently Scorsese had learned from the Paramount experience. So he and Universal kept the casting and North Africa filming details hush-hush in an attempt to keep concerned Christians off their back.

However, secrets in Hollywood are hard to keep—especially when hundreds of people and $15 million budgets are involved.[9] Someone with an entree into Universal's business affairs informed me of *The Last Temptation's* resurrection in October 1987. Immediately I asked American Family Association friends to contact MCA/Universal with gracious but firm protest calls and letters. And as per usual, they did—by the thousands.

Then in January 1988, just prior to my first major *Last Temptation*-related mailing asking concerned Christians to protest and pray, I received a phone call from Tim Penland. Tim is one of the few Christians I know who makes his living in the Hollywood entertainment business. A film promoter, he had spearheaded successful marketing campaigns directly to the Christian community for two fine films, *Chariots of Fire* and *The Mission*.

Tim was calling me to say that Universal Pictures was concerned about all the critical calls and letters they were getting. They had hired him to help Christian leaders understand that their movie, in stark contrast to the book, would *not* be blasphemous.

"Tom Pollack has assured me that Universal has no desire to

release a film defaming Christ," he noted. "In fact, Pollack says that this is going to be a faith-affirming film which honors Jesus."[10] Tim also quoted a letter Martin Scorsese had written indicating that it would be "a deeply religious film"[11] and depict Jesus "as sinless, as deity and as the Savior of mankind."[12]

Then Tim explained that Universal was willing to strike a deal. If I agreed not to protest the movie, Universal would arrange a private screening for me, Billy Graham, Jerry Falwell, James Dobson (Focus on the Family), Bill Bright (Campus Crusade for Christ) and a handful of other Christian leaders. Tim promised we would be shown the actual movie, not a work in progress, and have an opportunity to offer suggestions.

This screening, he continued, would be set up well in advance of the October release date. That way, if we found portions of the film to be offensive, and Universal refused to take corrective action, we would still have time to alert like-minded Christian friends.

Tim's proposal sounded almost too good to be true, so I readily agreed to Universal's terms. I did so not because I trusted Universal (I didn't). I agreed because I trusted my fellow Christian, Tim Penland, who assured me that if the film did indeed defame our Lord, he would break his ties with Universal and join the protest.

I only had one condition: that Universal agree to schedule the screening in May or early June at the latest. That way, even if Pollack and Scorsese were playing the same game network executives like to play (i.e. saying whatever is in their best interest, whether or not it's true), I figured I'd still have four months to mobilize a protest effort and MCA/Universal boycott.

To make a long story short, Universal, Tim Penland and I later agreed to schedule the screening no later than June 10. In fact, in letters addressed to concerned Christian leaders appealing to their "sense of fairness,"[13] Universal referred to this advance screening as just one of several reasons why the film should not be prejudged. Consequently with Universal publicly promising, in writing, to uphold their end of the bargain, I felt comfortable putting *The Last Temptation of Christ* issue on the back burner throughout the winter and spring of 1988.

However, by the end of May I developed a strong feeling that Universal might not be playing by the rules. Tim Penland had repeatedly asked to see a script, a rough cut of the film, selected scenes, anything. But each time Universal executives, in a nice way, had said "request denied."

It seemed rather odd to me that Universal would purposely keep the man they had hired to, in their own words, "help build bridges to the Christian community,"[14] in the dark about the actual content of this "faith-affirming film." I know Tim felt that way too. Yet, since he had arranged the special June 10 screening, which as far as he knew was still on, Tim, like me, maintained a wait-and-see attitude.

As it turned out, we didn't have to wait much longer. On June 2, Universal publicity director Sally Van Slyke told Tim that Martin Scorsese would not have the film ready for screening until late July at the earliest, maybe even August.[15]

I smelled a double-cross. But in good faith I had Tim tell Universal that I'd hold off my protest efforts if they'd agree to delay the movie's fall release in proportion to their screening delay. However, when Universal replied "absolutely not," I suspected that this "unexpected delay" had been carefully planned far in advance.

I theorized, based upon past experience with giant entertainment-related corporations, that this was Universal's first move in a projected cat-and-mouse game designed to keep me and other Christian leaders from seeing the film until just before its release. That way, we'd have no time to organize an effective protest based upon the *actual* movie content. Instead, our well-publicized comments would create just enough controversy at the last minute to fill theaters everywhere. Tim Penland, if my theory proved to be true, was viewed by Tom Pollack and Martin Scorsese as little more than a guinea pig—someone whose trust could be exploited for Universal's ultimate financial gain.

A few days later I discovered that my suspicions about Universal's behind-the-scenes maneuverings were fairly accurate. The June 4 edition of the *Philadelphia Enquirer* featured an article on the "trouble" Martin Scorsese anticipated when he released *The Last Temptation of Christ*. "In the spring, he [Scorsese] signed on a Christian marketing expert [Tim Penland] to shepherd the movie past possible objections of religionists," the *Enquirer* reported.

"Now comes word that he has scheduled a series of secret New York screenings. . . . "

Not long after that Marian Billings, head of Scorsese's New York publicity firm, candidly told a *Los Angeles Times* reporter, on the record, that Tim Penland was indeed just "a decoy."[16] I also learned that one of the "secret" screenings the *Philadelphia Enquirer* mentioned took place less than a week after June 10. At that time Universal showed the completed movie, all two hours and 48 minutes, to their key distribution people. In other words, Universal had blatantly lied about the film not being ready for screening until "late July or August."

How do I know this? One of the handful of eyewitnesses was discreetly relaying detailed information about the movie's content to Tim Penland. Tim, who had made good on his pledge to resign and join the protest, also found out that Tom Pollock and company planned an early release to ride the crest of the free controversy-generated publicity they anticipated—possibly even before August's Republican National Convention.

Still, it wasn't the "secret" screenings and the exploitation of Tim Penland that ultimately convinced me that Martin Scorsese and MCA/Universal were up to no good. It was a copy of the movie script itself that I received in mid-June. Since Scorsese and Universal seemed to be keeping the few scripts in existence under lock and key, I won't reveal who sent it to me. But I will say that the securing of this script was an answer to the fervent prayers of many faithful friends.

Within seconds after pulling the 99-page screenplay from the Federal Express package, I got my first bitter taste of the printed poison that was to follow. Script writer Paul Schrader's introduction page included a two-sentence glimpse into the apostate theology of Nikos Kazantzakis. "It is not God who will save us," the Greek writer had stated. "It is we who will save God, by battling, by creating and transmuting matter into spirit."

I believed right then that Schrader and Scorsese had indeed succumbed to the same temptation that had consumed Nikos Kazantzakis. Since they could not accept the Jesus of the Bible, they had exercised what Kazantzakis believed to be "man's right (and duty) to fashion a new savior and thereby rescue himself from a moral and spiritual void."[17] To do that they had used the motion picture medium to create a false god which they could accept—a god who in almost every aspect is the antithesis of the Savior described in the New Testament.

By the time I had finished the first few pages I could clearly see why Martin Scorsese and Universal had resorted to premeditated deception to cover up their true intentions. In one of the opening scenes a mob of angry Jews are threatening Jesus (the carpenter) because he has betrayed them by building the crosses the Romans use to crucify Jewish zealots.

"Forgive my son, he's crazy!" Mary, Jesus' mother, shouts to the furious crowd. "He doesn't know what he's doing. He has problems . . . He's not well in the head."

According to Schrader's script Jesus eventually is crucified himself, not to pay for the sins of the world, as the Bible teaches, but to pay for *his own* sins. For instance, "Forgive me for being a bad son," are the last words Mary, his mother, hears him speak. Indeed between the opening mob scene and his death five years later (there is no resurrection), Jesus' tumultuous inner struggle with his own *sinful* ways and actions dominates the screenplay.

One early scene finds Jesus visiting Mary Magdalene, the prostitute. Magdalene, who "lies naked on a stack of blankets covered with . . . sweat" (several male customers have just left) asks, "What are you doing here?"

"I want you to forgive me," Jesus replies. "I've done a lot of wrong things. The worst things I've done are to you. Forgive me."

In another scene Jesus confesses to Judas that he is both "a liar" and "a hypocrite." "I'm afraid of everything," Jesus says. "I don't ever tell the truth. I don't have the courage.

"You want to know who my mother and father are?" Jesus continues. "You want to know who my god is? Fear!"

Rare was the page that did not include dialogue and/or action that I, as an evangelical Christian, did not find patently offensive. And George Gallup, the famous pollster, says there are 82.5 million of us in America![18]

I cringed as I imagined what Martin Scorsese's grotesque Last Supper scene would look like in larger-than-life living color. "As they do [take communion], the bread and wine transubstantiate into flesh and blood in their mouths," the script instructions specify. "Peter is the first to cough up the bloody flesh. The others, sickened, follow. They wipe their bloody mouths."

Some eight pages later, I wanted to cry as I read how this director of *American Gigolo* planned to film Jesus and Magdalene making "love on blankets spread over straw." According to the script, as Jesus "kisses her breasts and lips" he says: "Now I know; a woman is God's greatest work. And I worship you. God sleeps between your legs."

I figured Scorsese would endeavor to justify this pornographic sequence by pointing out that it's part of a dream. But as far as I was concerned, that argument would have little merit. Many moviegoers do not differentiate between what is postured as reality and what is supposedly fantasy. To portray Jesus of Nazareth having sexual intercourse is a high insult to anyone who loves and worships him. (According to the script, after Magdalene is murdered, Jesus lives with Mary and Martha, sisters of Lazarus. Apparently he has sexual relations with them both.)

By the time I reached the scene where Jesus calls the Apostle Paul a "liar," I literally felt sick to my stomach. In the sequence, Jesus, who now has several children, hears a man preaching in the village square near his home. So he goes to check out what the man is saying.

"Jesus of Nazareth . . . he was the Son of God," Paul exclaims. "He took on our sins, he was tortured, crucified—but three days later he rose again and ascended to heaven. Death was conquered and the Gates of Heaven are open to everyone."

So far so good. But then something happens that's not so good. Jesus, who "has been rising to a slow boil and can restrain himself no longer," shouts "Liar!" When Paul stops, Jesus says, "I'm Jesus of Nazareth. I was never crucified, never resurrected. I'm a man like everyone else . . . Don't go around the world spreading these lies about me."

Though once again I figured Martin Scorsese would respond to criticism by saying, "This scene is a part of Christ's dream," I believed that many undiscerning moviegoers would take Jesus' denial of the gospel message at face value. No matter how you slice it, to have a character named "Jesus of Nazareth" say that what the real Jesus of Nazareth said is "lies" is blasphemy.

Much to my relief I finally finished reading this sickening

script. Hurt, anger, shock, sorrow, depression—these adjectives all describe my feelings as I thought and prayed about what to do next.

Never in almost 12 years of fighting the media's bias against Christian values had I ever come across a more blatant attack on Christianity than this movie. I realized that if there ever were a time for Christians to let the Hollywood elite know that the entertainment industry's constant Christian-bashing should stop, this was it.

Launching the *Last Temptation* Protest

So I met with other AFA staff members and came up with a plan that would make *The Last Temptation of Christ* our biggest protest ever. Sure, we knew that our efforts would create the controversy MCA/Universal almost seemed to welcome. But we also believed that if millions of God's people said "enough is enough," we could make MCA/Universal's slandering of our Lord less than profitable.

First, we made 250 photocopies of the script and mailed them to influential Christian leaders (e.g., several dozen Catholic archbishops and bishops, two dozen United Methodist bishops, and top-level officials from more than 70 religious organizations and denominations). While our copy machine flashed almost nonstop, we recorded a three-minute *Last Temptation*-related radio spot that soon was airing on 800 Christian radio stations nationwide.

We also hurried to produce a 30-minute television program attacking the movie. It aired on more than 50 Christian television stations and cable networks. We urged people to protest by writing and calling MCA/Universal. Our AFA phone number also appeared so people could call and request a special petition asking local theater owners, out of respect for Christians in their community, not to show the film.

But that was only the beginning. In July I wrote 170,000 Christian pastors and asked them to promote the protest effort in their churches. I also sent out more than *three million* letters to Christian lay people. They were encouraged to pass the petition and protest before August 12 and to pass the petition and boycott MCA/Universal after August 12.

Why did I pull out all the stops to fight this movie?

As I've already mentioned, Martin Scorsese and Universal Pictures tried to turn Jesus into a figment of someone's imagination. Their Jesus Christ has nothing to do with the Christ of history and the Christ of Scripture. Contrary to his mendacious letter assuring Christians that in *The Last Temptation* Jesus is both "sinless" and "deity," Martin Scorsese portrays him as a sinful human and not the divine Son of God. (Hebrews 4:15 says that Jesus was "tempted in every way, just as we are—yet was without sin.")

Does the real Jesus Christ need defending? Of course not! The big problem with *The Last Temptation of Christ* is this: It intentionally lies about the One whom Christians hold precious and dear. Indeed, as Christians we owe everything to Jesus Christ. For someone (or some $3.5 billion company) to lie about him on purpose is offensive.

That's why the response to our protest campaign, as I briefly described earlier in this chapter, was so incredible.

Within a matter of weeks, American Family Association operators had fielded more than 10,000 requests for protest petitions and script highlights. (Or maybe I should say lowlights!) Since most people said they had difficulty getting through, I'm confident that we would have doubled or tripled that number if our phone system had more lines. Several other Christian leaders with their own radio programs (e.g., James Dobson, Marlin Maddoux, James Kennedy) were also inundated with requests when they offered sample petitions.

And speaking of Christian leaders, most who received the entire script that we sent were flabbergasted by what they found themselves reading. In fact, some heads of denominations were so irate, they made sure each of their ministers received a copy.

Campus Crusade for Christ President Bill Bright's comments were representative of the hundreds of letters and phone calls I received from pastors, church officials and Christian ministry executives. After explaining that he became so angry that he couldn't sleep, Bill Bright wrote, "This is absolutely the most blasphemous, degenerate, immoral, depraved script and film that I believe it is possible to conceive."

Dr. James Dobson of Focus on the Family didn't mince his words either. "It would appear to be the most blasphemous, evil attack on the church and the cause of Christ in the history of entertainment," he fumed.

As the rumblings from the Christian community grew louder, the national media began to realize that this strange movie about a make-believe Jesus was becoming both the entertainment and religion story of the year. Unfortunately most members of the Fourth Estate heard my name and in their ignorance assumed that the "fundamentalist extremists" had found another "superficial" issue to get upset about. Few seemed to believe that just as many, if not more, people from mainline denominations were taking action as people from conservative evangelical or fundamentalist churches and organizations.

Calling *The Last Temptation of Christ* "the most serious misuse of filmcraft in the history of movie making," Dr. Lloyd Ogilvie, pastor of Hollywood (California) Presbyterian Church, represented the feelings of countless Presbyterians. "This film will disturb and distort the life of Jesus for those who are thinking about Christianity," he continued. "It will hurt and destroy those who have begun the Christian life, and it will add to the moral decay of our time in history."

Cardinal Bernard Law, Roman Catholic archbishop of Boston, like many of his peers, urged Catholics everywhere to let their hurt be known to MCA/Universal because, "This film is morally offensive and repugnant to Christian belief."

About the same time, as strong statements like these from highly respected Christian leaders began appearing in the press, I made a big mistake. This mistake allowed Universal to successfully posture themselves as the innocent victims of, to quote one nationally syndicated columnist, "the Rev. Donald Wildmon and his pack of howling censors."[19] In late June Universal promised to let me and a few other Christian leaders see the film in mid-July. Knowing that we had been manipulated and lied to the first time, I discussed their offer with some of the other invitees and decided to join them in saying "no thanks." We all figured that just prior to the new screening date Universal would once again come up with some lame excuse for postponing or canceling the viewing.

We should have played along and said, "We'll be there." That's because our decision not to be exploited any longer opened the door for Universal to show the film to a group of carefully selected liberal ministers and religious officials (Universal even paid their expenses!). I believe that had we said yes, Universal would not have shown it to any clergy until the final few days before its release.

Soon after this July 12 screening, these hand-picked men and women of the cloth began popping up on talk shows and were quoted extensively in news stories. Their near-unanimous verdict? *The Last Temptation of Christ* is an uplifting spiritual experience and "should not be considered sacrilegious or blasphemous."[20]

"It's artistically excellent and theologically sound,"[21] said New York Episcopal Bishop Paul Moore. Rev. Charles Bergstrom, in his strong recommendation, noted that he was "not offended in any way Scripture was used and applied."[22] Bergstrom, a Lutheran minister, just so happens to be chairman of the executive committee for Norman Lear's People for the American Way.

And what about the sexual intercourse scene with Jesus and Mary Magdalene? It's in there, indicated Rev. David Pomeroy, a United Church of Christ minister and National Council of Churches media specialist, "But it is *tastefully done*"[23] (emphasis mine).

Not only did our "no thanks" give Universal an opportunity to unleash this propaganda team of Reverends, but it also gave credence to the much-quoted half-truth that "Christian leaders protesting the film were invited to a screening which they refused to attend." It seems like I read dozens of *Last Temptation* pieces in which the writer had assumed that ministers such as Bergstrom, Moore and Pomeroy represented most American Christians. Many of these journalists assumed that the film's primary opposition was coming from a handful of rabid radicals who shouldn't be taken seriously.

Fortunately Universal's much-publicized "clergy screening" was not a total disaster for our side. A few of the invitees who Universal had mistakenly assumed would be sympathetic were shocked by what they had seen. From their copious notes and eyewitness descriptions we determined:

A. Despite Martin Scorsese's claims to the contrary, the script I had read and the actual movie were remarkably similar.

B. Sometime between June 15 and July 12, Scorsese shortened the film by six to eight minutes. Apparently, thanks to our protest, he had cut almost the entire Jesus/Magdalene sex scene. The most gruesome part of The Last Supper scene hit the cutting room floor as well.

C. Still, some parts of the movie were actually worse than the script. To cite just one example, prior to asking Magdalene for her "forgiveness," the script calls for Jesus to wait outside in her courtyard while the prostitute finishes her business. In the movie, Scorsese has Jesus enter her brothel where he joins a room full of men who are lustily watching the naked Magdalene have sex with a paying customer. Her moans, groans and bobbing body are quite audible and visible to both Jesus and the movie audience.

All of this inside information allowed me and others to continue the fight against this film with renewed confidence.

In the weeks surrounding the movie's release, I accepted invitations to appear on ABC's *Good Morning America*, ABC's *Nightline*, CNN's *Crossfire, The Oprah Winfrey Show* and a host of nationally syndicated and regional radio talk shows. Though it meant having to answer the question—"How can you protest a movie you haven't seen?"—dozens of times, I made the media rounds because I desperately wanted to set the record straight. (I did see the film shortly after its release.)

Whenever possible, I explained that the furor over *The Last Temptation of Christ* had absolutely nothing to do with all the usual buzz words such as "the First Amendment," "censorship" and "rights" that Martin Scorsese and MCA/Universal had been feeding the press. In fact, I routinely emphasized that MCA/Universal had every right to release this movie. No one was saying they didn't.

The key issue surrounding *The Last Temptation*, I stressed, is *respect*, or rather, *a lack of respect*. By releasing the film, I explained, MCA/Universal demonstrated brazen disrespect and contempt for millions of Christians. MCA/Universal's insensitivity to the feelings of so many, I continued, is without parallel in the history of this country.

Of course, I realized that these were strong statements. But I had plenty of evidence supporting my case. For instance, one of the speakers at our huge August 11 rally was Dr. Richard G. Lee, pastor of Atlanta's Rehoboth Baptist Church. He and his parishioners were so saddened by what MCA/Universal planned to do to their Lord, they bought an advertisement in both the *Atlanta Constitution* and the *Atlanta Journal*. It simply said, "If You Stand Against This Movie, Sign This Ad."

Not surprisingly the ad triggered an amazing chain reaction. Thousands of north Georgia residents clipped and reproduced the petition, passing it from friend to friend. In almost no time Rehoboth Baptist had collected 135,000 signatures.

At the rally Dr. Lee told the huge throng what Universal had said when he inquired about delivering his signatures: "We don't care about your petitions. Leave them with the guards and we'll put them in the dump."

MCA President Sidney Sheinberg displayed the same arrogance in his response to the tidal wave of protest letters, petitions and calls. "Christians," he huffed to a group of Universal officials, "won't stop us from distributing this movie."

Whenever I could I did my best to point out what MCA/Universal seemed to be saying to all of Christendom: "We are going to recreate your Christ and make him a sinful man. So what if you are insulted? We care nothing about your feelings. So what if our movie isn't based on your Scripture or even the spirit of your Scripture? We care nothing about your holy Scripture. Our right to insult you is more important than your incorrect thinking about your God. We are going to do it and there is nothing you can do to stop us."

Would MCA/Universal Chairman Lew Waserman, Sidney Sheinberg and Tom Pollack release a film portraying Adolf Hitler as a great benefactor of the Jews? Hardly. Would MCA/Universal release a movie if the black community found it to be highly disparaging? No way. You better believe MCA/Universal executives would also think long and hard before they released a movie offensive to American Indians, Muslims, homosexuals or virtually any affinity group. Yet, to MCA/Universal a film which offends millions of Christians is fine and dandy. Why?

Patrick Buchanan, a nationally syndicated columnist who also hosts a Cable News Network television show, said it best in his column entitled, "Hollywood's War on Christianity." "We live in an age where . . . Christian bashing is a popular indoor sport," he said.

It is an age, Buchanan continued, where "Christians . . .

America's unfashionable majority, may be mocked; their preachers may be parodied in books and on film; their faith may be portrayed as superstitious folly. And secular society, invoking the First Amendment, will rush to the defense of the defamers, not the defamed.

"The battle over *Last Temptation*," Buchanan concluded, "is one more skirmish in the . . . struggle over whose values, whose beliefs shall be exalted in American culture, and whose may be derided."[24]

So who won this "skirmish," which I think can be better described as perhaps the biggest battle yet in "Hollywood's War on Christianity"? If you believe everything you hear on the television news and read in the print media, you probably think *The Last Temptation of Christ* was a resounding financial success.

After all, the brouhaha created by all of us "holier than thou twits," to quote Bob Emmers of *The Orange County* [California] *Register*, could only mean one thing: *Millions of people are going to flock to see this movie.* At least that's what most of the journalists who interviewed me believed.

These media members looked at the full-page ads Universal was running in big city papers. They listened to the positive statements made by the handful of liberal clergy who were proudly boasting that they had *seen* the movie. They read the mountains of media coverage, including a *Time* magazine cover story. They looked at the glowing *Last Temptation* reviews coming from many movie critics. Then, after the film premiered in seven U.S. cities, they looked at the flood of news reports which included statements such as "box office hit," "every show sold out," "Universal's victory" and "record-breaking opening weekend."

In their eyes Universal couldn't lose. And that's what most of them told listeners and readers. Unfortunately, by September, when the real winner in the *Last Temptation* battle became apparent, these print and broadcast journalists were nowhere to be found.

So let me give you the facts now!

Remember the Atlanta Baptist Church that collected 135,000 protest signatures? Well, that same scenario was repeated in virtually every city, town and village in America. Thousands of churches, representing the Christian community's entire spectrum, passed *Last Temptation* petitions through the pews during services. Tens of thousands of faithful friends filled petitions by going door to door or standing in shopping malls.

Though only God knows how many of his people made phone calls, wrote letters or signed petitions, I believe the total is somewhere in the multimillions. And here's the good news. While MCA/Universal was tossing with recalcitrance most of the material addressed to them in their dumpster, the vast majority of signed petitions were sent to, and accepted by, local theatre owners and theatre chains all across the land.

As a result, *every* major theatre chain in America, with the exception of MCA/Universal-owned Cineplex-Odeon, declined to show the film. Said a representative for United Artists, which operates 2,000 theaters: "The movie is tasteless and has a lack of concern for the religious sensitivity of a majority of film goers."

All totaled, MCA/Universal was only able to place the movie in about 80 first-run theaters.[25] And most of those were theaters they happened to own. That's less than one percent of the nation's 13,000 plus theaters. In fact, *The Last Temptation of Christ* was never even shown in many midwestern and western states. Is it any wonder that Universal Pictures fired their vice president for distribution when it became apparent that they were going to lose millions of dollars on the film?

How many millions? Well, on November 8, when the film's theater run was almost completed, it had taken in $7.9 million[26] with approximately $4 million of that amount going to Universal. Compare that to *Young Guns*, a moderately successful film ($42.7 million) which was released one week later. Since Universal spent somewhere between $15 and $17 million making and promoting *The Last Temptation of Christ*, it has "box office bomb" written all over it. In other words, Universal's theatrical loss was more than $10 million.

To put things in an even clearer perspective, one of the most publicized movies in Hollywood history was seen by only 1.5 million people (less than one percent of the U.S. population) during the first two months.

The Challenge to Turn the Tide
But more important than dollars and cents, I believe our side

won because multitudes of Christians decided they would no longer passively sit back and watch the entertainment industry's assault on their faith and values. Though many did no more than sign their names on a petition, at least they did something. That was more than they had done in the past. I had hopes that a sleeping giant might finally be waking up.

As I said in chapter 7, back in 1983 I concluded that this nation was in the throes of a great spiritual war—a war for the hearts and minds of its citizens. I also came to believe that the outcome of this war would determine whether or not the foundation of this nation, and indeed all of Western civilization, would continue to be rooted in the Christian view of man, or change to the humanistic view of man—a view that not only rejects God's rules of conduct and conscience, but also rejects God himself and seeks to eliminate the influence of those who love him and endeavor to live according to his standards.

This spiritual war was and is the greatest single issue facing Christianity today. Knowing that the entertainment industry, particularly television, was a primary battleground in this war (as is our education system), I realized that the organized church simply had to be mobilized to join the fight. Only the church has the capacity to fight and win this great spiritual war.

I shifted my focus to concentrate on recruiting top church officials to join the fight and lead by example. However, much to my disappointment, I found that this was easier said than done.

I learned that many church leaders were leery of having anything to do with the self-righteous, book-burning person they had read and heard so much about in the media. I also found out that many church officials feared speaking out against the secular humanist value system which dominates television. Afraid that they might be called "right-wing fundamentalist extremists" (or worse) like I had been, they did not want to risk their own personal credibility, or the credibility of their institutions on this cause. So, for the most part, they remained silent.

How well I remember a bishop in my own denomination who said, "Wildmon is right, but he can't win. He's fighting the media." I suppose this rationale makes sense to some people. Yet, such thinking goes against the very essence of the gospel message. I've always operated on the belief that God doesn't call us to be successful. He only calls us to be faithful.

I found that a large percentage of church leaders were oblivious to the spiritual war waging in society because their thinking centered almost entirely on the denominational structure or the activities in their local churches. In the midst of carrying out their many responsibilities they had turned their focus inward. In the process, they had forgotten that part of our role as Christians is to be leaven, salt and light to the world around us.

I also discovered that some church leaders had bought into the same humanistic ideals that I was challenging them to fight. For example, some actually believed that personal morality is strictly relative.

Typical of this thinking was one bishop of a major denomination. I had offered, at great expense to our ministry, to send approximately 3,000 Christian leaders who desired one a copy of the 570-page *Final Report of the Attorney General's Commission on Pornography*. This bishop requested a copy. Later, he wrote to me,

> Dear Rev. Wildmon:
>
> Thank you for the copy of the Attorney General's Commission on Pornography report. Although I find much of the report understandably biased from the outset, there are a few things about it which are worthy of commendation and which raise appropriate expressions of concern (e.g. exploitation of persons and especially the use of children in a pornographic context).
>
> However, there are a lot of things in our society which are more obscene than most of the concerns which are the focus of this report (e.g. the threat of the use of nuclear weapons, the lack of concern for the poor, the homeless, the hungry and the oppressed). I recall seeing a cartoon in *Playboy* magazine some years ago which said it well: Two aging ladies were depicted watching a protest demonstration against a local theater because it was showing an "obscene" movie, and the one was saying to the other, "My definition of 'obscenity' is when they put you in a rest home and never come to see you."
>
> I think your request that we protest Holiday Inn's Satellite Cinema offerings falls in that category. I frequently stay in Holiday Inns. I do not watch the offerings in question. But

I will not protest against the right of those who wish to do so, in the privacy of that hotel room, and who wish to pay the price.

I encourage the National Federation for Decency to concentrate on those issues which genuinely have to do with the degradation of human dignity and decency, and to stop dissipating its energy and resources on such innocuous issues as what TV fare is offered in the privacy of hotel rooms!

Thank you for taking time to stop and talk about what you're doing!

Sincerely,

P.S. We plan to hold a convention of our church in Holiday Inn next year!

Fortunately not everyone I talked to turned a deaf ear. Early in 1984 I was greatly encouraged when several top-level denominational officials attended a conference designed to educate them about the destructiveness of pornography. Not long after that, the Southern Baptist Convention urged their 14 million members to join our 7-Eleven boycott.

Slowly, ever so slowly, church leaders began to realize we were dealing with issues that couldn't be ignored. In the fall of 1985, 10 denomination leaders helped me draft a statement which let the networks know that the Christian community was tired of their gratuitous sex, violence, profanity and their pronounced anti-Christian bias. Eventually, approximately 1,600 Christian leaders signed the Statement of Concern and pledged their support in an effort of working for constructive television. In February 1986 Christian Leaders for Responsible Television (CLeaR-TV) grew out of that Statement of Concern.

CLeaR-TV constitutes one of the largest and most diverse groups of Christian leaders ever to participate in a single social concern—leaders such as the heads of 70 denominations, more than 100 Catholic bishops, 20 Lutheran bishops, presidents of 53 Christian colleges, 17 Episcopal bishops, 24 executive directors of state Southern Baptist Conventions, 24 United Methodist bishops, more than 200 Christian broadcasters and the heads of most of the large parachurch organizations in America. At a meeting at O'Hare Airport in Chicago, Dr. Billy Melvin, executive director of the National Association of Evangelicals, was elected chairman of CLeaR-TV. I was elected to serve as its executive director.

Actions and proposed actions by CLeaR-TV led to ABC's decision to cancel two programs—*Crimes of Passion II* and *Scandals II*—scheduled for May 1989. Sponsors, wary of being cited by CLeaR-TV as a top sponsor of sex and violence, weren't even biting as ABC offered rock-bottom, "distressed merchandise" rates.

Many of these same Christian leaders endorsed and supported The American Family Association's boycott against Holiday Inn motels. Holiday Inn is the largest distributor of in-room pornographic movies in the world.

All of this action by church leaders has certainly been a step in the right direction. Yet, for the most part, I've found that the Christian community, especially the local church pastors and local church congregations, are still pretty much as apathetic and silent as I found them to be in the late 1970s and early 1980s. Let me give what I believe are the two primary reasons for this apathy.

First, Charles Colson was right when he said, "The enemy is in our midst. We Christians cannot fight effectively against secularization because we are riddled with it ourselves."

Karl Menninger wrote a book several years ago entitled, *Whatever Happened to Sin?* It is an apt question. In many of our churches sin is rarely mentioned, and if it is, it is only in a general sense.

I think that perhaps we who have responsibility have forgotten that in addition to comforting the afflicted, the other role of the church is to afflict the comfortable.

Colson also said that we have emphasized recruitment more than repentance. Our efforts have been largely to get new members for our churches rather than call people to repentance. We have packaged Christianity similar to a social club and often judged it by the same standard the world uses to judge—size, power and riches.

I'm afraid that many pastors, for several reasons, have been unwilling to afflict the comfortable in their pews. We have, as my friend Steve Gooden, the black singer who tore up his recording contract, said, "bowed to the things of this world."

We have, nearly without a whimper, accepted television entertainment and movies which continually mock and belittle Christianity and Christians. We have allowed radio to air vulgar and violent music which Christians two decades ago would never have tolerated.

Second, I think we have neglected the centrality of the cross. Jesus said, "If any man would come after Me, let him take up his cross daily, and follow Me." The call is as valid today as it was 2,000 years ago.

At the very heart of the Christian gospel is a cross—the symbol of suffering and sacrifice, of hurt and pain and humiliation and rejection. I want no part of a Christian message which does not call me to involvement, requires of me no sacrifice, takes from me no comfort, requires of me less than the best I have to give.

Many times I have been told that all we need to preach is love, and the problem would be solved. That is true. But the question is, what kind of love? A love which will tolerate anything and everything? Christian love is tough—it got Christ crucified. So if we are to preach love, let us preach real love, not some cheap imitation.

Why have we failed to point out the centrality of the cross to the Christian faith? I guess that in an age of instant gratification, the cross isn't very attractive.

We must return to our first love—to Jesus—to the One who was bruised for our iniquities and chastised for our transgressions. The One who paid the ultimate sacrifice and carried the cross, literally instead of figuratively, because of his love for us. We must come to repentance, die to self and live for Christ.

If, when I began my fight for decency in 1977, you would have told me that in a little more than a decade I'd be writing about a Saturday morning cartoon character snorting cocaine; diabolical children's trading cards; pornographic filth almost beyond description being pandered by some of America's most "respectable" corporations; incest and homosexuality being postured as acceptable, wholesome and good on network television; a death toll in America's abortion clinics totaling approximately 25 million (since 1973); the end of civilization as we know it; and how, for the most part, with the exception of a blasphemous, counterfeit Jesus, the church has silently sat back and watched it all happen—I would have said it would never happen, that you've lost touch with reality. Yet, I believe that to be faithful to the God I serve, I have no choice but to speak the truth as he leads me to see it.

A big part of the reason why society's problems have become

so bad so fast is because the church has not been the church and God's people have not been faithful to his priorities. We must turn to God in humility and shame and ask him to have mercy, to forgive us for our indifference and to use us in this spiritual battle.

How? By praying, by fasting, by becoming educated and getting involved.

Do you recall the time Christ's disciples were unsuccessful at expelling a demon from a boy? When they came to our Lord he commanded the devil to leave the boy and it did so immediately.

The disciples asked why they were unable to cure the boy, and Christ, after saying it was due to their unbelief, added, "However, this kind does not go out but by prayer and fasting."

I believe we are too close to losing this spiritual war to turn the tide against the onslaught of humanism any other way. And it is God, working through his faithful servants, who will be able to turn the tide. We can't even begin to do it ourselves.

We must pray for our pastors and church leaders—those who have the responsibility for leading the flock and leading the charge into this battle. And we must pray that God will use our talents in the battle, that we will be instruments in his hand.

Jeremiah 23:2 says, "Therefore thus says the Lord God of Israel concerning the shepherds who are tending My people: 'You have scattered My flock and driven them away, and have not attended to them; behold, I am about to attend to you for the evil of your deeds,' declares the Lord."

Pray that the Christian community would turn back to our first love, put Jesus first, answer his call, pick up the cross, endure the suffering and follow him whatever the price to be paid.

Isaiah 55:7 says, "Let the wicked forsake his way, and the unrighteous man his thoughts; and let him return to the Lord, and He will have compassion on him; And to our God, for He will abundantly pardon."

I believe that if the church fails to rise to this challenge, then the freedom we have known in this country for more than 200 years—the envy of every nation in the world—will be over. The history of a nation which undergirded itself with Christian principles and Christian ethics, a nation which based its law and justice on the Christian concept of man, a nation which has been the most giving and forgiving nation in the history of civilization, will draw to a close. The chances that any nation can ever produce such a society again are nil. The future of our generation and all generations to come is at stake.

But to pray without action is hypocritical. We must get educated and involved, from the local church level to the very top in our various denominations. Christians must encourage their leaders to educate their flock, and call them to involvement. Individuals must *demand* that their individual denominations become involved. We must realize that there is a difference between the way of the world and the way of Christ.

And in it all we must remember that there will be criticism and rejection; that we will have to deny ourselves; that we will be different and act differently from non-Christians; and that we will suffer because of our faith.

There is no glory in fighting a war, even a spiritual war. There is only suffering and pain. Does the Christian community have what it takes to turn this tide, to stop the decay of Western civilization? Do we have enough Christians who are willing to carry the cross and make the sacrifices necessary so that they can provide the leadership needed in our pulpits, in our homes and in our communities?

About 40 years ago theologian Georgia Harkness wrote about a movement she called "the modern rival to Christianity." She called it "secularism." Many of those in the very top positions of leadership in her day—as those in our day—paid little if any attention to her words. Here is how she defined it:

> What, then, is Secularism? It is the ordering and conducting of life as if God did not exist. It is the placing of hedonistic and cultural goals above and in place of those of the Kingdom. It is characterized, not universally but in startlingly large areas of modern life, by a superficial optimism and inner despair—and it has almost wholly engulfed our culture.

Tragically, and at great loss, the church has basically ignored what Georgia Harkness called secularism. Today we call it humanism. And for the most part the leadership in the church—at all levels—either doesn't know it exists, doesn't know how to cope with it, is deathly afraid of addressing it, or agrees with it. Regardless, it has taken and continues to take its toll and make its mark.

Fifty years ago Will Durant wrote concerning what Georgia Harkness called secularism and modern man calls humanism.

> We move into an age of spiritual exhaustion like that which hungered for the birth of Christ. The great question of our time is not Communism versus individualism, not Europe versus America, not even East versus West; it is whether man can bear to live without God.

The church has silently watched while 2,000 years of maturing civilization has slowly and methodically begun to be dismantled. We have been content to withdraw from the public arena into the safety of our own confines. In the process our influence has dwindled and our impact has been nullified. Like Martha, we have worried and been troubled about many things while missing the one thing needed.

We have shifted to dealing with that nearest us—buildings, budgets and baptisms. "Sure there is moral decay around us, but we can protect ourselves and those we love from it," we say. But like a cancer spreading slowly through a body, the moral decay does not stop at some superficial wall we have established. It touches us and ours.

We have accepted, nearly without question, the creed of the secularist that freedom is free—a license; that left to himself man will naturally progress to his highest, and that what is holding him back are the restraints and restrictions placed on him by a "narrow-minded, intolerant" religion.

Historians will write, some hundreds of years from now, that the most damning and damaging thing the church did in the face of moral decay was to turn inward. Like the disciples following the Crucifixion, we hid behind the false safety of locked doors. We thus far have lacked the will to either purge or heal the cancer.

There is still time for the church to turn the tide. There is still time to preserve 2,000 years of the influence of Christ on Western civilization. To do so we must begin once again to lose our life for Christ. In the process we will find our life.

I still don't know if a sleeping giant, God's church, is finally awakening. The answer to that remains to be seen.

And in the balance hangs the future of Western civilization.

Notes

One

1. MTM, one of Hollywood's largest and most successful companies, has produced such hits as *The Mary Tyler Moore Show, Lou Grant, Hill Street Blues* and *Cheers*.

2. "Network Program Executives United Against Pressure Groups," *Broadcasting Magazine* (December 4, 1978), 30.

3. 8:00-11:00 p.m. eastern and pacific standard time; 7:00-10:00 p.m. central and mountain standard time.

4. An in-depth study in *The Journal of Communications* noted, "Contextually implied intercourse increased from no weekly occurrences in 1975 to 15 in 1977 and 24 in 1978; Sexual innuendos increased in frequency from about 1 reference per hour in 1975 to 7 in 1977, and to almost 11 in 1978. Direct verbal references to intercourse increased from 2 occurrences per week in 1975 to 6 references in 1977 and 53 in 1978.

". . . Allusions to prostitution increased more than four-fold, and allusions to aggressive sexual contacts increased three-fold from 1977 to 1978 ("Physically Intimate and Sexual Behavior on Prime-Time Television 1978-79," *The Journal of Communications* [The University of Pennsylvania]).

5. *1978 National Federation for Decency (NFD) Monitoring Report.* Results of the fall 1978 *NFD Monitoring Report* indicated that sexual intercourse, implied sexual intercourse and references to sexual activity had been presented 88 percent of the time outside of marriage (see chapter 3 for explanation). Monitoring began September 10 and ended December 2.

6. Pete Hamill, *Flesh and Blood* (New York: Random House, 1977), 157-160.

7. Eliot Asinof, "Some Oedipus, Some Danny Boy," *The New York Times Book Review* (November 20, 1977), 15.

8. Aljean Harmetz, "The Year TV Turned to Sex: It's Raising Eyebrows and Ratings," *TV Guide* (May 6, 1978), 4-10.

9. Gary Deeb, "What Does TV Have Lined Up For Us?" *National Federation for Decency Journal* (May 1978; reprinted from *Chicago Tribune*), 11.

10. "New Show Blasted by Stewardesses," *NFD Journal* (Oct. 1978), 2.

11. Deeb, "What Does TV Have Lined Up?" 11.

12. *TV Guide*, in their "The Year TV Turned to Sex" issue,

reported that many network executives would point to this fact when responding to their critics. Unbelievably, with a straight face they'd say, "There's no sex on television."

13. Harry F. Waters, "Sex and TV," *Newsweek* (February 20, 1978), 54-61.

14. Deeb, "What Does TV Have Lined Up?" 11.

15. National Federation for Decency Prime-Time Monitoring between Sept. 10 and Dec. 2, 1978 indicated that CBS movies contained 397 scenes of sexual intercourse and scenes referring to sexual activity (sexually suggestive comments). ABC movies contained 360 and NBC movies contained 328.

16. Deeb, "What Does TV Have Lined Up?" 11.

17. *Ladies' Home Journal*, ran an excerpt that fall (1978) from the book, *Betrayal of Innocence: Incest and It's Devastation*, noting that "one in twenty Americans" has been emotionally scarred by this sexual abuse. *Psychology Today* magazine has put the number of American incest victims at 15 million. See Elizabeth Stark, "The Unspeakable Family Secret," *Psychology Today* (May 1984), 41-46.

18. Marjorie Holyoak, CBS director of audience services; response to viewer complaints about *Flesh and Blood*, (February 1979; reprinted in *NFD Journal*, March 1979).

19. Les Brown, "Networks Try To Assuage Affiliates," *New York Times* (March 13, 1979).

20. Dave Zurawik, *Detroit Free Press* (October 14, 1977).

21. George Zurich, CBS director of communications; memo to all CBS affiliate station managers, March 27, 1979.

22. Art Toalston, "CBS Says Flesh and Blood To Be Terrific," *NFD Journal* (September 1979; reprinted from *Jackson [Mississippi] Daily News*, August 1979), 10.

23. John Weisman, "Tennis 'Deception' May Bring FCC Action Against CBS," *TV Guide* (April 1, 1978).

24. Jeff Jordan, "Flesh and Blood Latest to Shatter Timid Television View," *Omaha World-Herald*, October 16, 1979.

25. Harry F. Waters, "Does Incest Belong On TV?" *Newsweek* (Oct. 8, 1978), 101.

26. Marilyn Beck, "CBS Reworking Sequences of Flesh and Blood," *St. Petersburg Times* (August 14, 1979).

27. Ibid.

28. Jordan, "Flesh and Blood."

29. Cecil Hodges, "TV Station Apologizes For Flesh and Blood," *NFD Journal* (November 1979).

30. Crowd estimate by an Atlanta television station covering this news event.

31. Hodges, "TV Station Apologizes."

32. "NFD Supporters Win a Major Battle," *NFD Journal* (November 1979), 7.

Two

1. Gregg Lewis, *Telegarbage* (Nashville: Thomas Nelson, 1977), 45.

2. "What's Happening to American Morality?" *U.S. News and World Report* (October 13, 1975), 39-41.

3. "TV Actress Tops List of Students' Heroes," *Senior Scholastic* (February 10, 1977), 15.

4. Harry F. Waters, "Sex and TV," *Newsweek* (February 20, 1978), 54-61.

5. Lewis, *Telegarbage*, 18.

6. "When Norman Lear Raises the Flag, Nearly Everyone in Town Salutes," *People* (March 22, 1982), 102.

7. Frank A. Reel, *The Networks: How They Stole the Show* (New York: Charles Scribner's Sons, 1979), 107.

8. I say "had not been afraid" because I later learned why only older, well-established stars seemed willing to voice their criticisms of television sex and violence. Several younger, well-known actors have told me "off the record" that if they were to speak out, they'd virtually forfeit their chance to land future roles. In other words, you don't bite the hand that feeds you if you want to make a living as a television actor.

9. A two-block area in Manhattan where the ABC, CBS and NBC corporate headquarters are located.

10. Rustin's letter, which served as ABC's principal complaint letter reply, was still being sent to viewers as late as 1985. His many successors never even bothered to change the wording.

11. Reel, *The Networks*, xi.

12. Sally Bedell, *Up The Tube: Prime Time in the Silverman Years* (New York: Viking, 1981), 198.

13. Neil Hickey, "It's Being Called a Dance of Death: In Desperation, Programmers Are Taking Drastic Steps to Survive in the Ratings War," *TV Guide* (April 29, 1978), 33-40.

Three

1. After our initial fall, 1977 monitoring study was complete, we made some minor adjustments and expanded each of our monitoring teams to 42 people. That enables us to assign two monitors, working together, to each network every night.

2. Not many months later Sears reorganized their corporate structure to insure, among other things, more uniformity of advertising prac-

tices within their corporate-owned subsidiaries (i.e. Allstate Insurance, Dean-Witter-Reynolds Financial Services and Coldwell Banker Real Estate Services).

3. Tom Shales, "The Rebellion of the 'Fed-ups': TV Reformers Win a Skirmish . . ." *The Washington Post,* (May 15, 1978).

4. Edward R. Telling, chairman, Sears, Roebuck and Co. Letter to James H. Rosenfield, president CBS Television, May 3, 1978.

5. Shales, "The Rebellion."

6. Charles A. Meyer, Sears senior vice president of public affairs. Personal letter to NFD supporters, Mr. and Mrs. Walter Heckel, May 25, 1978.

7. Donald Deutsch, retired Sears public affairs executive, comment made during interview with Randall Nulton, October 29, 1987.

8. "Sex on Television: Networks Feel Heat from Advertisers," *TV Guide,* June 3, 1978, A1.

9. Sally Bedell, *Up the Tube: Prime Time in the Silverman Years* (New York: Viking, 1981), 231.

10. *TV Guide* (September 30, 1978), A5.

11. Bedell, *Up the Tube*, 231.

12. Walter Ames Compton, letter to Donald E. Wildmon, October 27, 1978.

13. Ronald E. Zier, letter to Donald E. Wildmon, July 1, 1981.

Four

1. *International Radio and Television Society*, 1988 membership brochure.

2. Gene Jankowski, "CBS Head Blasts National Federation for Decency," *NFD Journal* (April 1979), 1.

3. William F. Paley, address to CBS stockholders, April 16, 1980, New Orleans, Louisiana (*Accuracy in Media Report*, May 1, 1980).

4. The 400 member companies in the Association of National Advertisers account for an estimated 75 percent of all network TV advertising. See "Broadcaster Aligns with ANA on Clutter Issue," *Broadcasting Magazine* (December 4, 1978), 30.

5. James Rosenfield, speech to the Association of National Advertisers, Palm Beach, Florida, December 3, 1979; reprinted in *NFD Journal* (January 1980), 6.

6. John J. O'Connor, "TV: Hawthorne and Judith Krantz," *New York Times* (February 25, 1980).

7. James Rosenfield, speech to the Association of National Advertisers.

8. "Sex on Television: Networks Feel Heat from Advertisers," *TV Guide* (June 3, 1978).

9. "Broadcaster Aligns with ANA on Clutter Issue," *Broadcasting Magazine* (December 4, 1978), 30.

10. David Robb, "Boycott Blues: Shifting Sands of Discontent Sweeps Hollywood," *Hollywood Reporter* (December 28, 1981).

11. *NFD Monitoring Report*, Fall 1978; reprinted in *NFD Journal* (February 1979), 3.

12. Gary Deeb, "Tony Randall Blasts TV Programming," *NFD Journal* (July 1978; reprinted from *Chicago Tribune*), 7.

13. Harry F. Waters, "Gomorrah Revisited," *Newsweek* (April 5, 1976), 61.

14. I didn't expect Rich to admit that his made-for-TV movie about the famous Charles Manson slayings had been directly linked to *nine* copycat murders. *Newsweek's* Helter Skelter preview seriously questioned CBS's decision to bring it to "prime-time television, where the mass family audience tends to be lethargically captive to whatever it is offered." Then *Newsweek* prophetically wondered "whether commercial television—after 25 years of scientific data linking video violence with anti-social behavior—will ever accept the fact that it can be a deadly potent carrier?" See Harry F. Waters, "Gomorrah Revisited," 61.

15. Kenneth L. Wooward, "The Exorcism Frenzy," *Newsweek* (February, 11, 1974), 60-66.

16. Ibid.

17. Ibid.

18. Christopher Porterfield, "Pazuzu Rides Again," *Time* (July 4, 1977).

19. Donya Cannon, "Heart Cut Out to Chase 'Demon,'" *The Wichita Falls Times* (October 29, 1980).

20. Bill Keshlear, "Jurors Study Documents," *Wichita Falls Times* (June 3, 1981).

21. A few weeks after the incident I appeared briefly on Pat Robertson's "700 Club" show with CBS vice president for program practices Gene Mater. When I asked him to comment on Khunji Wilson's murder, he denied the link, shrugged his shoulders and said, "those things happen." Just before that he had said he felt no need to "apologize" for anything CBS has aired.

22. Peter Funt, "What's Allowed on TV. Pressures for Change Are Mounting," *New York Times* (September 27, 1980).

Five

1. John Cox, vice president of franchising and public affairs, Kentucky Fried Chicken, letter to Donald E. Wildmon, May 1978.

2. Stuart D. Watson, chairman, Heublein, Inc., letter to NFD supporter, Ray Cox, November 26, 1979.

3. Robert Bowden, "On Television," *St. Petersburg Times* (November 3, 1980).

4. Neil Hickey, "Will the Network System Survive?" *TV Guide* (May 6, 1978), 31-40.

5. Tom Shales, "Sex on TV: Open Season on Smut," *Washington Post* (December 7, 1980).

6. "Scramble Under Way for Clean TV Shows," *Advertising Age* (March 30, 1981).

7. Though they attended the press conference, the networks did not give the Coalition even one second of coverage on any of their news broadcasts.

8. Colby Coates, "ABC-TV Theme: Renewal," *Advertising Age* (May 11, 1981).

9. Rick DuBrow, "Behind the TV Boycott: How Networks, Minister are Vying for Control," *Los Angeles Herald Examiner* (June 10, 1981).

10. Gioia Diliberto, "Sponsors Run for Cover as TV Vigilante Donald Wildmon Decides It's Prime Time for a Boycott," *People* (July 6, 1981), 24-27.

11. Jack Thomas, "Moral Majority's Campaign of Censorship," *Boston Globe* (March 20, 1981), 49.

12. "Networks, Advertisers Respond to Different Kinds of Falwells," *Los Angeles Times* (May 12, 1981).

13. "Era of Intimidation Back in TV, Symposium Told; Religious Right is Blamed," *Variety* (May 11, 1981).

14. Howard Rosenberg, "Pressure Groups and TV—The Showdown Over Ojai," *Los Angeles Times* (May 13, 1981).

15. Ibid.

16. Gerald Clarke and Martha Smilgis, "Sanitizing the Small Screen: Proctor and Gamble Joins the Network's Sex and Violence Critics," *Time* (June 29, 1981), 83.

17. Colby Coates and James P. Forkan, "Networks Stand Firm in Opposing Boycott," *Advertising Age* (March 23, 1981).

18. "Closed Circuit," *Broadcasting* (May 25, 1981), 7.

19. Colby Coates, "Nets Set for Up Front Sales," *Advertising Age* (May 25, 1981).

20. Coates, "ABC-TV Theme."

21. Janet Neiman, "Advertisers Want 'Major Change' in TV," *Advertising Age* (March 8, 1982), 1.

22. "Media Drive Will Oppose Moral Majoritarians," *New York Daily News* (June 25, 1981), 42.

23. Maureen Orth, "Religion on TV: Norman Lear Tackles the New Hot Issue," *Vogue* (February 1982).

24. Christy Marshall, "4 A's Cool to TV Chiefs," *Advertising Age* (April 13, 1981), 1.

25. Ibid.

26. Ibid.

27. "Network Heads Refuse to Debate Issue Under Live, Uncensored Conditions," *NFD Journal*, (May, 1981), 3.

28. Clarke and Smilgis, "Sanitizing the Small Screen," 83.

Six

1. Daniel Ruth, "CBS President Defends 'Quality' Programming," *Tampa Tribune* (January 11, 1980).

2. John Carmody, *Washington Post*, (June 15, 1981).

3. I later realized that I had accidentally gotten *Gay Power/Gay Politics* confused with another program that had all but postured homosexuality as a positive alternative to monogamous, heterosexual intimacy within marriage.

Seven

1. Tom Shales, "Sex and TV: Open Season on Smut," *Washington Post* (December 7, 1980).

2. "And the Playmates Sing," *Playboy* (December 1981), 226-29, 280.

3. *NBC Broadcast Standards for Television*, 1979 edition, 1.

4. Ibid., 6.

5. Ibid., 7.

6. Ibid.

7. Robert O'Neil, NBC manager of communications services, letter to Donald E. Wildmon, May 9, 1984.

8. Derek Clontz, "TV Incest Uproar: Watchdogs Say Daring New Mini-Series Shows Too Much," *Globe*; (reprinted in *NFD Journal*, September 1983), 1.

9. Ibid.

10. E. Salholz, and K.L. Woodward, "The Rights' New Bogeyman," *Newsweek* (July 6, 1981), 48.

11. Linda S. Lichter, S. Robert Lichter and Stanley Rothman, "Hollywood and America: The Odd Couple," *Public Opinion Magazine* (January 1983).

12. Ben Stein, *The View From Sunset Boulevard* (New York: Doubleday, 1980), xiii.

13. Ibid., 102.

14. Ibid.

15. Mary Murphy, "The Aids Scare: What It's Done to Hollywood . . . and the TV You See," *TV Guide* (October 22, 1988).

16. Richard M. Levine, "Family Affair," *Esquire* (March, 1984), 225-26.

17. Linda S. Lichter, S. Robert Lichter and Stanley Rothman, "Hollywood and America."

18. Geoffrey Wolff, "Shortcuts to the Heart," *Esquire* (August 1981), 44-49.

19. Robert S. Alley, *Television: Ethics for Hire?* (Nashville: Abingdon, 1977), 140-41.

20. *Diff'rent Strokes*, NBC, (January 15, 1983).

21. Research and Forecasts, Inc., Connecticut Mutual Life Report on American Values in the 80s, The Impact of Belief, (New York: Connecticut Mutual Life Insurance Company, 1981, 201-3).

22. "Silverman to NBC Affiliates: Press Paints Distorted Picture of Network," *Broadcasting*, (May 25, 1981), 34-35.

23. Linda Lichter, S. Robert Lichter and Stanley Rothman, "Hollywood and America."

24. Stein, *The View From Sunset Boulevard*, 136.

25. Rick DuBrow, "Lear's Indirect Challenge to the Religious Right," *Los Angeles Herald Examiner* (February 22, 1982), c. 1.

26. Ibid.

Eight

1. Following a much publicized trial, Johnny Zinn, the man who ordered Linda's killing, received a life sentence and will not be eligible for parole for 45 years. Randy Pierce, the man who pulled the trigger, received a 65-year prison sentence. Thomas Sliger was sentenced to three years for rape and was eligible for parole after two years. James Scartacinni was released following a plea-bargain arrangement granting him total immunity in exchange for his testimony against the other three.

2. Both Dixie Gallery and Sandra Hunter later wrote their tragic stories for publication in my monthly *National Federation for Decency [now American Family Association] Journal*. To insure accuracy, quotes are taken from those written accounts.

3. Pure Life Ministries, P.O. Box 345, Crittenden, KY 41030.

4. Milton Moskowitz, Michael Katz and Robert Levering, eds., *Everybody's Business—An Almanac* (New York: Harper and Row, 1980), 118.

5. Larry Teitelbaum "Federation Will Picket Against Magazine Sales," *Burlington County Times* (Willingboro, New Jersey, August 7, 1984).

6. John Pearman, South Florida division manager, letter to an NFD supporter, Nov. 16, 1983.

7. "Hanky Spanky," *Penthouse* (May 1984), 12-20).

8. Jeffery C. Dahlstrom, letter to Don Wildmon, April 2, 1984.

9. Judith Reisman, "Images of Children, Crime and Violence in Playboy, Penthouse and Hustler Magazines," *Executive Summary* (Arlington, Virginia: The Institute for Media Education, 1986).

10. Hugh M. Hefner, "The Blacklist: The Meese Commission has Become the Tool of Evangelical Terrorists," *Playboy* (July, 1986), 3.

11. "No More Adults: 7-Eleven Bans Skin Mags," *Time* (April 21, 1986), 62.

12. Penny Sori, "Anti-Porn Group Plans to Picket Rite-Aid Store," *Syracuse Herald Journal* (April 19, 1985).

13. Hefner, "The Blacklist," 3.

14. Gary Levin, "Playboy Readies Comeback," *Advertising Age* (October 26, 1987).

15. United Press International wire service, March 18, 1987.

16. James E. Olson, chairman, AT&T, letter to Allen F. Wildmon, July 28, 1987.

Nine

1. Ann Landers, *Los Angeles Times Syndicate* (June 28, 1988).

2. "Garbage Pail Kids Condemned by New Jersey PTA," *Northwest New Jersey Daily Record* (November 1, 1987).

3. Ibid.

4. Ibid.

5. Diane Haithman, "The Lid's Not Quite Shut on 'Garbage Pail Kids' at CBS," *Los Angeles Times* (October 10, 1987), VI 1.

6. Dave Kaufman, "Garbage Pail Kids is Canned by CBS," *Daily Variety* (September 16, 1987), 1.

7. Mal Vincent, "Mississippi Minister Takes on Networks in a Duel of Decency," *Virginian-Pilot* (July 6, 1981), B1.

8. Haithman, " The Lid's Not Quite Shut," VI 1.

9. John Culhane, "Ralph Bakshi, Iconoclast of Animation," *New York Times Biographical Service* (March, 1981), 271.

10. Ibid.

11. Martin Kasindorf, "A Kind of X-Rated Disney," *New York Times Biographical Edition* (October 1973), 1589-93.

12. Charles Higham, "The R-Rated Cartoon World of Ralph Bakshi (Bambi It Ain't)," *New York Times Biographical Edition* (November 1974), 1529-1531.

13. Diane Haithman, *Los Angeles Times Calendar* (June 4, 1987), 9.

14. George Dessart, CBS vice president of program practices, letter to Donald E. Wildmon, June 7, 1988.

15. Dessart, letter to Donald E. Wildmon, June 8, 1988.

16. Ibid.

17. Rod Chandler, U.S. Congressman 8th District—Washington, letter to Lawrence Tisch, president and CEO of CBS, July 7, 1988.

18. Edward J. Stegemann, vice president, secretary and general council of Mars, Incorporated, letter to Lawrence Tisch, president and CEO of CBS, July 21, 1988.

Ten

1. MCA Records did indeed try to make Steve Gooden pay a heavy price for his action. First, they adamantly refused to let Steve out of his contract. After AFA supporters made thousands of phone calls and letters on Steve's behalf, MCA officials said they'd forget the agreement if Steve paid them $11,000. Since those terms weren't satisfactory, I asked AFA supporters to make another round of phone calls and letters. Finally, after seven months, they agreed to release Steve from his contractual obligations for nothing.

2. Russell Chandler, "25,000 Gather at Universal to Protest Film," *Los Angeles Times* (August 12, 1988), 1.

3. Larry W. Poland, *The Last Temptation of Hollywood* (Highland, CA: Mastermedia International, Inc., 1988), 91.

4. Ibid.

5. Nikos Kazantzakis, *The Last Temptation of Christ* (New York: Simon and Schuster, 1960), 145.

6. Ibid., 146.

7. Dale Pollack, "To Scorsese, 'Comedy' Is Not Funny," *Los Angeles Times* (March 15, 1983), VI. 1.

8. *New American Standard Version*, John 14:6.

9. "MCA, Inc.—Universal Pictures Upcoming Theatrical Releases," *Investext* (July 29, 1988), 1.

10. Poland, *The Last Temptation of Hollywood*, 16.

11. Steve Rabey, "Producer Tries to Dim Fears Over Movie," *Christianity Today* (March 4, 1988).

12. Poland, *The Last Temptation of Hollywood*, 27.

13. Ibid., 38.

14. Ibid., 202.

15. Ibid., 50.

16. Ibid., 201.

17. Kazantzakis, *The Last Temptation of Christ*, "A Note on the Author and His Use of Language," by P.A. Bien, 505.

18. "Religion in America: Report No. 259," *The Gallup Report* (Princeton, New Jersey: April 1987), 28.

19. Mary Anne Dolan, "Wildmon's Intolerance Lends a Bad Name to Religion," *The Appleton [Wisconsin] Post Crescent* (August 23, 1988).

20. Mary Beth Murphy, "Minister Endorses Controversial Film," *The Milwaukee Sentinel* (July 16, 1989).

21. "Religious Leaders Happy with Movie," *Warsaw [Indiana] Times Union* (July 15, 1988), 4.

22. John Dart, "Some Clerics See No Evil in Temptation," *Los Angeles Times (July 14, 1988), VI, 11.*

23. James Dobson, *Focus on the Family Newsletter* (Pomona, California: September 1988), 4.

24. Patrick Buchanan, "Hollywood's War on Christianity," *Washington Times* (July 27, 1988).

25. Universal also placed *The Last Temptation of Christ* in approximately 60 second-run and art theatres. Located mostly in large cities, second-run theatres primarily show films that have passed their peak. As a result, they only need to pay major film studios such as Universal Pictures a fraction of the amount first-run theatres must pay for each viewer. Hence, second-run theatres normally charge about $2.00. Art theatres, primarily in hard to reach neighborhoods, specialize in avant-garde American films and foreign films.

26. "The Week at the Box Office," *The Hollywood Reporter* (November 8, 1988), 43.

Index

Acknowledgments

Naming everyone who helped provide information or prayer support for this book simply isn't possible. However, special thanks must go to Tim Wildmon and Forrest Ann Daniels, for diligently assisting with scores of details; Gary Morton, for helping to place some of the writing in sharper focus; Kiki Miller and Max Myers, for faithfully "standing in the gap." And there's Dorothy Nulton, Virgil Nulton and Lynda Wildmon, without whom. . . .